£17.99

D1345116

Art therapy in palliative care

This comprehensive and accessible introduction to the practice of art therapy in palliative care includes accounts from both therapists and clients in a variety of settings. The first section of the book introduces the basic concepts of art therapy and discusses its application in the palliative care context. The second section provides analysis of the practice and results of art therapy with different client groups, in settings within and beyond the hospital or hospice.

The case studies presented, which include examples of client artwork, demonstrate that the opportunity to explore personal issues and emotions through artwork has a positive effect on patients' health and quality of life. Discussing work with both individuals and groups contributors explore the power and value of the creative experience in helping clients regain a feeling of control in their lives. There is also significant discussion of griefwork with children who have been bereaved, and the contribution that art therapy makes to this work.

Based on the experience and expertise of professionals who have pioneered this important application of art therapy, this book is essential reading for anyone wishing to gain a fuller understanding of psychotherapeutic techniques and their potency in the palliative care setting.

Mandy Pratt is Senior I Art Therapist at St Helena Hospice, Colchester. **Michèle J.M. Wood** is Senior I Art Therapist at Mildmay Mission Hospital and Charing Cross Hospital and visiting lecturer at Goldsmiths' College, London. They are both founder members of The Creative Response, a professional association of art therapists who specialise in work in palliative care and loss.

Contributors: Ann Bartholomew; Val Beaver; Simon Bell; Camilla Connell; Jackie Coote; Elizabeth Hall; Peter Kaye; Paola Luzzatto; Sheila Mayo; Barbara Morley; Mandy Pratt; Gill Thomas; Michèle J.M. Wood.

Art therapy in palliative care

The creative response

Edited by Mandy Pratt and
Michèle J.M. Wood

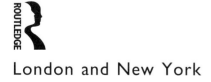

London and New York

First published 1998 by Routledge
11 New Fetter Lane, London EC4P 4EE

Simultaneously published in the USA and Canada
by Routledge
29 West 35th Street, New York, NY 10001

© 1998 Mandy Pratt and Michèle J.M. Wood for the collection
as a whole; individual chapters © the authors

Typeset in Times by Florencetype Ltd, Stoodleigh, Devon
Printed and bound in Great Britain by Biddles Ltd, Guildford
and King's Lynn

British Library Cataloguing in Publication Data
A catalogue record for this book is available
from the British Library

Library of Congress Cataloging in Publication Data
Art therapy in palliative care: the creative response /
edited by Mandy Pratt and Michèle J.M. Wood.
p. cm.
Includes bibliographical references and index.
1. Art therapy. 2. Palliative treatment. 3. Terminal care.
I. Pratt, Amanda, 1952– . II. Wood, Michèle J.M., 1960– .
4. Terminally Ill–psychology. 5. Bereavement. WM 450.5.S8
A78388
1998]
RC489.A7A773   1998
615.8'5156–dc21
                                                97–51524
                                                  CIP

ISBN 0–415–16156–8 (hbk)
ISBN 0–415–16157–6 (pbk)

Contents

Foreword by Dame Cicely Saunders   vii
Preface by Dr Michael Kearney   viii
Introduction   ix
Acknowledgements   xii

PART I   xiii

1 What is art therapy?   1
   Michèle J.M. Wood

2 What is palliative care?   12
   Michèle J.M. Wood

3 Art therapy in palliative care   26
   Michèle J.M. Wood

4 Some images of illness: the place of art therapy in the
   palliative care team – a doctor's perspective   38
   Peter Kaye with a Postscript by Elizabeth Hall

PART II   51

5 Getting started: introducing the art therapy service and the
   individual's first experiences   53
   Jackie Coote

6 What lies within us: individuals in a Marie Curie Hospice 64
   Gill Thomas

7 The search for a model which opens: open group at the
   Royal Marsden Hospital   75
   Camilla Connell

 8 Will the kitchen table do? Art therapy in the community   88
    Simon Bell

 9 The story board: reflections on group art therapy   102
    Sheila Mayo

10 A narrow ledge: art therapy at the London Lighthouse   115
    Ann Bartholomew

11 The butterfly garden: art therapy with HIV/AIDS prisoners   127
    Val Beaver

12 The body as art: individual session with a man with AIDS   140
    Michèle J.M. Wood

13 The invisible injury: adolescent griefwork group   153
    Mandy Pratt

14 From psychiatry to psycho-oncology: personal reflections
    on the use of art therapy with cancer patients   169
    Paola Luzzatto

15 Sunbeams and icebergs, meteorites and daisies: a cancer
    patient's experience of art therapy   176
    Barbara Morley

    Appendix I: Complications to grieving   186

    Appendix II: Psychological defences and the mourning
    process   188

    Appendix III: Childhood bereavement   189

    Appendix IV: The Barcelona Declaration on Palliative Care   191

    Glossary of terms   193

    Useful addresses   195

    Index   198

Foreword

During the thirty years of the Hospice and Palliative Care Movement, a key phrase for many has been 'Watch with me'. This has signified a readiness to be present, often in silence, waiting for the words that may come out of that silence. Over the years, skills have been gained in helping with the expression of questions and of helping people to search within themselves, sometimes for answers, but more often than not for the readiness to live with the questions.

Increasingly, forms of creativity have taken their place within this climate of discovery. The choice of art and decoration in hospice units has been important and has often let to unexpected responses. More important still has been the move towards encouraging people facing persistent illness to create their own art, their own writing and craftwork. Perhaps nowhere has this been more vividly seen than in art therapy, either in groups or individually. Healing, a new discovery of wholeness, has come through honesty unleashed in this way.

These very personal pilgrimages may have taken place at the end of life where every day may still bring reconciliation or, indeed, adventure. In these descriptions of the different spheres of such work we are reminded once again of the resilience and originality of the human spirit.

Dame Cicely Saunders, OM, DBE, FRCP
Chairman, St Christopher's Hospice, London

Preface

Some years ago I came across the following words of psychotherapist David Findlay describing what is possible when helping another towards healing, 'The most we can do is to prepare and hold the space where the miraculous may happen.' I believe this is also an accurate description of what we hope to achieve with palliative care. Through the efforts of a multiprofessional team effectively controlling distressing symptoms, opening up blocked channels of communication and working with the family, with the patient at the centre, as the unit of care, space is created in chaos and suffering; a space for being and for deepening one's experience of living.

Healing is also about diving deep and involves being embraced by what is deepest in ourselves. While this process happens silently and naturally for most individuals approaching death and while it is greatly facilitated by 'good enough' palliative care, for others, such efforts alone are simply not enough. There are some who become trapped in their dying in a prison of fear and meaninglessness, cut off from those in the world and that in themselves which can bring solace in their distress. It is particularly individuals like this who may benefit from an approach like art therapy which, by creating a safe place to be in one's suffering, can encourage a gradual opening to the healing depths within. Such an encounter with depth can bring calm in the midst of fear and a sense of significance and hope in the midst of what seems like the blackest night of the soul. Paradoxically, these individuals may then begin to live more fully, becoming more incarnate and more fully themselves in the process, even as their physical body begins to fade away.

While symptom control is rightly credited with being the cornerstone of palliative care, it is also only a starting point and a beginning in the healing journey. This book on art therapy in palliative care outlines an invaluable approach which must been seen for what it is: an essential part of any palliative care service and a healing skill that intertwines with other traditional medical interventions in palliative care like the snake coiling around the rod of Asklepios, Greek god of healing.

Dr Michael Kearney, MB, FRCPI
Consultant in Palliative Medicine
Our Lady's Hospice and St Vincent's Hospital, Dublin

Introduction

When someone first learns they have a life-threatening illness, they can be devastated, overwhelmed by the intensity of their emotions. They may feel unable to talk to those around them or unwilling to burden close friends and family with their concerns. This book explores how the opportunity to work with art materials provided by an art therapist can precipitate a profound exploration of personal issues which positively affects the individual's health and quality of life. Art therapists are trained to provide the help and encouragement necessary to facilitate what may be a difficult process, thus providing the possibility of release and resolution. Exploring the creativity latent in us all not only allows for insight and discovery of our personal strengths, but also vastly enriches our lives with new beginnings at a time otherwise filled with endings.

Health establishments are increasingly commissioning exhibitions of paintings, prints, photographs and sculpture. This reflects an awareness of the impact of aesthetics in the environment on those that work and receive care within it. On a more direct and personal level there is a growing recognition of the contribution of arts therapies to physical and mental health and our overall quality of life. Art, music, drama and dance movement therapists are now working in a wide range of healthcare settings. The importance of creativity to our sense of well being has received much exploration and examination by writers and thinkers over the centuries. The contribution of creative experience to the quality of life of individuals who are sick is the foundation for the use of the arts in healthcare. This reflects an awareness of the continuity between psychological and physical well being that underpins our present emphasis on a 'holistic', patient-centred approach to healthcare. The environmental, social and personal applications of the arts in healthcare are linked by the recognition that there is an inherently life-promoting force at work here.

This growth in interest in art and art therapy in the provision of holistic healthcare has coincided with the formation of a professional association of art therapists who specialise in working in palliative care and loss. This association, known as The Creative Response, is a subgroup of the British Association of Art Therapists. Regular study days enable its members to pool their experience and offer information and support. Since its formation, The Creative

Response has received a steady flow of enquiries. What is art therapy? Where and how does it work? Who would it be appropriate to refer? How can we contact an art therapist in our area? This book is intended to answer many of these questions and also to provide an opportunity for us to share some of our experience and thus give a greater appreciation of the contribution art therapy has to make to this area of healthcare.

The book is divided into two parts with a central gallery of patients' images. These are examples of images made in art therapy sessions and include any title or comments given by the patient when created. In this gallery we hope the patient's experience 'speaks' directly without being mediated by any introduction by an art therapist. The images presented throughout the book are constrained by reproduction in black and white, which cannot do justice to the richness, and variety of work we are privileged to share.

Part I of the book provides a historical overview of the origins and theory of art therapy (Chapter 1) and palliative care (Chapter 2) to familiarise readers new to either field with some key concepts and issues. Chapter 2 also gives a brief introduction to art therapy in griefwork. In Chapter 3 we highlight the benefits of art therapy in this area and raise some important questions concerning the development of art therapy practice. We also provide an overview of the literature on the use of art therapy in palliative care as a way of providing a context for subsequent chapters. Part I then provides an account of our past – how art therapists came to work in the field of palliative care – and starts to explore what each discipline may have to offer the other. Part I ends with reflections from Peter Kaye and Elizabeth Hall on the position and value of art therapy in the multidisciplinary team.

Part II moves the reader into the present as ten art therapists (demonstrating a range of theoretical approaches) present examples of their current practice in a variety of palliative care settings. There is groupwork from a large London teaching hospital (the Royal Marsden) where art therapy is offered as part of the rehabilitation unit; at St Catherine's Hospice where the group takes place in the middle of a busy open ward; at the London Lighthouse where the composition of the group is quite fluid, changing from week to week; and from a Scottish prison where boundaries are, by contrast, completely rigid (these last two groups for people with AIDS); and a griefwork group for adolescents at St Helena Hospice. Individual sessions are also described with an in-patient at a Marie Curie Centre; with the Macmillan Nursing Service, where art therapy is delivered in a patient's own home; in a single session at Mildmay Mission Hospital and at St Christopher's Hospice Day Centre as the art therapy service is first introduced. There is also an account of work in New York at the Memorial Sloan Kettering Cancer Center that demonstrates a degree of convergence in practice in this field not always evident in work from the US with other client groups.

Part II gives the reader a unique opportunity to sample the variety of challenges art therapists meet at 'the cutting edge' of practice in new territory. It also illustrates the flexibility and scope of art therapy as well as the singular affinity this therapeutic approach has with palliative care. The reader is invited 'through the art therapist's door' to witness a rich variety of ways in which clients of all ages have employed their time to remarkable effect.The last word rightly goes to Barbara Morley, who provides a very intimate account of coping with the diagnosis and treatments of a life-threatening illness aided by art therapy.

It is clear, both from those areas of controversy requiring critical self-appraisal raised in Part I and from the accounts of reflective and ground-breaking practice given in Part II that art therapy has a great deal to offer the future development of palliative care services. Through the generosity of the Omega Foundation, a database will be available by 1999 detailing all the arts therapies (art, music, drama and dance movement) available throughout the UK to people of all ages with a life-threatening illness. This will be a tremendous resource for research, enabling us to explore appropriate and sensitive measures to document the value of art therapy to people facing life-threatening illnesses. It will also enable professionals, carers, families and patients themselves to speedily access art therapy services. This book constitutes an important first step in demonstrating that we have much to contribute to the future development of a palliative care system that is genuinely patient-led.

Mandy Pratt and Michèle J.M. Wood

Acknowledgements

In a sense this book came about thanks to the mounting number of enquiries into the work of art therapists in palliative care; perhaps its very existence will prove thanks enough for many. More specifically we would like to thank Judith Ennew and Penelope Hall for the creative weekend that made us feel we could do it. Special thanks go to Yvonne Archdale, Michael Channon, Nicolas Cherniavsky, Julia Cleves Mosse, Carol Feldon, Andrea Gilroy, James and Jo Kay, Peter Kaye, Christine Korreski, Shirley Lunn, Elaine Sandon, Mary Spence and Joan Woddis for their encouragement, practical help and useful comments on early drafts of some of the chapters. To Alan Smith, Penny Healey and Colin Pratt who patiently read and re-read manuscripts – thanks for their invaluable comments and support. Thanks also to Jan Clough, Millie Hare and Jo Bint for their endless enthusiasm and support. Particular mention goes to Dave Rogers who is pioneering the work of art therapy with people who have suffered profound head injuries and who contributed much to the early shaping of this book. We would also like to acknowledge the helpful advice of the Society of Authors.

Thanks to Patrick Wood and Colin Pratt for their support, encouragement and assistance at all stages and innumerable thanks to Emily, Benedict and Madeleine, Thomas, Christopher and William for their tolerant forbearance of the time and energy focused on the book – rather than on them!

And finally our sincere thanks to Martin Huggett who has unhesitatingly helped and supported the entire project.

Part I

Chapter 1

What is art therapy?

Michèle J.M. Wood

INTRODUCTION

The combination of the words 'art' and 'therapy' are frequently greeted with incomprehension by people encountering art therapy for the first time. They often have an intuitive sense that art activity can be 'therapeutic' in some way, but are not sure how this extends beyond relaxation and recreation. In this chapter I would like to describe what art therapy is, and indicate the ways in which it works. (A more detailed description of the use of art therapy in palliative care will be given in Chapter 3.)

Put simply, art therapy is the use of art materials for self-expression and reflection in the presence of a trained art therapist. The creation of an image or artefact provides the client and therapist with a concrete form depicting something of the client's experiences, with which both client and therapist can engage.

The art-making activity is facilitated by the art therapist in a number of ways according to the needs of the client, the setting in which they are meeting and the therapist's style. The art therapist uses his or her understanding of the client's interactions with their artwork and with the therapist to bring about a greater self-awareness within the client. This involves noting the client's responses to the art materials available, the client's choice of media and the manner in which the artwork is executed. The thoughts and feelings evoked in the therapist by the client's artwork and those observed in and reported by the client all comprise the substance of the therapeutic encounter. If the art therapy is taking place within a group context then the effects of the relationships with other group members and their artwork are also considered by the art therapist. In other words art therapy involves not only the artwork produced but also the process by which it is made.

The overall aim of art therapy is to enable the client to change and grow on a personal level. Art therapy is often wrongly assumed to be a form of distraction or diversion from personal difficulties. This is not the case. In fact the opportunity for expression and communication without recourse to words can enable a person to see more clearly the nature and extent of the problems with which they struggle. Thus art therapy provides an alternative to spoken language as a means of representation and communication. In the making of a picture or artwork previously unacknowledged feelings can be given form which may lead to these feelings being reflected upon and then spoken about with the art therapist. The client's artwork is a container for a rich breadth of issues, which may be contradictory, contentious or even bizarre and which may be difficult for them to articulate in any other way. The possibility of depicting something personal which can be changed and developed in a series of images is a very useful part of the therapeutic process, as is the permanence of the artwork, for it allows a continued exploration, reflection and comparison over a number of sessions whereas words can be more easily forgotten or denied. The fact that the client can represent themselves in their own terms through their artwork can strengthen and validate their sense of identity.

The use of verbal and non-verbal processes in art therapy and the concrete nature of art making means that art therapists are able to work with a diversity of clients. Adults with a range of mental health problems have benefited from art therapy. For example, Dalley, Rifkind and Terry (1993) provide an account of the process of art therapy with a man suffering depression. Murphy (1984), Luzzatto (1994), Mahony and Waller (1992), Rust (1994), Levens (1995) and Schaverien (1995) document their work with people who have addictive and self-destructive behaviours. Art therapy has been used with people who have learning difficulties (Stott and Males 1984; Strand 1990; Tipple 1994; Stack 1996), and many art therapists have written about their work with people with psychotic illnesses (for example Charlton 1984; Killick 1991; Killick and Greenwood 1995; Crane 1996). Art therapy is also used with children who may have educational, behavioural or emotional difficulties or may have suffered traumatic experiences (Wood 1984; Case and Dalley 1990; Arguile 1992). Art therapy has been undertaken with people who are elderly (Miller 1984; Byers 1995), and with those who are chronically or terminally ill (Szepanski 1988; Malitskie 1988; Wood 1990; Connell 1992; Thomas 1995).

Art therapists, therefore, can be found working in many different settings, from community-based facilities such as schools, child guidance centres and day centres to residential establishments such as hospitals and prisons. Obviously the methods used by art therapists vary according to the particular needs of their clients and the context of their work. We can, however, identify the features which are distinctive to art therapy practice thus (based on Waller 1991):

- Art therapy is a means of representing inner feelings.
- Art therapy involves three parties: a therapist, a client (or clients if in a group) and artwork.
- In art therapy the client should have easy access to a variety of mark-making and plastic media.
- Art therapy should take place in an environment designated for that purpose.
- Art therapy is distinct from art education since the art therapist offers no technical assistance or advice beyond what may aid the client in achieving an intended communication.

THE LOCATION

The location in which art therapy occurs has a considerable influence upon the therapy. It provides a tangible expression of the boundaries of the therapeutic relationship. The choice of furniture and its position in the room convey to the client what is to be expected from the therapist and how they are to behave. Clients need to feel that the space for art therapy sessions will allow what is made and discussed to remain confidential to the therapist, or other members if in a group. Consequently, soundproofing and storage of artwork are factors to be considered. All art therapy rooms need a sink, for without access to water paints and clay cannot be used, and the client will be severely restricted in their ability to make a 'mess'.

Art therapy rooms which are set up as art studios and in which the client may position themselves at a distance from the art therapist will have a different effect from rooms in which therapist and client are seated close together and where the therapist has a clear view of the client's work as it is being made. Many art therapists working in large hospitals built in the last century have had the advantage of generously proportioned rooms which they have filled with patients' artworks and plants to provide a creative and stimulating atmosphere. Such rooms have also benefited from having large windows which provide ample sunlight and good views. In this way art therapy has provided an environment which counters the sterile institutional atmosphere that is often found elsewhere in these enormous hospitals.

With the current relocation of services into the community, art therapists have found themselves sharing rooms with other professionals, often in cramped conditions not conducive to art activity. The issue of where art therapy can take place is described in the chapters in Part II. Whatever the practical constraints surrounding the location of art therapy sessions, the art therapist's task is to ensure that the surroundings allow enough privacy for a client to get on with their work (see Case and Dalley 1992 for a fuller discussion).

THE ART MATERIALS

There must be a large enough range of art materials from which the client can choose, as each medium lends itself to certain kinds of emotional communications. Several writers have argued that the perceived world of sensations and objects (animate and inanimate) are imbued by humans with expressive qualities (Arnheim 1954 and Rycroft 1985). For example, the marks made by a 'screeching' pencil will convey a different emotional quality to thick paint that is stroked onto the paper with care. Objects from the client's own environment may be brought to art therapy and incorporated into mixed media pieces, to convey perhaps some intimate symbolic meaning. The therapist must ensure that the client can explore the materials provided and use them without unnecessary obstacles. For clients with a physical disability this may require ingenious support on the part of the therapist.

THE AIMS OF ART THERAPY

As we have seen, art therapy is a flexible tool and as such has extensive aims. These can be summarised as Creativity, Control, Communication, Catharsis and Change (based on Luzzatto and Gabriel 1998, p. 750).

Creativity

The challenge of a blank sheet of paper and a variety of art media can stimulate the creative forces within individuals who come for art therapy. Creativity is an aspect of experience which transcends notions of 'art' or 'science' and which can be seen in the lives of individuals, groups and cultures. Definitions of creativity are many, but in relation to art therapy we would suggest that the enjoyment of the individual's own creative thinking and experience, through the art materials, provides a means of movement on a psychological level. In this way creativity enables the person to make connections with the material and social worlds in which they exist. Implicit in the definition of creativity is the notion of change; a creative act always brings into existence something new.

Although creativity is assumed to be implicit in art making, this is not always the case. Mann (1990) has argued that art activity, rather than being an expression of creativity, can in fact be a means of defending the individual from a truly creative experience. He defines creativity as the capacity to experience change and suggests that this involves an individual in moving from something 'known' towards something that is as yet 'unknown'. This transition from known to unknown brings with it some anxiety. According to Mann an individual's ability to persevere in the face of such feelings is an essential part of creativity. Considered in this way creativity is understandably no easy matter and so the emotional support of the art therapist is vital for clients who, for a variety of reasons, may find creativity a difficult venture. In this respect the art therapist's focus on the value of the art-making *process* as well as the eventual *product* is crucial to facilitating an authentic creative experience in the client.

Art and craft activities with clients are provided by professionals who are not art therapists and these are without doubt of great value in contributing to the aesthetic experiences of the client and enhancing many positive feelings. Two organisations which promote the use of arts in healthcare in the UK are Hospital Arts and Hospice Arts. Artists, sculptors, writers, poets and musicians are variously employed as artists-in-residence, or as project workers providing workshops to encourage patient participation (Frampton 1986). The creative activities promoted by such arts agencies are aimed at improving the milieu and enhancing patients' quality of life. For Hospital Arts, healthcare settings also provide opportunities for the work of artists to reach wider audiences (Kaye and Blee 1997). Arts activities and art therapy have a common goal in the encouragement of patients' creativity, and a shared outcome in the increased value placed upon creativity by other members of the staff team and patients' families. However, the two approaches are different, with art therapists able to work with the barriers to creativity and able to provide support on emotional and psychological levels.

Control

The freedom to use art materials in art therapy provides the client with a tangible way to develop control of and to enjoy some mastery over the media. By splashing, pounding, tearing, sticking, scratching or smoothing the materials the client is able to order and symbolically represent their experiences. The opportunity of using the art materials to exercise and experience personal choices and control in a symbolic way can be enormously valuable for people with difficulties in this aspect of their lives.

Communication

Through the process of using the art materials and through the resulting imagery or marks the client can find a means of communication. The use of shapes, colours or symbols can provide expression for previously ill-understood issues or feelings. Contrary opinions, thoughts or desires can be communicated both to the client and to the art therapist. The result is that the client can gain a greater understanding of themselves. Many clients who benefit from art therapy have physical, psychological or emotional difficulties which make verbal communication problematic. Some people may be highly articulate and yet unable to communicate on an emotional level. For them, the non-verbal processes of art therapy can provide a non-threatening means of communication. At the other extreme are those who do not have the capacity to use speech (for example, those with aphasia or with severe learning difficulties), but who can use art materials for communication. The receptive presence of the art therapist is a crucial part of the communication.

Catharsis

Sometimes the use of materials can bring with it an expression of strong feelings so that the experience becomes a cathartic one. Powerful feelings are thereby accessed and discharged through the art materials. In this way the client can find a way of releasing 'dangerous' feelings. The use of striking colours, and substances like paint and clay which are strongly associated with the body and its fluids, can be used to convey feelings in a more socially acceptable way. The recognition of this element of art therapy raises anxieties amongst some health-care professionals who fear that art therapy will uncover a torrent of frightening feelings which will overwhelm the client and those around them. In fact the client's manipulation of the materials during the art making requires him or her to maintain a level of control which mitigates the feeling of being 'out-of-control'. The therapist's skill in keeping the boundaries of the therapy ensures that these feelings are contained and the client (and therapist) are kept safe.

Change

As described earlier, art therapy provides a client with the opportunity to expe-rience and make changes that will have a beneficial effect on all aspects of their life. The strengthening and integration of the client's personality that comes through art therapy enables them to cope with the inevitable changes that are part of life. This is certainly one benefit of using art therapy with people who are living with progressive terminal illness, and is demonstrated in the many cases presented in Part II.

WHAT IS AN ART THERAPIST?

Art therapists hold a postgraduate qualification in art therapy. They are usually mature people with experience of working in healthcare settings prior to their training in art therapy. Most art therapists work in statutory or voluntary agen-cies, often as part of a wider team of professionals. Some art therapists work in private and independent practice.

The training of art therapists usually follows a first degree in art and design or fine art, together with a minimum of one year full-time relevant working experience. In practice people have often worked for a number of years in various capacities with disturbed or distressed clients. A small percentage of applicants with degrees in other subjects, such as psychology, social sciences or history of art, are also admitted for training. Training currently takes place over two years full time or three to five years part time. It involves the consideration of different theories in psychology, psychotherapy, psychiatry and art therapy and a practical experience through placements in different art therapy settings. An awareness of inter-personal dynamics is gained during training through experiential groupwork and an increasing appreciation of the art process is developed through the continued experience of the trainee's own art making. It is recognised that art therapy training is demanding on a personal level and trainees are required to undertake their own therapy for the duration of the course.

There are at present five training establishments in the UK offering courses leading to the postgraduate diploma in art therapy (or art psychotherapy) (see Useful Addresses, p. 195).

Following qualification art therapists can be registered with the British Association of Art Therapists (BAAT). The association ensures that the therapist has attained an academic standard that meets its approval and that the therapist works in accordance with BAAT's objectives and constitution and in line with its Code of Ethics. At the time of writing, there are almost 1,000 art therapists in Britain, and a small number of British-trained art therapists working overseas. There are also associations of art therapists in the US, Canada, Switzerland and Australia. In Italy (Cagnoletta 1990; Waller 1992), Bulgaria (Waller 1995), Hungary (Vasarhelyi 1992) and the Netherlands art therapy training is also being developed. There are, however, significant differences between the training in Britain and those abroad.

In the UK a career structure for art therapists was introduced into the NHS in 1981 and there has been an art therapy advisor to the Department of Health since 1989. In 1997 art therapy became a state registered profession.

THE ROLE OF THE ART THERAPIST

The role of the art therapist has been hinted at in the above description of art therapy. The art therapist's task is to ensure a comfortable and safe environment in which a client can feel relaxed enough to use the materials to express themselves. By carefully attending to the client's direct and indirect communication the art therapist works with them in acknowledging, understanding and resolving important personal issues. The therapist also works within the context of their employing institutions and is often a valued member of the multidisciplinary team. The art therapist will usually be involved in liaison with other professionals, and where appropriate with the families and carers of their clients.

In common with many healthcare professionals supervision of the art therapist's work (usually by another art therapist) is considered good practice. This allows the therapist to reflect upon their part in the therapeutic encounters with clients.

HOW DO ART THERAPISTS WORK?

Art therapists work with individuals, with groups of people and with families. They may also do joint work with colleagues from different professional backgrounds. As described earlier, art therapists work with the spontaneous art making of their clients and they can use different methods to facilitate this. Some art therapists give clients themes from which to work. Others leave it entirely up to their clients in the belief that whatever comes up is worth exploring.

The most commonly used model for understanding the therapeutic process at work in art therapy is the psychodynamic one. It assumes that there is a constant dynamic interaction at work between aspects of an individual's personality and the world in which they live. This model supposes that the individual's personality is shaped by their childhood relationships with their caretakers (usually parents) and that these relationships in turn are a product of the culture into which the person is born. The tension and conflict between different aspects of the individual's personality are assumed to be repressed and held out of awareness (in the unconscious) when they become unbearable. However, the resulting contents of the unconscious need to find expression and may do so through physical symptoms, recurrent behaviour and relationship patterns, and dreams. Art therapy is considered to provide an arena in which the unconscious elements of the individual's personality can become apparent (Dalley 1987). In this model a situation is seen as unhealthy when elements of the personality are unable to interrelate, with the resulting conflict causing a repression or a 'splitting off' of some aspect. The aim of therapy is to recover these 'lost' parts and to bring about some form of integration (Nowell Hall 1987; Schaverien 1992; Rust 1992). The roots of psychodynamic thought are found in the theories of Freud and Jung and in the work of those who have developed their ideas during the current century (for example Melanie Klein, Donald Winnicott, Marion Milner).

Another model that is used by art therapists comes from humanistic and existential ideas of psychology. While the psychodynamic and psychoanalytical traditions emphasise the destructive capacity of human beings, the humanistic position is to promote the individual's capacity for self-actualisation. The focus of art therapy in this view is on the generation of new facets of identity rather than the recovery of those that have been 'lost'. The focus is on how the person's actions and experiences in the present can guide and create their future rather than on how the past has determined where they are now (Arnheim 1966; McNiff 1981, 1992). This approach can be seen in some of the literature on arts therapies with people suffering life-threatening illness (for example Aldridge 1993).

The art therapist's understanding of his or her relationship with the client, and whether it can itself become a tool for therapy, will depend on which orientation the therapist favours most. This is described in terms of the 'transference', where the client's early relationships unconsciously determine their responses to the therapist. It has been proposed by some art therapy theorists (Schaverien 1992; Luzzatto 1994) that transference also occurs towards the client's artwork. By understanding the transference, and working with it, unconscious conflicts can become more conscious and thereby can move toward resolution (Case 1994).

Art therapy is a developing professional and academic discipline. Its practitioners bring to their encounters with clients not only insights gained from various psychological theories but also knowledge of their own art making and life experiences, and the understanding gained through their previous clinical work. A point made by Embleton Tudor and Tudor (1994) in relation to psychotherapy is worth making here: whatever the therapist's orientation, the characteristics of spontaneity, flexibility, openmindedness and creativity must enliven the techniques of their profession in order to provide clients with a genuinely therapeutic experience.

ART THERAPY RESEARCH

Research is one way in which art therapists can evaluate their work and the theories which relate to it; although the body of research in this field in Britain is still quite small. Gilroy and Lee (1995) reviewed the art therapy research in the UK and found it to be focused mainly on issues relating to the professional development of art therapy or to the exploration of clinical practice using case study-based research. They found little evidence that art therapists were interested in researching the outcomes of art therapy. The situation in the US is somewhat different. Gilroy (1992) points out that art therapy research is fairly commonplace in the US, due in part to the inclusion of research methodologies as part of the basic art therapy training. (This is in contrast to British art therapy courses where research skills are taught only at an advanced training level.) A substantial amount of art therapy research emanating from the US concentrates on developing diagnostic tools for 'reading' clients' artwork, and in the use of clients' art for assessment purposes. Gilroy (1992) is critical of this approach and wonders at its relevance to the clinical application of art therapy, and particularly to the ensuing therapeutic relationship.

There is much scope for the development of art therapy research both in the UK and abroad. The publication of the first British book on art therapy and music therapy research (Gilroy and Lee 1995) and the growing number of art therapists registered for research at master's degree level would indicate a profession now willing to examine itself critically. There are signs that research is being encouraged by employers too.[1] The increasing pressure within British healthcare to audit clinical services may, as a by-product, increase art therapists' skills and confidence in research techniques and encourage them to join a steady stream of art therapy researchers.

NOTE

1   The secondment of an art therapist (Simon Bell) for the purposes of developing a research post with Trent Palliative Care Centre is an exciting development in this direction.

REFERENCES

Aldridge, D. (1993) 'Hope, meaning and the creative arts therapies in the treatment of AIDS', *Arts in Psychotherapy*, vol. 20, pp. 285–297.

Arguile, R. (1992) 'Art therapy with children and adolescents' in D. Waller and A. Gilroy (eds) *Art Therapy: A Handbook*, Buckingham and Philadelphia: Open University Press.

Arnheim, R. (1954) *Art and Visual Perception*, Berkeley, CA: University of California Press.

Arnheim, R. (1966) *Towards a Psychology of Art: Collected Essays*, Berkeley and Los Angeles, CA: University of California Press.

Byers, A. (1995) 'Beyond marks. On working with elderly people with severe memory loss', *Inscape*, vol. 1, pp. 13–15.

Cagnoletta, M. della (1990) 'Art therapy in Italy', *Inscape*, Summer, pp. 23–25.

Case, C. (1994) 'Art therapy in analysis: advance/retreat in the belly of the spider', *Inscape*, vol. 1, p. 3–10.

Case, C. and Dalley, T. (1990) *Working with Children in Art Therapy*, London and New York: Routledge.

Case, C. and Dalley, T. (1992) *The Handbook of Art Therapy*, London and New York: Routledge

Charlton, S. (1984) 'Art therapy with long stay residents of psychiatric hospitals' in T. Dalley (ed.) *Art as Therapy*, London and New York: Tavistock/Routledge.

Connell, C. (1992) 'Art therapy as part of a palliative care programme', *Palliative Medicine*, vol. 6, pp. 18–25.

Crane, W. (1996) 'A consideration of the usefulness of art therapy for psychotic clients with artistic identities', *Inscape*, vol. 1, no. 1, pp. 20–28.

Dalley, T. (1987) 'Art as therapy: some new perspectives' in T. Dalley, C. Case, J. Schaverien, F. Weir, D. Halliday, P. Nowell Hall and D. Waller *Images of Art Therapy*, London and New York: Tavistock/Routledge.

Dalley, T., Rifkind, G. and Terry, K. (1993) *Three Voices of Art Therapy: Image, Client, Therapist*, London and New York: Routledge.

Embleton Tudor, L. and Tudor, K. (1994) 'The personal and the political: power, authority and influence in psychotherapy' in P. Clarkson and M. Pokorny (eds) *The Handbook of Psychotherapy*, London and New York: Routledge.

Frampton, D.R. (1986) 'Restoring creativity to the dying patient', *British Medical Journal* 20/27 December, vol. 293, pp. 1593–1595.

Gilroy, A. (1992) 'Research in art therapy' in D. Waller and A. Gilroy (eds) *Art Therapy: A Handbook*, Buckingham and Philadelphia: Open University Press.

Gilroy, A. and Lee, C. (eds) (1995) *Art and Music: Therapy and Research*, London: Routledge.

Kaye, C. and Blee, T. (1997) *The Arts in Health Care*, London: Jessica Kingsley.

Killick, K. (1991) 'The practice of art therapy with patients in acute psychotic states', *Inscape*, Winter, pp. 2–6.

Killick, K. and Greenwood, H. (1995) 'Research in art therapy with people who have psychotic illnesses' in A. Gilroy and C. Lee (eds) *Art and Music: Therapy and Research*, London: Routledge.

Levens, M. (1995) *Eating Disorders and Magical Control of The Body. Treatment through Art Therapy*, London and New York: Routledge.

Luzzatto, P. (1994) 'The mental double trap of the anorexic patient' in D. Dokter (ed.) *Arts Therapies and Clients with Eating Disorders: Fragile Board*, London and Bristol: Jessica Kingsley.

Luzzatto, P. and Gabriel, G. (1998) 'Art psychotherapy' in J. Holland *et al.* (eds) *Psycho-oncology*, Oxford: Oxford University Press.

Mahony, J. and Waller, D. (1992) 'Art therapy in the treatment of alcohol and drug abuse' in D. Waller and A. Gilroy (eds) *Art Therapy: A Handbook*, Buckingham and Philadelphia: Open University Press.

Malitskie, G. (1988) 'Art therapy with kidney patients', *Inscape*, Spring, pp. 14–17.

McNiff, S. (1981) *The Arts and Psychotherapy*, Springfield, IL: Charles C. Thomas.

McNiff, S. (1992) *Art as Medicine: Creating a Therapy of the Imagination*, Boston and New York: Shambala.

Mann, D. (1990) 'Art as a defence mechanism against creativity', *British Journal of Psychotherapy*, vol. 7, no. 1, pp. 5–14.

Miller, B. (1984) 'Art therapy with the elderly and terminally ill' in T. Dalley (ed.) *Art as Therapy*, London and New York: Tavistock/Routledge.

Murphy, J. (1984) 'The use of art therapy in the treatment of anorexia nervosa' in T. Dalley (ed.) *Art as Therapy*, London and New York: Tavistock/Routledge.

Nowell Hall, P. (1987) 'Art therapy: a way of healing the split' in Dalley *et al.* (eds) *Images of Art Therapy*, London and New York: Tavistock/ Routledge.

Rust, M. (1992) 'Art therapy in the treatment of women with eating disorders' in D. Waller and A. Gilroy (eds) *Art Therapy: A Handbook*, Buckingham and Philadelphia: Open University Press.

Rust, M. (1994) 'Art therapy in the treatment of women with eating disorders' in D. Dokter (ed.) *Arts Therapies and Clients with Eating Disorders: Fragile Board*, London and Bristol: Jessica Kingsley.

Rycroft, C. (1985) *Psychoanalysis and Beyond*, London: Chatto and Windus/Hogarth Press.

Schaverien, J. (1992) *The Revealing Image*, London and New York: Routledge.

Schaverien, J. (1995) *Desire and the Female Therapist: Engendered Gazes in Psychotherapy and Art Therapy*, London and New York: Routledge.

Stack, M. (1996) 'Humpty dumpty had a great fall', *Inscape*, vol. 1, no. 1, pp. 1–13.

Stott, J. and Males, B. (1984) 'Art therapy for people who are mentally handicapped' in T. Dalley (ed.) *Art as Therapy*, London and New York: Tavistock/Routledge.

Strand, S. (1990) 'Counteracting isolation: group art therapy for people with learning difficulties', *Group Analysis*, vol. 23, pp. 255–263.

Szepanski, M. (1988) 'Art therapy and multiple sclerosis', *Inscape*, Spring, pp. 4–10.

Thomas, G. (1995) 'Art therapy and practice in palliative care', *European Journal of Palliative Care*, vol. 2, no. 3, pp. 120–121.

Tipple, R. (1992) 'Art therapy with people who have severe learning difficulties' in D. Waller and A. Gilroy (eds) *Art Therapy: A Handbook*, Buckingham and Philadelphia: Open University Press.

Tipple, R. (1994) 'Communication and interpretation in art therapy with people who have a learning disability', *Inscape*, vol. 2, pp. 31–35.

Vasarhelyi, V. (1992) 'Visual psychotherapy: the Hungarian challenge', *Inscape*, Winter, pp. 21–34.

Waller, D. (1991) *Becoming a Profession*, London: Routledge.

Waller, D. (1992) 'The development of art therapy in Italy', *Inscape*, Winter, pp. 9–17.

Waller, D. (1995) 'The development of art therapy in Bulgaria: infiltrating the system' in A. Gilroy and C. Lee (eds) *Art and Music: Therapy and Research*, London and New York: Routledge.

Wood, M. (1984) 'The child and art therapy' in T. Dalley (ed.) *Art as Therapy*, London and New York: Tavistock/Routledge.

Wood, M.J.M. (1990) 'Art therapy in one session: working with people with AIDS', *Inscape*, Winter, pp. 27–33.

Chapter 2

What is palliative care?

Michèle J.M. Wood

Palliative care aims to preserve a person's dignity and quality of life in the face of incurable illness. In this chapter I shall present an overview of what such care entails and shall look at some of the current issues for palliative care in Britain. First of all, however, it is important to make a distinction between a life-threatening illness and a terminal one, since the two terms are used with some degree of overlap throughout this book. For a person with a diagnosis of cancer, treatment through chemotherapy, radiotherapy and surgery may offer the possibility that the cancer will be removed. In such cases the person is described as going into 'remission' and there is a hope that the cancer will not recur. For someone in this position the term palliative care may not be strictly appropriate since it refers to care provided when illness cannot be cured. The work of art therapists described in this book is intended to illustrate a way of working with individuals who have had to face their own mortality and associated losses whether or not death will be the outcome. This issue is explored in the final chapter by Barbara Morley, who used art therapy following her own diagnosis of cancer.

INTRODUCTION

The network of facilities which provide palliative care is complex and growing. There are now hospice and palliative care services in over seventy countries of the world. There are in-patient hospices, day hospices, children's hospices and services which offer hospice care in the patient's own home. In January 1996 the Hospice Information Service established that there were 3,215 hospice beds available, provided for by a total of 217 different in-patient units in the UK. They also identified that there are about 56,000 admissions to hospices annually, with 100,000 patients each year being seen at home by palliative care nurses. In addition to the range of services for patients, the palliative approach includes an educational remit to provide and extend its aims throughout the health service. Establishments which offer hospice and palliative care also provide training for professionals working in their own and other areas of healthcare provision. This ranges from informal teaching sessions for locally based groups to professionally accredited courses at diploma and degree level.

Patients and their families do not have to pay for palliative care services. These are funded partly through the National Health Service (NHS) and partly through charitable giving. The majority of hospice and palliative services are provided by registered charities which operate in the voluntary or independent sector.

The range of ways in which palliative care is delivered is made even more impressive by the fact that this field has only developed in the last thirty years.

The beginnings of palliative care: the modern hospice movement

In 1967 Dame Cicely Saunders started the first hospice, St Christopher's, in Sydenham, London, and instigated a world-wide movement. The notion of 'hospice' was not new but dated back to the fifth century when monks would provide shelter for travellers and those in need. Working as a nurse and social worker in NHS hospitals, Cicely Saunders was appalled at the marginalisation of those who were dying by a medical establishment which was preoccupied with 'curing'. In such a climate those who could not be cured were regarded as 'medical failures' and little point was seen in taking time to address their needs for adequate pain relief or support in the process of dying. In pioneering what was to become the modern hospice movement Saunders aimed to combine compassionate care with the best scientific techniques available for controlling physical symptoms. Amongst her many ideas Saunders conceived of the one which is central to palliative care's holistic approach – 'total pain'. This is the recognition that pain has emotional, psychological and social components as well as physical ones, and in order to adequately care for the patient all aspects of their suffering need to be addressed. The foundation upon which palliative care has been built has been described by Saunders (1996: ii) as 'the best in symptom control and the understanding of emotional and family needs'. The aim of hospice care favours quality of life over quantity, but as many working in this area point out increasing quality of life for the individual may well result in an increase in its length also.

Cotter (1981) maintains that the hospice movement should be regarded as a human rights movement for the way in which it advocates that patients should have an increased involvement in and responsibility for the circumstances surrounding their own deaths, and for the inclusion of family members in this process. This is in contrast to the notion of active euthanasia, which, if it were legalised in the UK, would allow individuals to request that their lives are deliberately brought to an end. The achievements of the hospice movement to control and ease suffering calls into question the need for euthanasia. In fact, Crowther (1993) contends that if the good practice developed in palliative care were universal there would be no need for active euthanasia. The promotion of palliative care on an international level can be seen in the recently signed Barcelona Declaration which is aimed at lobbying the support of governments through the world (see Appendix IV).

WHAT DOES PALLIATIVE CARE MEAN?

The National Council for Hospice and Specialist Palliative Care Services has defined palliative care as:

> the active, total care of patients whose disease no longer responds to curative treatment, and for whom the goal must be the best quality of life for them and their families. . . . It focuses on controlling pain and other symptoms, easing suffering and enhancing the life that remains. It integrates the psychological and spiritual aspects of care, to enable patients to live out their lives with dignity, as well as offering support to families both during the patient's illness and their bereavement. It offers a unique combination of care in hospices and at home.
>
> (Hospice Information Service 1996: iii)

From this we can see that palliative care endeavours to respond to the patient in a holistic way. The patient and their family are placed at the centre of a circle of care which is itself made up of the various professionals, agencies and informal carers most appropriate to provide for that specific patient. This model is described as patient-centred, patient-focused or patient-led care. There are subtle distinctions between these terms, particularly when the patient may no longer be able to direct their care (through cognitive impairment or during the terminal phase). However, the central point is that palliative care is tailored to meet the individual needs of a particular patient and those with whom they are in a close relationship. For palliative care to be most effective a cohesive team of formal and informal carers must be established. This will comprise professionals based in the patient's community and in the hospices or hospitals. Hancock (1993) has aptly described palliative care as a multidisciplinary subject.

Funding

The national charities which provide palliative care in the UK are Cancer Relief Macmillan Fund, Marie Curie Cancer Care and the Sue Ryder Foundation. These charities have funded in-patient units, day centres and home care teams. Marie Curie nurses, for example, provide round the clock nursing care for people in their own homes. Given these sources of funding, hospice and palliative care has traditionally been almost exclusively for people with cancers. However, this is now changing, with many units providing services for those with other life-threatening illnesses such as motor neurone disease and HIV/AIDS.

Meeting needs: the multidisciplinary team at work

The delivery of hospice and palliative care is essentially multidisciplinary through a cohesive team of professionals, volunteers and carers, at the centre of which is the patient and their family. Families and friends have an important role to play not only as part of the unit to be cared for (as mentioned earlier), but also as part of the team of care-givers.

Each palliative care facility has its own combination of professionals who make up the multidisciplinary team. However, the most usual members are: doctors, nurses, occupational therapists, physiotherapists, chaplains, social workers, counsellors, dieticians, day centre workers, art therapists, music therapists, complementary therapists (such as aromatherapists, massage therapists) and volunteers. In order to understand how the multidisciplinary team provides palliative care to the patient and their family let us take a brief look at the physical, social, emotional/psychological and spiritual aspects of care. It is important to bear in mind that these different aspects of a person's experience are not discrete and there are many overlaps and connections; the effective communication between team members ensures that these connections continue and that the integrity of the person is maintained by this integrated model of care.

The physical aspect

This element of a patient's care is managed by the co-ordinated efforts of doctors, nurses, dieticians and physiotherapists. The doctors' and nurses' aim is to control symptoms, alleviate pain and provide as much information to the patient and their family about what is happening to them as they wish to know. Explanations about the disease process are part of good symptom control (Kaye 1994). Nurses have regular daily contact with the patient and their family and are often the first to become aware of any needs which require help from other members of the team. Dieticians are often involved to help patients who have eating and swallowing difficulties, particularly when these are due to side-effects of medications. Dieticians also help to improve an individual's nutritional intake, which will significantly enhance their quality of life. Physiotherapists address issues of mobility and provide programmes designed to maximise an individual's function within the constraints of their illness.

The social aspect

Illness brings with it changes on many different levels. For adults employment will eventually cease to be possible and with this comes financial, and in some cases, accommodation difficulties. Certainly as the patient becomes increasingly unwell changes will need to be made to their accommodation. The tasks and roles usually fulfilled by the patient will be passed onto others creating a dependency which may be uncomfortable for them. Usually relatives step in, but some formal assistance may be needed such as home helps, foster carers for children, or regular visits from a district nurse. Social workers, based either in the community or as part of the palliative care team, are responsible for dealing with this aspect of a patient's care. They also work closely with voluntary agencies or charities who provide funding for holidays, furniture or other material needs. Social workers may also be involved in cases where state benefits need to be organised, and they may assist relatives in the tasks following a death. Social workers also provide a counselling service, and may be involved in co-ordinating palliative services for families.

The rehabilitative needs of the patient draw in other members of the team. Kaye (1994: 203) defines the aim of such help as 'enabling a person to achieve their maximum potential for living'. Nurses work with the patient to encourage self-care, and occupational therapists work with the patient on their capabilities to function in their own homes and in carrying out the necessary tasks of daily living. Issues relating to the patient's productive use of time and recreational interests are also addressed by occupational therapists in order to restore a sense of purpose to the patient and to increase their sense of self-esteem.

There may be other members of the multidisciplinary team who will be useful to the patient on a social level, such as volunteers and befrienders who can offer many different interests and activities to the patient on an informal level. Many of these services are provided by day centres, or on an out-patient basis. The possibility for patients to use day services also gives their partners and family a respite from daytime caring.

There are many staff in hospices, day centres and clinics who contribute to the patient's care. In discussing the workings of a team in an AIDS hospice Marcetti and Lunn (1993: 24) write: 'Next to the nursing staff the housekeepers are people who provide an important sense of continuity for hospice residents as they will be seen every day while providing practical services.'

The emotional and psychological aspect

The emotional and psychological adjustments that have to be made to illness and the multitude of losses that accompany it are immense. Consequently, emotional support needs to be available to the patient and their family from the time of diagnosis right through to the time when the patient is in the terminal phase. And bereavement support should be available to the family once the patient has died. Many hospices and palliative care services have counsellors, nurse counsellors, social workers, art therapists, music therapists and psychotherapists at hand to help the patient or family member explore and express their feelings. According to Kaye (1994) 50 per cent of hospice patients and their families actively seek counselling help for their emotions.

In one respect all members of the palliative care team need to recognise and respond to the emotional and psychological aspects of their patients' lives, since they inform every element of care. However, there are issues which benefit

from the involvement of a professional trained to provide emotional or psychological support, for example, in areas around changing body image, pain control,
relationships and death and dying. In many hospices or palliative care teams
there are often good links with outside psychiatric or psychological services
which can be called upon when needed. In many hospitals there are also advi-
sory services which offer emotional support (as well as information on pain
relief and symptom control).

The spiritual aspect

The holistic view of the individual that characterises the palliative care approach
supposes that human nature contains physical and spiritual elements. However,
the spiritual is not to be confused with religious beliefs and practices, for it is
argued that whilst everyone has a spiritual part of themselves not everyone
expresses this in a religious way.

Spirituality is concerned with an individual's sense of themselves in relation
to the history of their culture, the world in which they live and the meaning
they attribute to this position. It is expressed in many ways regarding relationships with others, with the environment and in ideas about the future.
Religion is regarded as the framework of beliefs and rituals which represent
spiritual concerns and through which these are made manifest. The inevitable
journey towards death, of which we are all aware whether consciously or not,
and which becomes particularly clear at times of illness, will give rise to spiritual considerations. Spiritual pain is thus recognised as a struggle with existential
questions – Why? Why me? Why this illness? Why now? (Kaye 1994).

Spiritual pain is seen in a person's search for meaning in their situation, and
in their re-evaluation of their lives. Illness and the realities of death may threaten
an individual's system of beliefs and challenge their sense of personal meaning
and self-worth. There is an appreciation amongst palliative care staff that spiritual support can be provided in times of 'ordinariness', such as those found
in moments of routine care. Kaye (ibid.: 216) writes: 'Spiritual distress has a
habit of emerging in intimate and relaxing moments such as provided by a bed-
bath or a hair-do or a massage.' Although this attitude of respect and support
may inform the most practical of contacts with a patient, there are specific ways
in which spiritual support is offered. These include, imagework, art therapy and
reminiscence, all of which are to be undertaken by therapists trained in these
areas (ibid.).

The expression of spiritual pain and a subsequent search for meaning can
lead people who have held no religious belief to consider theological explanations. All hospices have chaplains on their staff and usually have access to
authorities or leaders from other religious communities (Buddhist, Hindu,
Muslim, Sikh, Jewish, for example).

For some patients religious rituals are very important, particularly as they
approach death. Patients and their partners and family are encouraged (if they

are willing) to discuss the rituals they wish to have at the time of death and some patients are keen to be involved in plans for their funeral arrangements.

As described at the beginning of this chapter, hospices and palliative care services are predominantly voluntary sector agencies which have a religious, particularly Christian, foundation. In this respect they have been able to put spirituality on the agenda for the care of those living with incurable illness. However, one criticism levelled at them is that they can appear to be white, middle-class, Christian institutions. There is evidence that many palliative care establishments are engaged in a continual exploration of the spiritual needs and spiritual care of all those facing death. The opening of a multi-faith hospice in London (The North London Hospice) is one example of a development in this area.

When someone dies: ways of understanding loss and bereavement

The changes brought about by loss of any sort can produce profound insecurity and a resulting loss of self-esteem. Grief over the death of someone close is a special case of loss characterised by a range of physical, emotional and psychological reactions. The insecurity and diminished self-esteem produced by grief can be devastating and the changes it brings constitute a huge challenge of adjustment. Mourning is the term used to describe the process of adaptation to life without the deceased. Grief and mourning are natural, normal responses to an extraordinarily difficult and painful experience. The range of physical, psychological and emotional reactions associated with straightforward grief have been described by Parkes (1986), Bowlby (1980) and others as following a pattern. It has been observed that immediately after the death the bereaved experience numbness, shock and disbelief (even where the death was anticipated). Gradually this gives way to a period of suffering characterised by a complex assortment of feelings and physical symptoms. These range from trembling, loss of appetite and disturbed sleep to acute anxiety as memories of early loss are reawakened. Visions and obsessively replaying the events around the death are not uncommon but can give rise to fears of mental illness. Searching or yearning for the deceased can result in profound sadness or despair. Emotions such as anger, guilt, shame and fear which cannot be directed at the deceased may generate difficult behaviour which only serves to increase isolation. Eventually the time arrives when this suffering becomes noticeably more tolerable and a gradual reorganisation becomes possible. Ideally the bereaved can adapt to a life re-structured to provide a new sense of security which in turn reflects a new found self-esteem.

The concept of psychological defences offers an explanation for the behaviours seen in people who have suffered a significant loss. These defences are regarded as a necessary means by which the individual is prevented from being overwhelmed by the anxiety and psychic pain of grief (see Appendix II). These enable the full impact of the loss to be deflected until the person is gradually able to accept what has happened. These defences as such are a healthy coping strategy, a necessary part of the grieving process which should not be challenged during the weeks and months immediately after the death. However, for some individuals whose grief is complicated by other factors (see Appendix I) these defences may eventually become unhelpful. They may become integrated into the person's behaviour, preventing a re-adjustment to life without the deceased. In such cases the involvement of a trained counsellor or therapist may be helpful. The timing of such interventions is critical. Recent research indicates that, particularly for those affected by traumatic loss, immediate intervention may actually deepen the trauma and constitute an unwarranted assault on the individual's defences (McEwan, personal communication).

The pattern of grief and mourning described so far suggests a linear progression leading to an emotional detachment from the deceased as the only truly healthy outcome. Worden (1993) points out that the process of mourning is not so much linear as that of making a number of adjustments which he summarises as 'tasks' of mourning. The first task is to accept the reality of the loss, then to work through the pain of grief, then to adjust to an environment in which the deceased is missing and finally to emotionally relocate the deceased and move on with life. This model is often used by griefwork counsellors.

Walter (1996) takes issue with the view that the purpose of grief is to emotionally detach from the deceased. Instead he proposes the creation of what he terms a 'durable biography' of the dead. This is constructed through discussion with others who knew the deceased as a means of integrating the memory of the dead into the bereaved person's ongoing life. Walter points to the difficulty of undertaking the enterprise of a durable biography in contemporary society unaided by tradition. He describes a society peopled by individuals who 'become self-referential, continually having to construct and reconstruct their identity' (1996: 15). The insecurity produced by grief and many of the emotions that come in its wake are not easily set aside. Sharing memories must inevitably evoke feelings and may even serve to intensify the sense of isolation the mourner feels if these are not validated. Indeed, in his account of the sharing of memories that followed the death of a friend, Walter refers to others who had fallen out with her and concludes 'How they struggled to make sense of things I know not' (ibid.: 13).

One example of support offered to whose who have been bereaved is griefwork groups, which are described by Mandy Pratt in Chapter 13, where art therapy offers individuals the opportunity to tell their stories and to integrate memories in a constructive and supportive setting.

Staff support

Hospice and palliative staff teams are often referred to as communities of care. This implies that staff are expected to embody the palliative care philosophy and display an attitude of respect for the patient, whose illness is never allowed to overshadow who they are as a person. Inevitably this involves a degree of emotional attachment between staff and their patients. Staff are not exempt from the feelings of grief associated with the many deaths of those whose lives they have shared. Some research by Baker and Seager (1991) shows that hospice staff find it more stressful working with patients who are younger than the average hospice patient who is generally past middle age or elderly. This is presumably linked to a sense of the 'natural order of things' in which the young are not expected to die before their elders. Many hospices recognise the importance of staff support and provide staff counsellors and staff support groups. In many settings the speedy organisation of staff debriefing meetings following particularly difficult situations also helps to address the stress of the work head on. In discussing the literature on staff stress and burnout in palliative care Vachon (1995) observes that teamwork is one of the most important coping mechanisms for hospice staff. She points out that staff support programmes and team development were high priorities from the beginning of the hospice movement, and that the literature indicates that they continue to contribute to the management of stress within staff teams. One use of art therapy within hospices has been to provide staff support groups with team building exercises. This will be discussed in the next chapter.

Informal carers

Formal carers are those professionals who are paid to provide a service to the patient. However formal carers only give part of the overall care received by the person who is dying. Informal carers such as the family, friends and neighbours play a vital role. In fact much of the bereavement support characteristic of hospice care is provided by trained volunteers and relatives. Wilkes (1993) points out that the incorporation of volunteers into hospices in the early days of the movement was a deliberate attempt to deprofessionalise the care of the dying and was not (as might rather cynically be assumed) a money saving measure. The involvement of close family and friends in all aspects of the patient's care is unquestionably an essential aim of good practice. This, however, puts the family in an unusual position of being part of the identified unit of care and part of the team of caregivers. Neale (1993) points out that this can be problematic when the carers' needs are lost under a pressure to continue to care, particularly when formal agencies are relying on them. There is a danger here if family members continue to care to a point where they exhaust themselves, and Neale alerts the palliative care team to be sensitive to carers' needs much earlier.

ISSUES WITHIN PALLIATIVE CARE

The complex needs of individuals facing the final phases of life with an incurable condition and those of their families raise many issues worthy of consideration.

I would like to briefly discuss three which have an impact on all those working within palliative care as well as on the nature of the care they are able to provide. These are: cultural and lifestyle differences; the apparent increasing medicalisation of care; and the auditing of palliative care.

Cultural and lifestyle differences

One area that has received very little attention despite the enormous expansion of services is how best to respond to the religious, cultural and lifestyle differences of the people who could benefit from palliative care facilities. Britain is now recognised as being a multicultural society and so there is a great imperative for healthcare professionals to ensure their practice is informed by an understanding of this cultural diversity. Firth (1993) points out that a person's cultural background will determine the way in which they respond to treatment and choose to die. She suggests three factors which can make it difficult for a dying patient from a non-British culture to receive the religious and emotional support they need, particularly in NHS hospitals. These are: problems in communication, racism in care providers and a lack of facilities. The use of young children or family members to act as interpreters for the patient is one way in which some establishments attempt to overcome problems of communication. However, many practitioners regard this as inappropriate and not in the best interests of the patient as they may become dependent on those with a limited understanding or with whom they are emotionally involved and who may censor the information passed on. It is suggested that trained patient advocates and link workers from ethnic minorities are used instead. Ideally, states Firth, interpreters should be familiar with the patient's language, medical terminology and the culture of both parties. She cites several writers who suggest that a lack of sensitivity and the prevalence of assumptions about a patient's capacity to understand are unhelpful and a manifestation of racism. To overcome this Firth suggests that workers should be encouraged to take time to find out about social and religious needs relating to issues such as women, modesty, food and rituals for the time of death. She suggests that facilities within hospitals and hospices need to be made available for relatives to conduct the rituals that are an important part of their cultural obligations. As an example she describes the Hindu belief that death should ideally occur on the floor, with the person's head placed to the north as it is believed their soul will be released more easily. She cites cases where elderly Hindu patients have been lifted back into their beds by nurses unaware of what they were attempting to do. Firth emphasises that ceremonial acts not correctly undertaken at the time of death are believed to have negative consequences for the bereaved family in many cultures. Thus the provision of special facilities for these purposes, such as rooms for ritual washing or mourning, or a mattress on the floor, can be crucial for the relatives' long-term peace of mind.

However, Firth maintains that it is important for professionals to view patients as individuals who need to be consulted on the particular religious practices they wish to observe, rather than make assumptions about what is required based on stereotypes. This may be particularly true for second and third generation members of ethnic groups who may have distanced themselves from many traditional practices. Firth points out that the holistic approach which is central to high-quality palliative care should be available to all sections of the community.

There has been very little discussion in the palliative care literature in relation to lifestyle differences between professionals and their patients and the impact this has on the care provided. The advent of AIDS has brought a much younger population of patients into palliative care services (and as mentioned earlier it can be stressful for staff working with younger patients). The initial prevalence of HIV amongst marginalised subgroups within British society (homosexual men, injecting drug users and people from the African continent) has challenged the agencies who provide palliative care to adjust and develop a model that takes into account many new issues. Same sex partnerships challenge notions of 'family', difficulties of pain control in injecting drug users can cause management problems and working with the secrecy surrounding sexuality and HIV status add up to a very complex picture of needs for the palliative care team to respond to.

An increase in the medicalisation of palliative care?

The acceptance of palliative medicine by the Royal College of Physicians as a sub-speciality of general medicine has been regarded by many (for example Ahmedzai 1993) as a move away from the community towards hospital-based medicine where the 'medical model' is prevalent. Along with this there have been tremendous medical advances in the management of difficult symptoms seen in the terminal stages of life. This pulls away from the holistic palliative approach which is essentially not dominated by the medical view. This apparent medicalisation has given rise to fears that the process of dying may be overshadowed by the increasing expertise in palliative techniques now able to relieve difficult symptoms right into the terminal phase. The emotional and spiritual care which could be offered at an earlier stage may therefore be relegated to the sidelines by the thrust to alleviate symptoms. Biswas (1993) is concerned that an increasing medical perspective of palliative care (uncoupled from the other aspects) reduces death to yet another symptom to be relieved. The sharing of care between formal and informal carers which is characteristic of the palliative care approach seems threatened too. Wilkes (1993) describes the significant advances in medicine as having the unfortunate effect of deskilling and diminishing the confidence of ordinary members of the community who would normally deal with matters of death. This issue is linked to the next one, that of auditing.

Auditing palliative care

Many practitioners are faced with the challenge to audit their practice in order to describe, measure and evaluate what they do. This has been linked with setting standards of care which provide a benchmark of good practice, and such standard setting is in turn linked to the funding of the services in question. This has led to a pressure to develop auditing techniques. Finding techniques that are sensitive to all the elements of palliative care is a real challenge, particularly for those that are the most subjective, that is the emotional and spiritual aspects. Physical symptoms are more amenable to measurement and are therefore easier to produce for audit purposes. Some writers (for example Biswas 1993) are concerned that with funding being linked to auditing, services may become less multidisciplinary and more medically 'led'.

It is interesting at this point to reflect upon the development of the hospice movement in the US. Although this was inspired by the work of Saunders and others in Britain, the delivery of current hospice care in the States contrasts with our system notably around the issue of payment of fees. The health insurance schemes, and the American healthcare reimbursement schemes (for those individuals who do not have a private insurance), will not reimburse certain basic hospice services. One example given by Lunceford (1981) is that of bereavement visits by hospice staff. Wilkes (1993) describes difficulties in the American system arising from restrictive funding and a conflict between hospices and physicians who are in competition for funds to treat the same patients. Consequently hospices in the US are primarily community-oriented with an emphasis being placed on volunteers and self-help activities. Wilkes describes the correlation between the influence of general physicians in hospice care and their interest in treatments which can be seen to be profitable. He cites as an example of this the intravenous feeding of dying patients, a practice that would cause concern in Britain.

With the current changes in the National Health Service in the UK and the implementation of the NHS and Community Care Act 1991, hospices are now having to re-think their previous position of autonomy and independence in relation to the NHS. Hospices or voluntary agencies offering hospice care must now enter the 'marketplace' and negotiate for contracts with health authorities willing to purchase their services. As described earlier, hospices are funded partly from charitable giving and partly from the NHS which in the past has been in the form of specially designated (ring-fenced) funds. Clark (1993) points out that, given fund-raising difficulties in a period of economic recession in the UK and the loss of ring-fenced monies from central government, the financial future for hospices may be at risk.

The challenge to audit palliative care is one that needs careful and creative consideration so that the essence of the multidisciplinary approach to living the ending of life well and dying with dignity are not lost.

To conclude, palliative care is concerned with maintaining the integrity of an individual's experience of themselves in the face of incurable physical illness and eventual death. It is concerned with enabling the person to achieve and enjoy an optimal quality of life that is free from physical pain and to enable them to die with dignity. Palliative care recognises that the person who is sick is in relationship with family, partners and friends and whilst these people provide care for the patient they too need the attention and support of the palliative care team.

REFERENCES

Ahmedzai, S. (1993) 'The medicalization of dying', in D. Clark (ed.) *The Future of Palliative Care: Issues of Policy and Practice*, Buckingham: Open University Press.

Baker, N.T. and Seager, R.T. (1991) 'A comparison of psychosocial needs of hospice patients with AIDS and those with diagnoses', *The Hospice Journal*, vol. 7, no. 1/2: 61–69.

Biswas, B. (1993) 'The medicalization of dying: a nurse's view', in D. Clark (ed.) *The Future of Palliative Care: Issues of Policy and Practice*, Buckingham: Open University Press.

Bowlby, J. (1980) *Attachment and Loss: vol. 3. Loss*, London: Hogarth Press.

Clark, D. (ed.) (1993) *The Future of Palliative Care: Issues of Policy and Practice*, Buckingham: Open University Press.

Cotter, Z.M. (1981) 'Hospice as a human rights movement' in C. Saunders, D.H. Summers and N. Teller (eds) *Hospice: The Living Idea*, London: Edward Arnold.

Crowther, T. (1993) 'Euthanasia' in D. Clark (ed.) *The Future of Palliative Care: Issues of Policy and Practice*, Buckingham: Open University Press.

Feakins, A. (1993) 'Impact of caring for HIV/AIDS patients upon staff', unpublished essay for Diploma Social Work, St Helena Hospice, Colchester.

Firth, S. (1993) 'Cultural issues in terminal care' in D. Clark (ed.) *The Future of Palliative Care: Issues of Policy and Practice*, Buckingham: Open University Press.

Hancock, B. (1993) 'Foreword' in D. Clark (ed.) *The Future of Palliative Care: Issues of Policy and Practice*, Buckingham: Open University Press, pp. x–xi.

Hospice Information Service (1996) *The Hospice Directory*, St Christopher's Hospice, Sydenham, London.

Kaye, P. (1994) *A to Z of Hospice and Palliative Medicine*, Northampton: EPL Publications.

McEwan (1996) Personal communication.

Marcetti, A. and Lunn, S. (1993) *A Place of Growth: Counselling and Pastoral Care of People with AIDS,* London: Darton, Longman and Todd.

Lunceford, J. (1981) 'Hospice in America' in C. Saunders, D.H. Summers and N. Teller (eds) *Hospice: The Living Idea*, London: Edward Arnold.

Neale, B. (1993) 'Informal care and community care' in D. Clark (ed.) *The Future of Palliative Care: Issues of Policy and Practice*, Buckingham: Open University Press.

Parkes, C.M. (1986) *Bereavement. Studies of Grief in Adult Life*, London: Tavistock.

Saunders, C. (1996) 'Introduction' in Hospice Information Service, *The Hospice Directory*, St. Christopher's Hospice, Sydenham, London.

Vachon, M.L.S. (1995) 'Staff stress in hospice/palliative care: a review', *Palliative Medicine*, vol. 9: 91–122.

Walter, T. (1996) 'A new model of grief: bereavement and biography', *Mortality*, vol. 1, no. 1: 13.

Wilkes, E. (1993) 'Introduction' in D. Clark (ed.) The *Future of Palliative Care: Issues of Policy and Practice*, Buckingham: Open University Press.

Worden, J.W. (1993) *Grief Counselling and Grief Therapy*, London: Routledge.

FURTHER READING

Parkes, C.M., Laungani, P. and Young, B. (1997) *Death and Bereavement Across Cultures*, London: Routledge.

Sheldon, F. (1997) *Psychosocial Palliative Care. Good Practice in the Care of the Dying and Bereaved,* Cheltenham: Stanley Thornes.

Chapter 3

Art therapy in palliative care

Michèle J.M. Wood

In the previous chapters I have outlined what art therapy is and have described the principles of palliative care. In this chapter I will look directly at how art therapists have used their skills in providing care for those who are physically ill or dying. I shall begin by saying something of how art therapy developed in this area, before going on to outline its benefits to palliative care. Some mention will also be made of issues that need further thought and exploration. In this way I hope to provide a backdrop against which the chapters in Part II can be read.

A BRIEF HISTORY

Art therapy in Britain began in the 1940s with a few artists using their skills to work with hospital patients suffering with a physical or terminal condition (Waller 1991). The most famous of these was Adrian Hill, an artist recovering from tuberculosis, who found that his own artwork helped in his recovery and who went on to work with patients in a similar condition. Other links between art and medicine were being forged at a similar time with research being undertaken by neuro-psychiatrists into the art of psychotic patients and in the collation of artwork made by psychiatric patients (one famous example of the latter is Prinzhorn's collection of pictures).

The successful work of the early pioneers of art therapy gave a certain credence to the idea of art as therapy (see Waller, ibid., for a thorough description). However, with the demise of the TB sanatoria, these artists moved into other areas of healthcare, particularly those which offered psychological treatments. It was out of their innovative work, amid a climate of interest and growth in psychological therapies and the arts, that the profession of art therapy grew, becoming formalised with the creation of the British Association of Art Therapists (BAAT) in 1964.

Art therapy practice continued to develop with an ever increasing range of clients, although predominantly in mental health and mental handicap (later to be re-named 'learning disability') settings (see Chapter 1). It was not until the 1980s that art therapists appeared to be working again with people with terminal illnesses. Miller (1984) detailed his work with the elderly and terminally ill, and in 1988 *Inscape*, the journal of the British Association of Art Therapists, devoted an entire issue to the subject. In 1987 an unpublished paper by Sumaya McIntyre outlined a research project exploring the use of art therapy with people who had leukaemia. Over the next few years art therapists were gradually employed to develop services in hospitals, hospices and other palliative settings around the UK.

The need for mutual support and a forum for the exchange of ideas led to regular meetings for this dispersed collection of art therapists. These meetings became study days and the number of their participants grew until it was decided to formalise what had now become an identifiable group of practitioners. In 1993 the group became a special interest group within BAAT and called itself 'The Creative Response'. Since then more posts have been created for art therapy in palliative care settings. In 1994 The Corinne Burton Memorial Trust established the first studentship at Goldsmiths' College, University of London, specifically aimed at training art therapists for work in palliative care. It is envisaged that 1999 will see the publication of a database of arts therapies available nationwide for all those with a life-threatening illness.

And so we can see that art therapy has come full circle, returning to the clients who first demonstrated the therapeutic benefits of using art during times of extreme physical illness. Fifty years later art therapists are equipped not only with a training in art (like their artist forebears), but also with the insights gained during a postgraduate training in art therapy and the evolution of theory and practice during the last half century.

Since the early 1980s there has been a slowly growing body of literature on the use of art therapy, music therapy and creative arts therapies in palliative care. The majority of writers use case studies to describe their work. The literature comes mainly from the UK, Canada and the US and there are significant differences in the way in which art therapy is practised either side of the Atlantic. In addition there is evidence of work being carried out in Germany (Aldridge 1993; Herrmann 1996) and Italy (Belfiore 1994).

In looking at the literature on art therapy (and in some cases arts therapies) I would like to examine three questions. First, in order to gain a sense of the sorts of people and places that have responded to art therapy, I ask – where has art therapy been provided and for whom? Second, what do those writing about their work consider to be its benefits? Lastly, what important ideas are emerging for consideration from the interchange between art therapy and palliative care?

WHERE AND WITH WHOM IS ART THERAPY BEING USED?

Art therapy has been used with those suffering a life-threatening illness and their loved ones in several settings: hospices (Bekter McIntyre 1990;

Wood 1990; Thomas 1995; Mayo 1996; Pratt 1997), hospitals (Rosner David and Sageman 1987; Connell 1992; Feldman 1993), schools (Herrmann 1995), community facilities (Miller 1984; Spearman 1992; Herrmann 1996) and prisons (described by Val Beaver in Chapter 11). It is also used with adults and children who have been bereaved (Simon 1981; Baulkwill and Wood 1994; Pratt 1997, and Chapter 13 in this volume). Kaufman (1996) describes the artwork she made in response to the death of her 5-year-old son due to AIDS. Art therapy is also being carried out within people's own homes (see Chapter 8).

Not surprisingly, therefore, art therapists are working with people who have a wide range of life-threatening and terminal conditions and at different stages of illness. Several articles detail art therapy with people suffering from different forms of cancer and with AIDS-related illnesses. There is evidence that art therapy is useful to those with multiple sclerosis (Szepanski 1988), cystic fibrosis and motor neurone disease (see Chapter 5).

Work with children who have an incurable illness has been documented by relatively few writers, some of whom have used art, but in the contexts of education or child psychotherapy (for example Bach 1966; Furth 1988; Judd 1989; Bertoia 1993; Moore 1994; Sourkes 1996; see Chapter 5 for a description of a single session with a 10-year-old boy). Art therapy with bereaved children is more frequently reported, sometimes in the context of peer groups (for example, Baulkwill and Wood 1994; Davis 1996; see Chapter 13) and sometimes on an individual basis (for example Simon 1981; Case 1987; Bekter McIntyre 1990). Art therapy with children living with HIV and AIDS (both infected and affected) has also been documented (Lunn et al. 1995; and Moss et al. in preparation).

Different locations for art therapy determine how the client is named – prisoner, resident, service user, patient or client. Such names reflect a particular view of the person who is ill and may reflect something of the art therapist's approach, and the opportunity for the client to direct the service; for example the contrast between the patient-centred palliative care approach and the custodial care of a terminally ill prisoner (compare Chapters 9, 10, 11 and 12, all of which describe art therapy with people who have HIV and AIDS). Some institutions appear to favour groupwork (day centres, drop-in community facilities and prisons), while individual work is most likely to be offered in hospice or terminal care settings. Certainly work in the client's own home suggests individual or family work. The location of the art therapy session is an interesting question. As described in Chapter 1, art therapy generally occurs in a specially designated space in which the client can work with some ease and privacy. This space is usually set up and maintained by the art therapist who guards against any interruptions and who 'holds' the boundaries. However, from the literature (including the work described in Part II) art therapy in palliative care is also conducted at the patient's bedside, in their hospice bedroom, in a waiting area of a clinic or at their kitchen table. This shifts the dynamic between client and therapist and creates a situation in which it can be unclear who is responsible for keeping at bay influences external to the therapeutic encounter. (Simon Bell describes this in some detail in Chapter 8.)

The physical condition of the patient also presents a challenge which requires a flexible approach from the therapist. Feldman (1993) identifies the importance of working within the physical limitations of the patient. This may mean having shorter sessions when the patient is tired or nauseous. It may mean providing a special selection of art materials which are left with the patient or thrown away at the end of a session to avoid cross-infections between patients. Patients who have lost or are losing their sight may need to work with particular materials that are textured or have definite tactile properties. The issue of time is central to this area of work and is discussed in Chapters 6 and 12, and also by Wood (1990) and Connell (1992).

The position of art therapy within the structure of an institution will determine many factors of the service. This issue is discussed in Chapters 8 and 11. Art therapists have worked quite hard to educate their colleagues about their practice and its benefits, and this has resulted in their inclusion in the multidisciplinary team in many centres. The evidence is that in most cases art therapists (both in Britain and the US) hold a position of respect within their staff teams and there is much mutual support and sharing of ideas. In fact most contributors to this book have been sought out for the training, education and support of other palliative care staff, indicating art therapy's contribution to palliative care team work.

THE BENEFITS OF ART THERAPY TO PALLIATIVE CARE

The benefits of art therapy to those who have a life-threatening condition are wide ranging. For some patients art therapy provides an opportunity to adjust to the effects of their diagnosis and to the ways in which illness has changed their lives. Specific issues such as coming to terms with changes in body image due to hair loss, weight loss or the disfigurement caused by skin lesions have been tackled through art therapy. The management of pain is another area in which art therapy has been described as having an important role; Thomas (1995) points out that when a person is suffering emotionally they have a lower pain threshold and will therefore feel more physical pain. She suggests that by releasing emotions and anxieties through art therapy a patient can work towards psychological rehabilitation and an increased sense of well being.

The possibility of coming to terms with the feelings of isolation caused by illness has been identified by Rosner David and Sageman (1987). They see art therapy as enabling their patients to gain an increased sense of autonomy and confidence which consequently strengthens the patients' ability to cope with illness. The value of art therapy in facilitating the expression and release of unacknowledged feelings in relation to a patient's diagnosis of AIDS has been described by Wood (1990).

On a more general level, art therapy has been outlined as helping to maintain the individual's sense of identity in the face of illness. For example, Connell (1992) regards art therapy as making a contribution to a person's well being by fulfilling a fundamental human need to be creative. She advocates that art therapy can support the patient's own search for an understanding of their situation. Aldridge (1993), a music therapist, describes in some detail the ways in which the arts therapies have a significant role to play in the care of people with AIDS. He suggests that by increasing the patient's quality of life there is an increase in hope, which he identifies as a meaningful coping strategy. In this way hope provides a motivation within the patient to achieve their inner goals. For Aldridge, the arts therapies provide patients with the capacity to transcend seemingly hopeless situations which can help them to gain new perspectives on themselves and their lives.

Feldman (1993) asserts that one primary aim is to provide reassurance and support to the patient on his or her journey towards death. As an expressive therapist (a profession not known in Britain) Feldman uses a combination of art, craft and music that seems to span occupational therapy and art therapy. There seems to be much agreement amongst those writing about their practice that art therapy is an intervention aimed at improving the patient's quality of life.

Art therapy has not only been used to come to terms with issues related to illness. Some writers describe their patients using art therapy as a means of reflecting upon and resolving events that pre-date their diagnosis (for example, Jansen 1995), indicating that the crisis brought about by illness brings too the motivation to resolve other important personal issues. In addition the value of art therapy in facilitating the grieving process in those who have been bereaved is emphasised in the literature (for example Simon 1981; Case 1986; Zambelli *et al.* 1988; Bekter McIntyre 1990; Orton 1994).

One important benefit of art therapy is the opportunity to shift from a passive to an active role through art making for people who are increasingly losing their independence due to illness. For those in the terminal stages art may be one of the few productive activities they are able to engage in. Several writers point out the value of the patient's art making as tangible evidence of their vitality and capacity to control their bodies. Simon (1981) maintains that art therapy allows the patient to assert their identity to the very end of their lives. The possibility for individual expression and a validation of personal experience through art is highlighted by all art therapists working in this field.

One final benefit of art therapy to palliative care can be seen in its use with staff rather than patients. The importance of staff support has already been mentioned in Chapter 2 and this is being provided in a variety of ways. Art therapy is seen as an attractive tool for team building because it combines practical and creative activity with emotional expression in a way that is accessible to every member of the staff team. The present author has used art therapy in this way for staff from a variety of backgrounds. One example is given by Belfiore (1994) who describes the use of art therapy to prevent burn-out in staff providing home care to terminally ill patients in Italy.

The role of the art therapist and the nature of the therapeutic relationship

This is an important aspect of art therapy and one which is often described but which has not been fully explored in the literature. One writer on the subject is Sally Skaife who raises several questions about the therapeutic relationship (Skaife 1993). These questions will be examined in passing below, and are discussed in detail in Chapter 12. I would first like to highlight some of the issues which need to be considered.

The physical limitations placed on a patient by their condition have been mentioned already. The therapist must have an adaptable approach and be prepared to alter the therapeutic environment to ensure the patient is physically comfortable enough to use the art materials. Many other people with whom the patient will interact may need to make similar alterations, but in the art therapist's case, given his or her brief to attend to the patient on an emotional level, getting the working space ready may be laden with meaning. The power differential between an apparently healthy therapist and a physically weak or restricted patient touches upon the losses with which the patient is faced. Feelings of envy (Skaife 1993) and disempowerment may compound any existing feelings within the patient that the therapist is an 'expert', a 'good artist' or like other health professionals 'will do something to me'. The possibility is that these difficult feelings will be part of the art therapist's encounter with the patient. How the therapist works with these feelings will depend upon many factors – the context in which patient and therapist are meeting, the number of sessions available to them, the health of the patient and the therapist's particular style of working.

Many writers (for example Lago and Thompson (1996) who discuss cultural issues in counselling) point out that there is always an imbalance of power in therapeutic relationships, with the client invariably being in the weaker position. Skaife (ibid.) suggests that the fact of a power differential in the relationship needs to be acknowledged by the therapist (but not necessarily directly with the patient) in order to keep open the full range of emotional options for the patient, who may be finding it hard to share negative feelings with family and other carers who are 'doing their very best'. However, the presence of art materials, their use and the products which result provide the means for the balance of power to swing the other way, enabling the patient to move from a passive to an active position and providing the patient with a way of representing themselves in their own terms. One function of the art therapist is to facilitate an experience of empowerment through the art materials, and when this is achieved the patient becomes 'the expert' in the telling of their own story. In a sense the patient is able to double their presence through their images. Connell (1992) and Jansen (1995) emphasise that the value of the artwork lies in its capacity to contain layers of meaning which carry the experiences, thoughts and concerns of its creator. The importance of facilitating the patient's own meanings for their artwork is crucial. Jansen (ibid.) argues that a therapist immobilises an image by fixing its meaning with his or her own interpretation. This she regards as an abuse of the power relationship between therapist and client, resulting in the client's subjectivity being undermined. The capacity to recognise and work with the subtle and often covert communications around this element of the encounter between therapist and patient distinguishes art therapy from other situations in which the patient will engage in art activities. The art therapist's attention to emotional detail opens up the possibility for the patient to explore on a deep level within themselves (Wood 1990; Connell 1992; and throughout Part II).

There are many facets to the relationship between the therapist and the patient that contribute to what has been identified here as a power differential. Age, gender, ethnic and social background are imbued with cultural meaning and are accorded different levels of respect in different cultures. Although there is not space enough here to fully explore the meanings of these characteristics it is true to say that they greatly inform exchanges between people. Men may be taken more seriously than women, older people may command more respect than younger people, those who are white may be listened to more willingly than people who are seen as 'non-white'. The match between the age, gender and background of the therapist and their patient will influence the type of relationship that is formed. This does not mean that difference is an obstacle to therapy, it could in fact be beneficial. What it does mean is that since difference exists the health professional needs to be aware of its potential for being a barrier to forming a good working relationship (this relates to the point made in Chapter 2) and must seek ways to address it in themselves and when appropriate with the patient in therapy. Mayo (1996) gives one example of art therapy taking place between an older white English woman and a young Ugandan woman. Both were familiar with each other's culture, the white art therapist spoke Swahili and was familiar with the stories of East Africa, the Ugandan patient spoke English and enjoyed the writings of Shakespeare. The therapist's ability to work with the differences and similarities of culture with someone who was being cared for in a country that was not her own shows the importance of addressing these issues.

The similarities in ages between themselves and their clients is recognised by some therapists as having an impact on the therapeutic relationship. There is a growing awareness of cultural, age and gender differences upon counselling, art therapy and psychotherapy and as we have seen in Chapter 2 such questions are also being considered in palliative care services.

PALLIATIVE CARE AND ART THERAPY: DEVELOPING THE VIEW BOTH WAYS

Neither art therapy nor palliative care are static quantities but have evolved, and continue to do so in relation to the political, social and ideological influences of their time. In this respect it is exciting to consider the impact that art therapy can make on the development of the palliative care approach and also exciting to consider the challenges raised by work in palliative care to art therapy theory and practice. This is potentially a vast and rich domain and it is very much hoped that the current trends for research and audit will encourage practitioners across the disciplines (and perhaps more importantly those who hold the purse strings) to invest in its exploration. I would like to end this chapter by discussing three examples of interchange between art therapy and work with those who have a terminal or life-threatening illness.

The patient's artwork

The artwork is the point on which the wheels of art therapy turn. Its influence can extend beyond the individual who created it, and beyond the relationship they may have with the therapist, out to other members of the professional team and family and friends. It has been observed (and is described in Chapters 5 and 6) that the patients who make images are viewed more positively by doctors, nurses, family members and friends. This may be due to many factors, such as the carers own need to see the patient engaged in something 'productive', but more likely (particularly when the patient is engaged in art therapy and the artwork is therefore more personal) it would seem as though the image maintains and conveys something of the continuing humanity of the person.

The artwork may even touch the lives of people who are complete strangers to the patient/artist in the form of exhibitions or as part of a collective Group Notebook as described by Camilla Connell in Chapter 6. Patients' images are also used to convey information about art therapy and patients' experiences when training staff in this area.

Issues of confidentiality are important to mention here as all work made in therapy is considered confidential. Any arrangement to show a patient's work is negotiated with the patient. The patient is at liberty to keep their work and to show it to whoever they please, though this usually follows some discussion with the art therapist. The need to leave something of oneself behind for relatives or staff when one is dying is a powerful element within the artwork.

How much can be 'read' from the patient's pictures? This is a question that concerns some therapists, particularly in the US where images are more commonly used for diagnosis. Two practitioners in the field of terminal illness who have endeavoured to develop frameworks for 'reading' pictures are Susan Bach (1966) and Greg Furth (1988). Bach was one of the pioneers of art therapy in Britain who went on to train as a Jungian analyst. Her research and extensive work on children's drawings seem to be primarily concerned with the use of pictures to diagnose, treat and make an early prognosis in sick children. This approach to the artwork of terminally ill children appears to be aimed at benefiting the patient indirectly once the 'correct' diagnosis has been made. Furth (ibid.) has also developed an interpretative framework for 'reading' pictures made by the terminally ill. He proposes that individuals can be restored to a harmonious relationship of mind and body through the accurate interpretation of a picture. The use of patients' artwork as a means of revealing something otherwise obscured to the professionals involved in the case has occupied several art therapy researchers (Russell-Lacy *et al.* 1979; Williams *et al.* 1996). However, the efficacy of making such interpretations has not been clearly validated. Certainly Bach and Furth have been criticised for viewing a person's images based on the diagnosis of a terminal illness and consequently missing other possible meanings. Jansen (1995) criticises Bach for not giving any data to support the recognition of certain images as significant, and questions Furth's exclusion of his own assumptions and value judgements from his analysis of the artwork. Jansen wonders how much Furth's conclusions are informed or confirmed by what the clients have said about their art.

Both Bach and Furth work from an assumption that there are fixed meanings linking the symbols within the images produced by seriously ill individuals to death and dying. This is an avenue for further research, although its interest may be more theoretical than applied to work with clients. The danger in this sort of approach can be seen in the commonly voiced misconception of art therapy from patients: that the therapist and not the patient will interpret the artwork. This, as has been made clear already, is not art therapy.

In describing how he began working with drawings, Furth outlines his attempts to help terminally ill patients educate their medical staff into finding better ways of caring for them. Perhaps the palliative approach of listening well to the patient reduces the necessity for the patient's art to be a go-between in this way.

The 'bodyliness' of art therapy

The contribution made by art therapy to a patient's experience of their ill or failing body is often mentioned by those working in the field. This is particularly seen in the activity or process by which a person engages physically with the materials. The notion of linking bodily experiences and art therapy is not new, but has found favour with art therapists working with psychotic clients and those with eating disorders (Levens 1995; Killick and Greenwood 1995).

The interdependence of mind and body as a dynamic unity rather than a duality (mind versus body) has been eloquently discussed by Erskine and Judd (1994). They point out that, although easy to accept in theory, this interrelationship of body and mind is extremely difficult to experience. Something of this unity can however be glimpsed in artwork produced in therapy. The physicality of art materials along with their symbolic capacity enables word-less layers of experience to be rendered in concrete form, with the very resonances between the two being regarded as therapeutically powerful. The mechanisms which link bodily/psychological experience and art making are of great interest and need further exploration, particularly when it preserves a holistic view of an individual or where it is linked to pain control.

Recent ideas in neurocognitive research suggest different ways in which experiences are stored in memory (Grigsby, Schneiders and Kaye 1991, cited by Moore 1994). Moore (ibid.) states that some experiences (stored in 'non-declar-ative memory') are never available for verbal recall. Instead they are reflected in behaviour, and may be depicted graphically. How much of our sense of self is damaged or remains intact once we lose parts of our bodies (through illness or amputation) is an interesting question. The role of art either as an attempt to symbolically repair the damage or to work towards the creation of an altered configuration of self has been seen clinically; with rigorous consideration there could be interesting developments in this area.

Boundaries

The usual boundaries adhered to in art therapy practice with other client groups are firmly shaken when working in palliative care. The urgency of the patient's changing health, the brevity of admissions to hospital or hospice and the limitations of the locations for the sessions demand different boundaries. The creativity of art therapists in this area have given rise to new ways of working, for example Connell's Group Notebook – the recognition of a single session as a viable therapeutic intervention and the development of art therapy in patients' homes.

As discussed in Chapter 2 the holistic approach of palliative care is being threatened by increasing pressures for management to become more medically focused. Art therapy as part of the palliative package, given enough resources (including research opportunities), can go some way towards counterbalancing this pull by maintaining and underlining the total personhood of those who come for care. Art therapy touches upon all aspects of the person's being. Its contribution to palliative care lies here, in providing an experience which can address physical pain, can facilitate a search for meaning, can provide an outlet for strong feelings and can enhance the person's quality of life. The patient's artwork is also a record of their struggles with illness, and their view of themselves and all that is important in the final phases of life.

REFERENCES

Aldridge, D. (1993) 'Hope, meaning and the creative arts therapies in the treatment of AIDS', *The Arts in Psychotherapy*, vol. 20: 285–97.

Bach, S. (1966) 'Spontaneous paintings of severely ill patients', *Acta Psychosomatica*, vol. 8: 1–66.

Baulkwill, J. and Wood, C. (1994) 'Groupwork with bereaved children', *European Journal Of Palliative Care*, vol. 1, no. 3: 113–15.

Bekter McIntyre, B. (1990) 'Art therapy with bereaved youth', *Journal of Palliative Care*, vol. 6: 16–23.

Belfiore, M. (1994) 'The group takes care of itself: art therapy to prevent burnout', *The Arts in Psychotherapy*, vol. 21, no. 2: 119–26.

Bertoia, J. (1993) *Drawings from a Dying Child*, London and New York: Routledge.

Case, C. (1986) 'Hide and seek: a struggle for meaning', *Inscape*, Winter: 20–4.

Case, C. (1987) 'Loss and transition in art therapy with children', in T. Dalley, C. Case, J. Schaverien, F. Weir, D. Halliday, P. Nowell Hall and D. Waller (eds) *Images of Art Therapy*, London: Tavistock.

Connell, C. (1992) 'Art therapy as part of a palliative care programme' *Palliative Medicine*, vol. 6: 18–25.

Davis, C.B. (1996) 'The use of art therapy and group process with grieving children', in S.C. Smith and Sister M. Pennells (eds) *Interventions with Bereaved Children*, London: Jessica Kingsley.

Erskine, A. and Judd, D. (eds) (1994) *The Imaginative Body: Psychodynamic Therapy in Health Care*, London: Whurr.

Feldman, E. (1993) 'HIV dementia and countertransference', *The Arts in Psychotherapy*, vol. 20: 317–23.

Furth, G. (1988) *The Secret World of Drawings: Healing Through Art*, Boston, MA: Sigo Press.

Grigsby, J., Schneiders, J. and Kaye, K. (1991) 'Reality testing, the self and the brain as modular distributed systems', *Psychiatry*, vol. 54: 39–54.

Herrmann, U. (1995) 'A Trojan horse of clay: art in a residential school for the blind', *The Arts in Psychotherapy,* vol. 22, no. 3: 229–34.

Herrmann, U. (1996) *Aus Unserer Sicht/From Our Point of View*, Hanover, Germany: Hannoversche AIDS Hilfe e.V.

Jansen, T. (1995) 'Art therapy with terminally ill individuals', *The Canadian Art Therapy Association Journal*, Winter, vol. 9, no. 1: 13–24.

Judd, D. (1989) *Give Sorrow Words*, London: Free Association Books.

Kaufman, A.B. (1996) 'Art in boxes: an exploration of meanings', *The Arts in Psychotherapy*, vol. 23: 237–47.

Killick, K. and Greenwood, H. (1995) 'Research in art therapy with people who have psychotic illnesses', in A. Gilroy and C. Lee (eds) *Art and Music Therapy and Research,* London and New York: Routledge.

Lago, C. and Thompson, J. (1996) *Race, Culture and Counselling*, Buckingham and Philadelphia: Open University Press.

Levens, M. (1995) 'Art therapy and psychodrama with eating disordered patients', in D. Doktor (ed.) *Arts Therapies and Clients with Eating Disorders: Fragile Board,* London: Jessica Kingsley.

Lunn, S., Sattaur, A. and Wood, M.J.M. (1995) 'Working with children at Mildmay Mission Hospital', in *HIV/AIDS NO TIME TO WASTE*, London: Barnado's Publications.

Mayo, S. (1996) 'Symbol, metaphor and story: the function of group art therapy in palliative care', *Palliative Medicine*, vol. 10: 209–16.

Miller, B. (1984) 'Art therapy with the elderly and the terminally ill', in T. Dalley (ed.) *Art as Therapy*, London: Tavistock/Routledge.

Moore, M. (1994) 'Reflections of self: the use of drawings in evaluating and treating physically ill children', in A. Erskine and D. Judd (eds) *The Imaginative Body*, London: Whurr.

Moss, V.A., Sattaur, A., Chambers, J., Wood, M.J.M. and Anscombe, B. (forthcoming) 'A day nursery in an AIDS palliative care setting: can this be appropriate?', manuscript in preparation.

Orton, M. (1994) 'A case study of an adolescent mother grieving the death of her child due to sudden infant death syndrome', *American Journal of Art Therapy*, vol. 33: 37–44.

Pratt, A.J. (1997) 'The creative response', *Palliative Care Today*, vol. 5, no. 4: 148–9.

Rosner David, I. and Sageman, S. (1987) 'Psychological aspects of AIDS as seen in art therapy', *American Journal of Art Therapy*, vol. 26: 3–10.

Russell-Lacy, S., Robinson, V., Benson, J. and Cranage, J. (1979) 'An experimental study of pictures produced by acute schizophrenic subjects', *British Journal of Psychiatry*, vol. 13: 195–200.

Simon, R. (1981) 'Bereavement art', *American Journal of Art Therapy*, vol. 20: 35–43.

Skaife, S. (1993) 'Sickness, health and the therapeutic relationship: thoughts arising from the literature on art therapy and physical illness', *Inscape*, Summer: 24–9.

Spearman, J. (1992) 'Drawing out the fear on a journey onto the unknown', *Guardian*, 27 July.

Sourkes, B. (1996) *Armfuls of Time: The Psychological Experience of the Child with a Life-Threatening Illness*, London: Routledge.

Szepanski, M. (1988) 'Art therapy and multiple sclerosis', *Inscape*, Spring: 4–10.

Thomas, G. (1995) 'Art therapy and practice in palliative care' *European Journal of Palliative Care*, vol. 2, no. 3: 120–1.

Waller, D. (1991) *Becoming a Profession: The History of Art Therapy in Britain 1940–82*, London and New York: Tavistock/Routledge.

Williams, K., Agell, G., Gantt, L., Goodman, L. and Goodman, R. (1996) 'Art-based diagnosis: fact or fantasy?', *American Journal of Art Therapy*, vol. 35: 9–31.

Wood, M.J.M. (1990) 'Art therapy in one session: working with people with AIDS', *Inscape*, Winter: 27–33.

Zambelli, G., Clark, E.J., Barile, L. and Jong, A.N. (1988) 'An inter-disciplinary approach to clinical intervention for childhood bereavement', *Death Studies*, vol. 12: 41–50.

Chapter 4

Some images of illness

The place of art therapy in the palliative care team – a doctor's perspective

Peter Kaye (with a Postscript by Elizabeth Hall)

INTRODUCTION

At first glance the concepts of 'art' and 'illness' do not seem to go together. Art and creativity are active, whereas illness seems passive. In fact, art therapy is a legitimate and very helpful discipline, and it is of particular value within hospice and palliative care. Art therapy is about helping individual patients, but it is also relevant to reflect briefly on the place of art and art therapy in the wider context of medical care. This chapter briefly considers:

- the medical model of care
- the crisis model
- the spiritual needs of patients
- art in hospices
- art in hospitals
- art therapy in illness
- art therapy for staff
- art therapy in bereavement

THE MEDICAL MODEL OF CARE

Expectations about suffering have changed. Before this century there were few effective treatments, 25 per cent of babies died before reaching a year of age, and people lived with the constant presence of death and disease. As recently as 1840 a labourer in Britain could expect to live on average only 22 years! But we now live in an age of scientific miracles (spacecraft on Mars, the internet, organ transplants, test-tube babies, gene therapy). Nowadays we expect to be well. Many of us assume that if we are ill at all, it will be for a short time, before modern medicine cures us.

Modern medical care is rightly focused on diagnosis and cure, and patients are often willing to suffer in pursuit of that cure. In a study of patients with cancer most patients were willing to consider very unpleasant and severe treatments even if there was only a 1 per cent chance of cure (whereas most doctors and nurses wanted a 50 per cent chance of cure to consider enduring the same side-effects).[1] However, the present medical model does not seem to meet all the needs of patients. It seems ironic that as modern medicine has developed more and more therapeutic power, public dissatisfaction with doctors has increased. Complaints against doctors continue to rise. Malpractice suits more than doubled between 1975 and 1985, whilst alternative and complementary therapies have flourished. But what happens when cure is not possible? Have all our medical advances reduced suffering? Indeed, expectations of cure may even be increasing suffering and existential distress in the face of diseases we are still powerless to control.

The medical model of care (Figure 4.1) is an external model, describing the modern doctor's perspective on the management of *disease*. But a parallel internal model is needed, that looks at the experience of *illness* from the patient's perspective. A lot of medical care, especially palliative care, is concerned with crises (and their prevention) and a model of care based on crisis intervention can be helpful in understanding patient's needs.

THE CRISIS MODEL

The crisis model (Figure 4.2) is a good way of understanding the needs of patients adjusting to illness. Illness often involves facing a series of crises. A crisis can be defined as a temporary inability to cope with change. Faced with a crisis, two main things happen simultaneously for the patient:

1   A search for information – to solve new problems
2   An emotional reaction to loss of control

Crisis intervention is often the most appropriate way of offering help because it leaves the patient in control of the decision-making (and the patient is the expert in their own situation). The professional carer aims to:

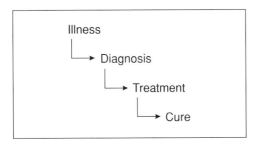

Figure 4.1 The medical model

- provide necessary information
- offer a forum for problem-solving
- discuss pros and cons of options
- remind the patient of their strengths and weaknesses
- remain realistic

Problem-solving breaks a problem into small and manageable behavioural steps. In teaching the steps of problem-solving, a patient often begins to feel more in control, and can begin to see more clearly. Just starting this process will often promote creative thinking and can lead on to intuitive solutions even before all the steps are completed. However, the patient often has times of emotional exhaustion, when more intensive support is needed for a time, and when decision-making is not possible.

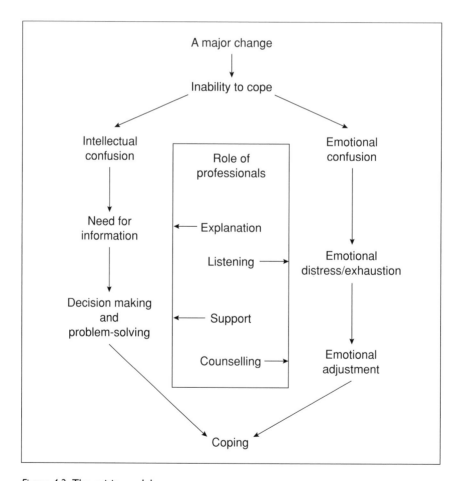

Figure 4.2 The crisis model

Both the intellectual process (problem-solving) and the emotional process (adjustment) can be facilitated by art therapy or other approaches that offer a person time and space to reflect on, and adjust to, bad news or powerful feelings. We tend to think of a crisis in negative terms, but a crisis can be an opportunity for personal growth. In her book *Death and the Family* Lily Pincus wrote:

> A crisis is not an abstract imposition from without, but a high point in the life of the person concerned . . . a dynamic interaction between a person and an extreme event'.[2]

Other life crises, in addition to medical crises (Figure 4.3), often occur simultaneously. These may be physical (for example injury), developmental (child leaving home, retirement), emotional (argument, bereavement) or social (promotion, burglary).

SPIRITUAL NEEDS OF PATIENTS

In 1954 the psychologist Abraham Maslow proposed a theory of motivation and personal fulfilment in which he described a person's 'hierarchy of needs' – which should be kept in balance.[3] This is a useful idea when considering the needs of patients. Once basic needs (food, shelter and physical comfort) are

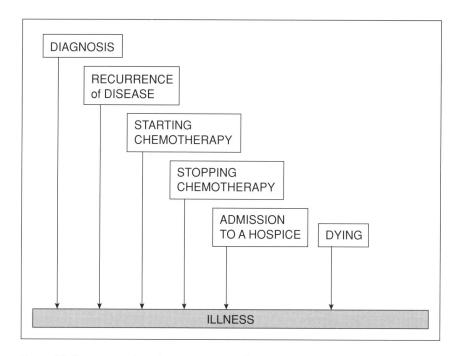

Figure 4.3 Some examples of common crises for cancer patients

met, an individual is free to fulfil other needs such as social contact, a sense of security, a sense of belonging, love and self-esteem. Finally, for complete fulfilment, a person's highest needs are a sense of meaning and a spiritual awareness about their life.

Spiritual distress in the context of illness has been described as 'The experience of dis-ease and the search for meaning within it'.[4] The spiritual needs of the sick continue to be neglected. Recently at a weekend seminar a group of 100 Macmillan nurses (specialists in palliative care) were asked to do a brainstorm to consider the needs of patients living with advanced cancer. They came up with a final list of forty needs. The group produced a good and comprehensive list, as far as it went. But only two categories related to spiritual issues: 'to have time alone' and 'spiritual support'. The needs they listed were all very important, but the list emphasised to me that the perspective of doctors and nurses (even those specialising in an area known to be sympathetic to spiritual needs) is mainly practical and physical.

The way professional carers can facilitate the spiritual support of patients still remains a largely unexplored area. In his recent book *Mortally Wounded*, Michael Kearney talks of soul pain, and describes a particular way of working with the deep, inner aspects of a dying person's own psyche that involves accessing and working with the patient's unconscious images, normally only experienced in dreams.

> This inner or depth work is essentially a co-operative venture with the healing forces of the person's own psyche. It is the essential complement to the outer care of the individual and may enable that person to find his or her own way through the prison of soul pain to a place of greater wholeness, a new depth of living, and a falling away of fear.[5]

Art therapy can work in a similar way, at a very deep level, but with real rather than imagined pictures, and may be especially helpful for patients who prefer to think visually rather than verbally.

It is to the spiritual aspects of patient care that art therapy has so much to offer. Hospice and palliative care services can now benefit from a wide range of complementary therapists, including art therapists, to enhance our awareness of the spiritual needs of patients, and to bring fresh perspectives and a variety of approaches to meet those spiritual needs.

ART IN HOSPICES

The founding of St Christopher's Hospice in South London by Dame Cicely Saunders in 1967 is a landmark in the medical history of this century. St Christopher's developed at a time when medicine was increasingly cure-orientated, and the wider needs of patients were being neglected. It is probably

no coincidence that the British Association of Art Therapists was also established around the same time, in 1963. St Christopher's was the first purpose-built
research and teaching hospice, and over the following thirty years it became
the model for many similar hospices across the UK, and across the world.
Saunders listened to patients dying on hospital wards and realised their needs
were not being met. One of the first patients she met said: 'I need what is in
your head, and what is in your heart.' Saunders developed a blueprint for an
organisation to meet those needs. From the beginning she appreciated the importance of having paintings and works of art in the hospice. Through looking
for suitable paintings to decorate the hospice, she met and finally married the
Polish artist Marian Bohusz, who became the artist in residence at St
Christopher's, where over sixty of his works are now displayed.[6]

St Christopher's became the model for most other hospices, which explains
the openness of many hospice services to the role of art therapy, painting, sculpture, poetry, music therapy and drama in the holistic care of patients.

The first hospices were voluntary, established outside the NHS, but in 1980
the first hospital-based support team was established to bring hospice principles back into the hospital setting, and there are now over 250 hospital-based
support teams in the UK. In 1987 palliative medicine became recognised as a
speciality within mainstream medicine, and the general public are beginning to
learn that 'palliative care' means skilled medical help and support even when
cure is not possible. The next challenge is to augment this acknowledged medical
specialism with methods of spiritual support such as art therapy in all palliative care settings.

ART IN HOSPITALS

Art therapy is about helping individual patients, but it is relevant to reflect
briefly on the role of art in the wider context of hospital care. The presence of
art in hospitals is now understood to be important, to create an environment
for healing.[7] Prince Charles once commented, 'It can't be easy to be healed in
a soul-less concrete box' and Florence Nightingale in her *Notes on Nursing*
said 'the effect in sickness of beautiful objects, and especially of brilliancy of
colour is hardly at all appreciated'.[8] The importance of art in hospitals was
formally acknowledged in 1988 by the Department of Health and Social Security
in its report *Buildings for the Health Service* which stated:

> Works of art should be incorporated into the architect's brief . . . hospitals
> should be beautiful as well as functional, attractive visually both internally
> and externally, because works of art enhance health.[9]

It is difficult to measure quality of life. How do we measure the uplifting effect
that art might have on a person's spirits? However, there is some evidence that

art might directly affect healing. An ingenious study by a geographer called Roger Ulrich at the University of Delaware compared the post-operative recovery of twenty-three matched pairs of patients and found that patients with vibrant surroundings and a view of trees and gardens from their hospital bed recovered faster, and needed fewer pain-killers, than those with dull surroundings.[10] But more needs to be done to improve the environment for patients in most hospitals. Perhaps art therapists have an ancillary role here, to raise the awareness of hospital managers to the importance of art in relation to healing.

ART THERAPY IN ILLNESS

One of the most helpful experiences for ill patients is that of empathy from another person. Empathy enhances a doctor's ability to diagnose and treat patients and is also the key component of spiritual support.[11] Empathy can be defined as: the attempt to understand (but not to feel) another person's feelings, and then to skilfully communicate that attempt back to the person.

Cicely Saunders' work in the 1960s coincided with that of Elizabeth Kübler-Ross, who revolutionised the psychological care of dying patients by her observations that talking with the dying about dying did not make them feel worse (as had been universally assumed up to that time) but actually made them feel better. Her book describing her findings, *On Death and Dying,* was widely read by the general public and helped to develop the hospice program in the US.[12]

Susan Sontag has described illness as like being a citizen in a foreign country:

> Illness is the night-side of life, a more onerous citizenship. Everyone who is born holds a dual citizenship, in the kingdom of the well and in the kingdom of the sick. Although we all prefer to use only the good passport, sooner or later each of us is obliged, at least for a spell, to identify ourselves as citizens of that other place.[13]

It is very difficult for those who are well to really appreciate the feelings of those who are sick, especially when the patient is from a different cultural background. The following case history illustrates that the palliative care of patients involves more than just physical medical care, and that the spiritual aspects of care can be more difficult and challenging, and can leave professionals feeling inadequate and helpless.

Some patients seem to need a great deal of time and attention to begin to face up to their situation. I can think of several patients admitted to our hospice who we, as a team, seemed to completely fail in terms of making contact with their spiritual distress (especially when there have been cultural and language barriers) and I wonder now whether an experienced art therapist might have been able to help. Very weak patients may be unable to participate in creative

A CASE OF DESPAIR

RS was a 33-year-old Indian woman, of striking beauty, who was married with two daughters aged 6 and 3. She and her husband had married outside their castes, and they had very little contact with either family. They were non-practising Hindus. She developed a rare cancer (of the bile duct) which was very small when it was removed surgically, and it was a mystery why it was not cured. Six months after the operation she started to complain of pain. All investigations were normal, and her pain was assumed to be 'post-operative'. Eventually she was found to have recurrent disease, and had more surgery to remove a secondary cancer from the liver, followed by radiotherapy. She felt too weak to finish the course and was admitted to the hospice. She then wanted to try chemotherapy, but after one course developed more pain, and asked to see the surgeon, who reluctantly operated again. After this operation she developed a fistula, with bile leaking out through the skin. This was repaired, but she later developed another fistula into the lung, and was coughing up bile, which was again eventually repaired. She spent most of the last year of her life as an in-patient in the hospice, complaining of weakness and severe abdominal pains that could not be fully controlled. She co-operated with the doctors, but refused all other help. She alternated between feeling weak and staying in bed for days or weeks, but would occasionally get up, dress up in glamorous clothes and go out for the evening or for a weekend, but then return and go back to bed, and seemed depressed and withdrawn. She always refused to discuss her illness in any terms other than that she wanted to be cured, and hoped to be cured. She described even the gentlest attempts to discuss the real situation as 'depressing'. She also refused to discuss her illness with her daughters. She died without any change in her attitude that she did not believe she would die. She never talked to her children about her dying.

activity, but even drawing the simplest of things can link a person to childhood experiences, and can be a way to see things differently.

ART THERAPY AND STAFF SUPPORT

Patients have to rely on their professional carers. In addition to hoping for skill and competence, patients and their relatives ideally need emotionally mature carers who can still function effectively (and daily) in the face of, at times, intense emotional distress. A doctor who took his young daughter to hospital with an acute asthmatic attack wrote an article about his experiences, as several doctors dealt with the medical emergency and simultaneously tried to reassure him, as the child's father. He observed that the emotional reactions of the staff were often inappropriate, and concluded:

I do not believe that health professionals are trained at all in how to deal with these events. I was left feeling that the staff were not robust, not able to cope with the full impact of it all.[14]

Looking out for their own emotional health is an ongoing task for professionals working in the emotionally charged atmosphere of hospice care, where powerful negative feelings amongst the staff can affect working relationships, and sometimes even prevent optimal care of patients, and can be disguised as (and result from) 'chronic niceness', as described by Peter Speck:

> While there is little doubt that hospice staff are caring and dedicated people, one of the dangers which face them, and others who work long term with dying people, is that of 'chronic niceness', whereby the individual and the organisation collude to split off and deny the negative aspects of caring for the dying. There is a collective fantasy that the staff are nice people, who are caring for nice dying people, who are going to have a nice death in a nice place. This protects everyone from facing the fact that the relationship between carers and the dying can often arouse very primitive and powerful feelings which are disturbingly not-nice.[15]

It seems to me that art therapy could be one very useful way to help professionals explore and understand their own emotional reactions, and how to distinguish their own human needs and emotions from those of their patients and relatives.

A NURSE'S VIEW OF ART THERAPY – A WAY TO LEARN

Joan is a Macmillan nurse who vividly remembers working with an art therapist on a course about grief and loss, three years ago. She said:

> It was in the context of a weekend course that was well organised and felt very safe and supportive. First we were invited to draw aspects of our lives. It was skillfully introduced, which must have had something to do with it, but I found myself drawing pictures relating to the death of my grandmother when I was 11, which I had not thought about for years, and did not even realise was still an issue for me. Later we listened to the tape of a real patient talking about her reactions to her illness and to finding out that she was going to die. Then we were asked to paint our feelings as if we were that woman. I remember being shocked at how black and despairing my picture felt, although other nurses on the course were equally shocked that their pictures were so optimistic. It was a powerful way of gaining insights into my own feelings and communicating together about our own emotions.

ART THERAPY AND BEREAVEMENT SUPPORT

Children love to play, and often communicate their feelings through play. Many children instinctively love to draw and colour and paint. Hospice professionals find themselves working with children, from time to time, but often with little formal training in how best to facilitate communication with children at their different developmental stages. Young children visiting sick or dying parents or grandparents often draw pictures, and often give them to the patient. In our hospice the nurses often encourage children to draw pictures and then chat with them about what they show and why they have drawn what they have. One 12-year-old girl drew several pictures of her parents with huge mouths, which

---

A CHILD COMMUNICATES THROUGH ART

C was a 42-year-old woman, married with two young sons, who developed a brain tumour. She died whilst an in-patient in the hospice. She denied her illness, and always refused to discuss the real situation with her carers or her family. Two weeks before her death her son Darren (aged 6) had shocked his parents by suddenly announcing 'Mummy is dying, she will be dead before Christmas'. It turned out that Darren had been right. Later, about two months after C died, Darren's father phoned the hospice to ask for help. Darren's behaviour was disturbing. He had become aggressive and uncooperative. A meeting was arranged with the doctor and social worker. The room was equipped with ice cream, and paper and coloured pencils for drawing. As they came into the room, Tommy (aged 4), suddenly asked 'Can we see the bed where Mummy died?' The boys were taken there, but their father (an extremely shy man) refused to go. (Another patient was now in the bed, surrounded by paintings done by her grandchildren.) When they returned, Tommy announced he 'wanted to pee' so his father took him to the toilet. On the way back, Tommy led his father to the room where his mother had died, and showed him the bed. Then the boys had their ice cream, chatted and drew pictures. They were asked to draw a picture of where they thought Mummy was now. As he drew, Darren suddenly told a joke that he said he had made up, about a snowman who wanted a wife. Then he started to draw a snowman. When asked why, it emerged that his mother had given him a large poster of a snowman before she died, which hung above his bed. His father finally began to talk, and suddenly described how he had taken Tommy, the younger boy, to see his mother's grave. The doctor asked why Darren had not gone too. The father explained that the grave was in the village churchyard across a busy road, and he was worried Darren might try to go there by himself. The social worker asked Darren if he would like to visit his mother's grave and Darren said he would.[16]

was her way of communicating that the key problem in the family was all the shouting and arguing. Art therapists could play an important role both in working with bereaved adults and children, and in teaching some of their skills to other professionals, so the therapeutic value of drawing and art could be used more widely within the multidisciplinary team.

CONCLUSION

Hospices presently use a variety of approaches to support patients, including hypnotherapy, visualisation, massage, aromatherapy, music therapy, creative writing, sculpture and group drama. The use of all these approaches remains patchy, and they are still under-described.

Art therapy has a very useful role, especially in hospice and palliative care, in helping patients and relatives to make contact with and make sense of their deepest feelings, especially at points of crisis. It offers a very helpful method of providing emotional and spiritual support to patients and relatives and could usefully be extended to supporting staff working with the sick and dying.

Peter Kaye is a Consultant in Palliative Medicine at Cynthia Spencer Hospice where he has been for the past eleven years. He is a member of the Royal College of General Practitioners and a Fellow of the Royal College of Physicians. He has written several books on hospice and palliative care and has a particular interest in the psychological aspects of illness.

POSTSCRIPT – HELP US TO GROW

ELIZABETH HALL

My personal introduction to art therapy was in a half-day staff workshop bringing art therapy to the hospice for the first time. My lasting memory is of one exercise where we were invited to express our feelings about 'loss'. My first reaction was to feel a little irritated. I knew we encountered loss, but what about all the gains? My constant aim is to look positively at things! So my sheet of paper was divided into a big area of gains, but I did concede a small strip for losses. The gains part was soon filled with red, orange and yellow splodges – I can't paint – expressing my joy and excitement in all I have learned during my years working at the hospice. Finally I was forced to look at my losses and try to put things into this narrow column I had allowed myself. Suddenly it started to fill with all the things I no longer did or felt I easily had time for. Dressmaking and embroidery, walks in the country, going to the theatre, concerts, even a long soak in the bath.

I still use what I learnt from that short demonstration. I bought a wonderful tapestry of brilliant pansies – it will take me years, but since I cannot draw or paint I can enjoy its use of colour with my needle. Art therapy had helped me to re-introduce recreation and creativity into living. If one short exercise could do this, what potential might there be for change and personal growth in meeting the needs of patients and their families? I echo Peter's sense of having little to offer some people in distress – it was very like that for me before art therapy became available to families I had contact with. So when do I as a doctor think art therapy may be helpful? When have I noticed changes once it has been offered?

Susan had AIDS. She had been a bouncy, vivacious young woman, full of life and fun. She had a little girl, Jenny, though her husband was HIV positive too. She was weak and dependent, a degree of dementia made her forgetful and affected her speech, although she retained her sense of humour. Steroids had made her fat and bloated, her legs were swollen and weeping. She felt grotesque. She also felt sad and worried about the future for Jenny and her husband Peter. She asked the art therapist to help her make a self-portrait. The full size outline of her body was a delightful surprise – much slimmer than she had imagined. She 'dressed' it in leggings and trainers and laughed as she added nicotine stains to her fingers! Jenny now has this picture on her wall at home.

I met Mary in the radiotherapy clinic. She had had breast cancer diagnosed fifteen years before. Her liver secondaries had returned in spite of chemotherapy; the prognosis looked bad. Full of anxiety, she and her husband sat and told me of their concern about their only daughter's behaviour. Moody, irritable and inconsiderate, with a difficult, rude boyfriend, she had dismissed offers of counselling. She had been just 10 when her mother was first diagnosed and must have sensed that something was wrong again. Mary never discussed her symptoms in front of her and always put on a brave face. I spoke to them about how we work with young people, stressing that art therapy may offer her daughter a way of expressing the frustration and distress she couldn't otherwise share. Mary's condition deteriorated rapidly, but she found great reassurance knowing that her family would not be left unsupported and her daughter out of control.

A colleague tells me of a child whose mother committed suicide a year ago. He is about to be excluded from school for uncontrolled behaviour. His father is also in conflict with authority. I know our art therapist has worked with children and teachers in many similar situations and so I can suggest it now in the confidence that it will make a real difference.

I met Sophie on the children's ward. She had cystic fibrosis and felt trapped by her breathlessness, trapped in her child's body but with adolescent emotions. When I next saw her she drew my attention to a dolphin she had painted in her art therapy session. The dolphin too is trapped, needing both the ocean and air to breathe. She told me that what she most loved about dolphins though was that 'they leap and play just for the fun of it'. The next time I saw her she was laughing with the art therapist as she designed bright motifs to decorate her wheelchair. She had found release and a capacity to have fun too!

These few examples are just a fragment of what I have seen happen since I have been able to offer art therapy. I have seen increased self-awareness, a movement to see the future realistically and a re-evaluation of what it is still important to achieve. I have seen the dissipation of destructive, blocking feelings leading to a lift in mood and a focus on the possible. Above all I have seen people restore their self-esteem and find a sense of meaning that is able to sustain them until their last breath. So I see art therapy as a useful tool in some of the most distressing and frustrating situations that I meet. As a result I am confident that it would have had a real impact on those situations Peter described earlier in this chapter. For the despairing young woman unable to speak of her illness to her family and so alone; for children of all ages who find it so difficult to communicate their hopes and fears verbally; and for ourselves, the staff who almost daily encounter a sense of helplessness at our inability to do more.

Elizabeth Hall MB BS MRCS LRCP DRCOG is Medical Director at St Helena Hospice, Colchester, and is firmly committed to a holistic and interdisciplinary approach enabling patients and families to concentrate on living the life that's left. She believes the way forward in palliative care is through education and facilitation.

REFERENCES

1 Slevin, M.L., Stubbs, L., Plant, H.J. *et al.* 'Attitudes to chemotherapy: comparing views of patients with cancer with those of doctors, nurses and general public', *British Medical Journal*, 1990, 300: 1458–60.
2 Pincus, L., *Death and the Family. The Importance of Mourning*, London: Faber and Faber, 1974.
3 Maslow, A., *Motivation and Personality*, 1954.
4 Speck, P.W., *Being There – Pastoral Care in Times of Illness*, London: SPCK, 1988.
5 Kearney, M., *Mortally Wounded. Stories of Soul Pain, Death and Healing*, Dublin: Marino, 1966.
6 Wykes-Joyce, M., *The Art of Marian Bohucz*, London: Drian Gallery, 1977.
7 Behrman, P., 'Art in hospitals: why is it there and what is it for?', *Lancet*, 1997, 350: 584–85.
8 Nightingale, F., *Notes On Nursing: What it is and what it is not*, London: Harrison and Sons, 1859.
9 DHSS and the Welsh Office. *Buildings for the Health Service*, 14, London: HMSO, 1988.
10 Ulrich, R., 'View through a window may influence recovery from surgery', *Science*, 1984, 224: 420–1.
11 Neuwirth, Z.E., 'Physician empathy – should we care?', *Lancet*, 1997, 350: 606–7.
12 Kübler-Ross, E., 'On Death and Dying', London: Tavistock, 1970.
13 Sontag, S., *Illness as Metaphor\AIDS as Metaphor*, Harmondsworth: Penguin, 1991.
14 Weiner, A., 'Personal view: problems on the other side of the fence, *British Medical Journal*, 1993, 306: 661.
15 Speck, P., 'Working with dying people: on being good enough', in Obholzer, A. and Roberts, V.Z. (eds) *The Unconscious at Work*, London: Routledge, 1994.
16 Kaye, P. 'Notes on symptom control in hospice and palliative care, Connecticut MA: Hospice Education Institute, 1989.

Plate 1 Painted by a woman who continues to live with her diagnosis of cancer.

Plate 2 'I am very conscious of eyes, of people watching me. I watch my body all the time to see if it has changed.' Image by a man with AIDS.

Plate 3 'You can say things in clay you wouldn't get away with in words.' Heads made by a young man, HIV sero positive, serving a long prison sentence.

Plate 4 'What I love about dolphins is that they leap and jump just for the fun of it.' Crayon sketch by 15-year-old with cystic fibrosis. The dolphin who *must* surface to breathe was a constant motif in the last month of her life.

Plate 5 Painting by a bereaved six-year-old girl who used the three pigs story to explore her own fears. Here the wolf towers over her 'shaky little straw house'.

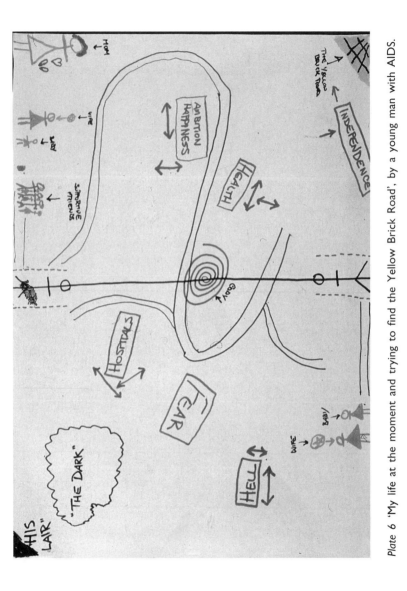

Plate 6 'My life at the moment and trying to find the Yellow Brick Road', by a young man with AIDS.

Plate 7 A 72-year-old man with cancer of the lung confronted his pain to produce this image in soft pastels. 'Once it is "out there" I can really know it.'

Plate 8 'The road of money and drugs, leading to illness and death, passes Leith docks, Edinburgh castle and the tenements until it reaches the hills beyond.' This is a group painting done by four men serving long prison sentences, all of whom were HIV sero positive.

Part II

Chapter 5

Getting started

Introducing the art therapy service and the individual's first experiences

Jackie Coote

In this chapter I shall be considering beginnings in the context of my position as art therapist in a large hospice in London. In an area of work where the focus is very much on endings, paradoxically, much of my work revolves around beginnings. My contact with patients is often brief, and I am weekly having to consider my approach to new patients. However, by beginnings, I shall not be referring to the practical necessities of set up procedures for the therapist, although this is a constant preoccupation. I am referring in particular to the myriad of beginnings for the patient, such as beginning something new, beginning a journey, and beginning to come to terms with the end. I shall use case studies throughout the chapter to illustrate this aspect of my work.

THE APPROACH

I am based in the day centre at the hospice, working with both day patients and in-patients on the wards. A limited budget allows only two and a half hours there a week. Considering the often brief time a patient has at the hospice, this inevitably limits the number of patients I will see. However, living very locally has made it possible for me to occasionally be flexible and vary my time at the hospice when necessary. Referrals come via the social worker attached to the day centre, but these are often scarce. I have found, during these scarcities, it is always helpful to approach ward staff for in-patient referrals. Their almost constant contact with patients means they have an up to the minute awareness of their state of mind and will often suggest that I approach a patient who has 'been a bit low lately', 'seems withdrawn' or they just feel it might be right for them. I trust their hunches, particularly as the staff usually know enough about the service to know what is and what is not an appropriate referral. For a vast majority of the people who enter a hospice, this is their first encounter with any of the lesser known therapy services, let alone any opportunity to use them. I feel it is therefore important to find ways to approach patients and introduce myself and the service in a way that makes it accessible to them. This, I have found, has come with experience through trial and error, gradually developing a sensitivity and awareness of a patient's needs. When introducing myself to the patient, I will explain who I am, what I am and that the patient's name had been mentioned to me as someone who may be interested in the service. It is often possible quite early on in the conversation to gauge whether or not the patient is attracted to this means of self-expression and to pursue the matter further. Responses vary, from immediate interest, or curiosity to know more, to some bewilderment that making pictures at a time like this could possibly be seen as helpful. Art therapy, to some, seems particularly obscure, and is often initially resisted on the grounds that the patient 'can't paint or draw' (despite anything I may have already said about skill not being necessary). For some, the idea of using colour and shape as a means of self-expression is just too alien to contemplate. Yet, for others, despite any reservations they may have expressed regarding their artistic skills, they become interested and accept the offer. Knowing that I have made certain to inform the patient during the course of our conversation as to the purpose of the art therapy session, I always trust the patient's decision to attend. Whatever their conscious reasons – 'I may as well – what else have I got to do?', or 'I think I'll give it a go' – I feel that an inner need is being recognised, and an attempt made to meet it. We will then agree the best time to meet – this may be straight away, or at a later time – and the best place. Some patients are in single rooms and prefer to stay there, some need to get away from their surroundings. Others are in a more public ward and would prefer to have a private space, which I then arrange.

THE FIRST SESSION

I often view starting in the first art therapy session as the biggest hurdle for a patient to overcome. Having agreed to attend, they often arrive at the session with reservations about the decision they have made and the session will frequently start with discussion about those reservations. Even patients who have specifically requested art therapy have been known to start their first session with 'oh dear, now I don't know what to do'. It is important, therefore, to offer the patient a comfortable, safe environment and, when necessary, reassurance about being there. Having done this, I encourage the patient to take some time to have a look at the variety of materials available. I then encourage them to start to experiment with them and explore their possibilities – trying out different colours and textures, discovering what they can and can't do with each medium and which colours and textures they like or dislike. I find this is a helpful way to encourage the patient to make those daunting first marks on the empty page without becoming too tied up with the idea that they 'can't think of what to draw or how to do it'. By taking the emphasis away from the idea of producing an image, the patient becomes less self-conscious about what is appearing. However, there are no hard and fast rules about how the patient gets started and I will respond to their needs in whatever way seems appropriate to help them make their first marks. The following case shows how this can happen.

EILEEN

Eileen, a woman of 52 with motor neurone disease, was referred to art therapy. The referral had come from nursing staff aware of her increasing depression since her admission to the hospice. Not only was she suffering an extremely debilitating illness, but she had also suffered several recent losses. Her husband had died in the previous year and there had been other problems in the family. Eileen was a fairly reserved, quietly spoken woman. Apparently, speaking about her difficulties did not come easily to her. She did, however, recognise that she needed help of some kind. For this reason, when she was told about art therapy, she decided to try it. Yet, when Eileen arrived for her first session, she became terrified at the thought of being there. Her anxiety about her inability to paint or draw and her concerns about expectations I might have – despite my reassurances – were causing her great distress. She became dumb-struck, unable to enter into even a gentle conversation. Eventually, she expressed regret at having agreed to come as she had no idea what to do or how to do it and asked to go back to the ward. It occurred to me at this point, given her distress, that perhaps I should consider taking her back, as she had requested. To keep her there against her will would have been unthinkable. On the other hand, she had recognised her need for help and, having learned about art therapy, had chosen to come. I commented on this and encouraged her to try and trust her initial decision to attend. She agreed to stay a little longer. It seemed at this point that in order for her to take her first step across the threshold, she needed some assistance. Deciding what materials to choose and where to start had caused her such anxiety, I gave her a piece of paper and took a large packet of felt tipped pens. I asked her to choose a colour which she felt might describe her right now. She chose a blue one. I then suggested she use any shape at all to put herself on the piece of paper. Without any hesitation, at the bottom centre of the page, she drew a house. It was quickly and simply drawn; a square with a triangular roof, two small upstairs windows, with a larger window downstairs on the right and the front door on the left. To the right of the house, attached to the side, she drew another square containing rows of flowers and vegetables (see Figure 5.1).

As she drew, she began to speak about her own house which she had recently had to leave, as it was no longer appropriate for her to stay there. Her youngest son had just left and moved to a flat. She imagined the house now and felt it must be cold, empty and abandoned. The garden was now untended whereas it had always been well cared for. She then proceeded to put curtains in the downstairs window, filling them in quite heavily, leaving a narrow gap down

Figure 5.1

the centre between them. She went on to explain that the curtains at home had been left partially drawn, with a timer on some of the lighting, so that it came on at regular intervals. Anyone outside would think everything inside was carrying on as usual.

I wondered if the image might also be saying something about her. She related to this immediately, saying that none of her family (she had several children) was able to acknowledge her illness and imminent death and refused to talk about it. One of the reasons her son had left home was his inability to cope with her illness. All this left her feeling abandoned, neglected and empty. Like the house with the curtains drawn, she had been unable to let anyone outside know what was really going on inside.

By now Eileen had become much more relaxed and felt able to move onto a second picture using a large brush and quite runny paint. She spoke much more freely about issues concerning herself and her family, things she had previously been unable to address.

For many patients, initial anxieties are a result of being faced with the unknown. They are at a point of departure but have no idea what lies over the threshold. They experience a sense of panic. Eileen was overcome by panic to the point where she wanted to flee. In the countertransference, I felt Eileen's panic and almost reacted to it myself by immediately sending her back to the ward. However, I also felt very strongly that her initial request for help must be trusted. Rather than assist in her 'flight' from the unknown, I felt Eileen needed someone to support and accompany her across the threshold into it. In the moment that Eileen chose the blue pen, she had taken the step over the threshold. Her image flowed from her – it seemed – without thought, apparently providing immediate release from her initial anxieties. Her image was both conscious and unconscious, providing her with a means to voice not only her immediate concerns about her home, but also giving her inner self a voice which enabled Eileen to recognise her own sense of abandonment and isolation. Having taken this initial step, Eileen found a release for her anxieties and was then able to move on to use paint much more freely. She enjoyed the sense of freedom it offered her, and trusted the 'voice' offered to her inner self.

In his book, *Hero with a Thousand Faces*, Joseph Campbell says:

> The adventure is always and everywhere a passage beyond the veil of the known into the unknown; the powers that watch at the boundary are dangerous; to deal with them is risky; yet for anyone with competence and courage the danger fades.
>
> (Campbell 1993: 82)

Eileen had the competence and courage to step over the boundary and the danger faded.

My experience in working with a cross-section of the general British public leads me to believe that the need to communicate through imagery is something the majority of people are out of touch with. The fact that my title contains the word art frequently causes my services to be seen as something other – a subject few people readily associate with. Yet, given the right circumstances, this powerful means of communication can be rediscovered and used to express sometimes overwhelming emotions. Its very unfamiliarity is often a bonus. Those less sophisticated in the uses of artistic grammar can often be less guarded about the images which surface. They have less control over what appears on the paper, thus giving the unconscious greater freedom of speech.

BOB

For instance, Bob, a man of 65 who had only recently received the news that he did not have long to live, came along to an art therapy session. He was constantly brimming with tears and having to wipe his eyes. He said since he had come to the hospice, he had been like a leaking tap. Always weeping. He felt sad – grief stricken at leaving his wife, whom he loved dearly, yet the crying seemed excessive and he couldn't understand why it wouldn't stop. Although he had agreed to come along to art therapy at the recommendation of a member of staff, he was so self-conscious about using any of the materials that for some time he resisted using them at all. Instead, he sat and talked, relating stories from his past. Then, out of the blue he described an incident which had occurred twenty years before. It was an occasion where he had been treated extremely badly at work. He told me he used to be a bus driver, and enjoyed his job. But some problems arose, and a judgement had been made on him which was unjust and undeserved. He described the fury he had felt toward the person who had made the accusation, and had ultimately returned to tackle him about it. In telling this story, the tone of Bob's voice changed and became very angry. When he finished, I felt the anger still hanging in the air. I commented on this. He agreed, and I wondered what might have reminded him of this particular incident. He gradually began to recognise the same sense of anger and injustice about his present situation. As he began to acknowledge these feelings, he became increasingly distressed. It was then that I suggested it might help to express these feelings, if not through words, which he was having trouble finding, then perhaps by using some of the art materials. He picked up a red felt tipped pen and began to cover the piece of paper in front of him in red lines and gashes, stabbing at the paper as he gave vent to his rage and his tears flowed. By the end of the session this man said he felt that a great pressure had been lifted from him. His 'leaking', having by now been recognised as tears of rage, had already begun to cease.

There were very few subsequent meetings with this patient. Those we had were brief and consisted mainly of conversation. He would, however, with a wry grin, occasionally refer to the time I 'very cleverly conned' him into recognising his anger. He never quite believed it was something he had allowed himself to do.

Once again, by agreeing to attend the art therapy session, the patient was recognising an inner need and attempting to meet it. Bob's unfamiliarity with any kind of art-making process was the cause of considerable self-consciousness. Having agreed to come, he then resisted making use of any of the art materials, choosing instead to use a more familiar and comfortable means of communication – conversation. Yet, he still found the opportunity to express his utter rage at his present situation. Initially this expression was indirect. Once he began to recognise his overwhelming anger, finding words to express it seemed impossible. Ultimately, the very medium he was so unfamiliar with came to his aid. The use of art materials offered him the opportunity to give immediate vent to his feelings in a way which did not necessitate searching for the right words. He seemed to find release through the use of colour and the sweeping and stabbing movements on the paper.

THE 'ONE OFF'

Having worked in a large cancer hospital and a hospice, I have found that, in both, I would frequently only see a patient once. In palliative care in particular, 'one off' sessions are common. This is not always due to the fact that a patient may have deteriorated rapidly between one meeting and the next, but sometimes because one session is all they need. One of the first things I noticed about working with people facing imminent death was the immediacy with which they seemed to 'plunge into the deep'. I still never fail to be impressed by the speed with which, very frequently in our first session, a patient can express extremely powerful, sometimes overwhelming emotions. It is as if the unconscious is fully aware that time is of the essence and there are pressing issues it is important to resolve before death. Once an opportunity to deal with these issues is offered, no time is wasted in taking it. Michael Kearney, consultant at Our Lady's Hospice in Dublin, states in his book, *Mortally Wounded*, 'It is as if the depths are ready and waiting for that individual to take even one small step in their direction' (Kearney 1996: 106).

TERESA

For instance, I was approached by ward staff about Teresa, a woman of 54. They felt they were having some difficulty helping her. She was very poorly and deteriorating rapidly. The nursing staff had found her very needy for some time. She wanted constant attention, yet they had trouble meeting her needs, as it was never really clear what the problem was. Nothing was ever quite right. She maintained a polite distance with staff, but was always full of praise for them – expressing extreme gratitude for all they were doing. Yet the staff were always left feeling that somehow they hadn't got it right for her.

To begin with, it felt the same in art therapy. She was full of praise, compliments and gratitude yet it was difficult to get anything quite right for her. First the seating was wrong, then she felt I was sitting on the wrong side of her, as she was having problems with one of her eyes and had difficulty seeing me. She was also suffering from nausea and vomiting and was concerned that the small bowl she had brought with her should be within reach.

Eventually, she became settled and chose to use the oil pastels. She spent fifteen minutes quietly drawing on a large piece of paper a woman's head which virtually filled the page. Teresa was familiar with using art materials and had been fond of painting and the likeness to herself that she had captured in such a short time was quite striking. However, the face in the picture was distraught, the eyes brimming with tears which poured down her cheeks. She just sat looking at it. I said 'The person in the picture looks very unhappy.' It was then that her own tears began to flow. She quietly began to sob and said 'Everyone is so kind to me, and I know I should be grateful . . .'. There was a long pause and I said 'But – ?' and she went on to express the bitterness and resentment she felt towards anyone she came into contact with, because, basically, they weren't about to die. She was. She expressed the desperate unfairness she felt, in that she had spent much of her life being health conscious – (it seemed) all for nothing. She was ultimately able to express the sheer terror and loneliness she felt – like a lost child.

Teresa found a powerful release for feelings she had until now been unable to admit to herself, let alone any one else. I received a call the next day to say that there seemed to have been a 'massive breakthrough' with Teresa and already she was much more relaxed and approachable. I was asked if I might call in and see her very soon, as she had found the session so helpful that she wanted a further meeting and knew she had little time left. I called in to see her on two more occasions very soon after our first meeting. She was indeed much more relaxed and although she produced one more drawing – this time of a row of medicine bottles representing all the 'disgusting concoctions' she was having to take and her anger about that and her illness, she preferred just to talk, as she was very tired. It felt to me that our first meeting had been the vital 'one off' which had enabled her to make the breakthrough to her deeper self and face her fear. Teresa died five days after our first meeting.

Kearney refers to the observation of depth psychologist Edward Edinger that, for those close to death, the individuation process can be accelerated and there is an 'urgency on the part of the unconscious to convey awareness of a metaphysical reality, as if such an awareness were important to have before one's physical death' (Edinger 1992: 224, cited in Kearney 1996: 107). The image Teresa had created offered her a reflection of her inner self. Once faced with it she could no longer deny her real feelings and responded accordingly. I felt that it was the terrified and lonely child in her who had been constantly wanting attention from the staff. Once Teresa had found a way to give her true feelings expression, the brave front fell away and she became 'real'.

BEN

In an ideal world an art therapist would have a room to offer a patient time and privacy without interruption. However, the fact that this seems to be a luxury many establishments can ill afford does not necessarily mean a useful session cannot still take place. As well as hospice work, I have also spent some time working in a large cancer hospital. Much of my time was spent visiting wards. Lack of available space and the condition of some of the patients often meant working with them by the bedside. This was how I met Ben, a 10-year-old boy on the children's ward. One of the ward staff suggested he might be interested in doing some drawing, as he seemed to need something to do. Ben was suffering from leukaemia, and was attending the hospital for yet more treatment. When I approached Ben he seemed quite active and 'giggly' – squirming around on the bed. Yet his laughter didn't seem that of a relaxed, happy child, more tense and anxious – almost angry. When I introduced myself, showed him the materials and asked whether he might be interested in using them, he nodded straight away, taking a further look at what was available.

As we were setting up to work together by his bed, he was approached by one of the nurses who had to administer antibiotics, which was a lengthy process taking about ten minutes. While this was happening, he said he would draw the nurse. He took a very soft, crumbly pastel, and what started to appear on the paper was a dragon, breathing fire. His hands became very messy and he showed them to the nurse while she was administering his medication, and threatened to touch her face with them. Although she asked him (very nicely!) not to, he did, eventually, touch her forehead, leaving a large mark containing all the colours of the dragon. After a short while, he rubbed off the mark, his treatment was completed, and she left.

During the course of drawing his picture, there were (as there often are when working on a ward) several more interruptions and with each one, something else would be added to the picture. For instance, the dragon's head became decapitated – a sword and slayer were added – the sword became more bloodied – the dragon grew and the fire from its mouth increased. As he continued to work I felt strongly that he was expressing his anger about his situation and all that went with it. He wanted to 'mark' the nurse with the dragon's colours, which he had on his hand. The further visits by other members of staff added fuel to his fire and the flames from the dragon's mouth grew. The fact that he said he was going to draw the nurse and immediately started drawing a dragon seemed to me to indicate that perhaps he saw his illness and all that went with it – hospital, treatment, staff administering it – as a huge, threatening dragon. A patient, whether child or adult, often feels disempowered in a hospital – somewhat at the mercy of medical staff actively administering treatment, while they have to passively lie back and take it. In his picture I felt that Ben empowered himself by killing off this whole threatening, frightening area of his life – albeit in fantasy. Far from being a passive patient who feels out of control of his situation, he seemed to channel his frustration and anger into this picture, where he was very much in control and taking action.

Although the setting and circumstances for Ben's session were far from ideal, I feel that the very intrusions and interruptions we experienced were the motivating force behind the picture. The need to find an outlet for his feelings of fear, frustration and anger seemed enormous and when the opportunity to do so presented itself, he took it. The medium in this instance was ideal for Ben. Not only was he able to express very powerfully through his image a wealth of feelings, by choosing a particularly messy medium, he could also take on the colours of the dragon, rather like taking on its power.

Ben had no wish to discuss his picture. Perhaps the breadth of feelings it contained could not be put into words at his age. It seemed enough for him just to do it. He did not want to keep it, but preferred me to take it away.

When I left him he was very calm – almost sleepy. Ben's stay for treatment was short, so I did not have the opportunity to see him again.

CONCLUSION

For many people, the idea of entering a hospice signifies only one thing – the end. This is often the reason why someone suffering from a terminal illness may initially reject the offer of hospice care. It is seen as giving up or admitting defeat, acknowledging their imminent death. In her book on art therapy with groups, Marian Liebmann discusses a group run at a cancer help centre and says 'they found it difficult to have any concept of the future without feeling that they were looking into their own graves' (Liebmann 1994: 78). Yet, for me, this powerful image of standing at a graveside, looking down into the darkness, can also be seen as standing on a threshold, looking into the unknown, something I have found myself witnessing with patients frequently.

Very often, a patient attending art therapy for the first time will have been looking anywhere but ahead, while at the same time, their unconscious is eagerly searching for a way to resolve deeper, darker issues. For the patients mentioned in this chapter, art therapy provided them with the means to focus fully ahead, into the darkness. Eileen was able to overcome her panic about facing the unknown, and move on to use her sessions to explore a variety of issues which were around for her. Teresa wasted no time in coming face to face with her real self. Bob was completely unfamiliar with the idea of using art as a means to express anger and a sense of injustice, yet, when the opportunity arose, his deep need to find an outlet for these feelings overcame any prior inhibitions and allowed them expression. Ben was able, in just one session, to respond immediately, through his images, to all that was going on around him.

Most of us go through life avoiding the reality of our own death and the fact that our time is limited, behaving more often as if we are immortal. Those suffering from a life-threatening illness are no longer able to avoid the fact and have to face up to the very thing most manage not to look at. 'Neither the sun, nor death can be looked at steadily', wrote La Rochefoucauld.

In my experience, it has become evident that the first session in art therapy is vital as a means to enable patients to step over the threshold from the known into the unknown and focus on what is directly ahead of them, with the urgency required to do so. Even after the diagnosis of a terminal illness, an individual's conscious self will frequently avoid facing the truth. Yet the unconscious self does recognise it and the immediate necessity to resolve pressing issues. In using the art therapy sessions to step over the threshold, from conscious to unconscious, the patients discussed in this chapter found immediate release from their present difficulties – fear, anxiety, anger and much else. For many patients, this release then enables them to move on, frequently embarking on a voyage of self-discovery and psychological rehabilitation.

BIBLIOGRAPHY

Cambell, J. (1993) *Hero With A Thousand Faces*, London: Fontana.
Kearney, M. (1996) *Mortally Wounded*, Dublin: Marino.
Edinger, E. (1992) *Ego And Archetype*, Boston and London: Shambala.
Liebmann, M. (1994) *Art Therapy For Groups*, London: Routledge.

Jackie Coote trained in art therapy at Goldsmiths' College. She has introduced the profession in several establishments for people with life-threatening or terminal illness, including St Christopher's Hospice, Sydenham. She works at the Royal Marsden Hospital, Sutton and 'The Junction' drop-in centre, Penge. She lives in London.

Chapter 6

What lies within us

Individuals in a Marie Curie Hospice

Gill Thomas

I have worked at the Marie Curie Centre in London as a part-time art thera-pist for over three years. It is a thirty-two bed unit with a very active out-patients' department and day centre. There is a very strong medical lead within the unit, which provides excellent palliative care. Over the period of time that I have been at the centre there has been some considerable change toward a more holistic approach to the care that is offered. We have a strong multidisciplinary team and there is a more open approach to psycho-social and emotional issues. I have developed my role so that I can work in a very flexible way and be as responsive to the needs of the patients as is possible within the time constraints.

Time has a huge bearing on both the nature of the work and the type of interactions that I have with the patients. When someone is so physically unwell it is important to be able to catch the moment when they are well enough to take part in a session. Time is a constant factor determining how many occa-sions I might see an individual. If a patient comes to the hospice for respite this might only be for two weeks. When a patient is at the end of their care then time is an unknown factor. If someone wishes to make an image or do a piece of work, I need to be able to respond as quickly as I can because their state of health might well fluctuate. Making an appointment time for the next day still has an element of uncertainty, as a person's state of health can deteriorate overnight leaving them unable to keep their time. Therefore the opportunity for them to make an image has been lost. At a time when they are dealing with so many losses, this additional one needs to be avoided.

I have two groups at the hospice each week, and I think it is very important that they run at the same time. Boundaries to a therapeutic relationship are often a difficult issue within this kind of setting; for example, I might have contact with a patient in a different context later in the day. The issue of intimacy has to be recognised; I might have a session with a patient who is in bed, who could require help in moving into a more comfortable position. With each new contact that I make with a patient we have to agree how this will work.

On one occasion I worked with a young woman who was unable to get out of bed and she did not wish her bedroom door to be closed, or to stop the flow of people who tend to come in and out. We agreed that, as she was working on a drawing board, if someone came into her room she would turn this over and it would be as if a pause button on a tape recorder had been pressed until the person had left. This worked well for her.

I have to be flexible and creative with each relationship. It is impossible to predict who or how many people will come to the groups each week. The things that are constant about it are myself and the timing of the session. As things work at the moment I do not have any visiting students or other staff in these sessions. I feel it important to keep these aspects of the boundaries secure.

Working with patients who know they are dying is challenging in many ways. Every patient that I meet has arrived at this point in their life having met with different sorts of difficulties, and is often feeling somewhat battle scarred. Their journey to this point has led them to deal with physical, emotional and spiritual issues. Offering someone the opportunity to explore these different issues at this time using a creative process needs to be approached with care and respect. The patient will often feel very exposed when asked to make a mark on a piece of paper. Some patients leap to the suggestion with an eagerness that can feel potentially all consuming. Many patients can seem reluctant, or express huge inhibitions. They feel that their drawing skills are going to be inadequate.

Some patients instinctively know how to use the process of art therapy, making links between their image and their feelings. They are able to work at a deep level very quickly. They understand the process of using metaphors and symbols, and are comfortable with this way of working. Most patients seem to gradually evolve a relationship with the process. Some begin by talking of coming to an art class, other patients take more time before being able to talk about their images, and are content to allow the image to speak for itself. A person who has cancer is feeling so out of control because of what the disease is doing to their body that I feel it imperative that they are able to reclaim some sense of control within the frame of their drawing and the session. If someone is already feeling vulnerable, it is important that I do not add to this feeling. I want to provide a place that feels safe, where issues that may be painful or disturbing can be explored.

INDIVIDUAL JOURNEYS

Patients can use an art therapy session to explore many feelings. Often they feel that they are travelling with their disease, and coping with the fallout from it. I often refer to the opportunity of making an image as the beginning of a journey – you can move to a different place and maybe see things from a different perspective. And by moving to a different place you can gain through the experience along the way, acquiring an insight or some new kind of understanding. Some patients require different amounts of support in order to begin. This is the point at which I have felt most challenged as a therapist. I have been required to change my approach in order to allow each person to be able to begin on their own individual journey, in a way that feels right for them. I need to find a way in joining the patient at their own starting point. I would not want someone to feel stuck and feel that they did not know how to begin to make a mark on a piece of paper.

WORKING FROM FOUND IMAGES

For some patients, working from what I call 'found images' can prove to be a most valuable place to begin. I have discovered that having a box full of assorted postcards of paintings and places for people to look through is a 'safety net' that a person might need in order to make their first mark. A found image might well be a photograph or picture that a patient has discovered for themselves outside of the group. These found images may stimulate an idea or feeling for an individual. By picking up the cards and sorting them each person is responding to them in a very different way. I make it very clear that I am not suggesting that they copy from these cards but merely look through them and see which ones they are attracted to. For some patients working from a found image can act as a bridge that allows them to cross the gulf to the unknown in their own image.

I suggest that they look through the box and see if there is a colour or a shape that they are attracted to. Is there a mood suggested by a picture? What feelings does a particular image evoke? Would they like to bring pieces or parts from different images together. Somehow having something physical to hold and look at can take away some of the anxious feelings that are related to the beginnings of this creative journey. I have been amazed at what can develop.

One lady, having picked a postcard of San Francisco, began to draw a quiet country scene which she said was in the Lake District in the north of England. It was a memory of when she had last been on holiday with all her family and had felt well. Her image did not resemble the card she had picked visually, but clearly a feeling had been evoked. This lady like so many others was then able to make other images of her own without the use of the 'safety net'.

CREATING THE SPACE

The elements that make up my way of working are sometimes difficult to piece together. There is the time, place and space; the opportunity to engage with the art materials and a non-judgemental attitude to what is produced; a calm reflective stillness, that can hold or contain often a turmoil of feelings. Again I am drawn back to the issue of time, and how important it is for patients to find a reflective space. I find this quote by Murray Cox very powerful, and it has deep echoes in the way that I work – 'attend, witness, wait, discern, formulate, reflect, attend, witness, wait'.

images that she made twenty-five colour copies of it to send to relatives around the world.

Toward the latter stages of her care she arrived at the group holding a picture of a ginger kitten gleaned from a magazine. This was of the 'chocolate box' variety. I have to admit to having some difficulty with this picture as a place for her to begin. Sarah had never made a verbal link with her feelings and the images that she made. My reaction to the kitten was that it was going to feed into her belief that this was an art class not a therapy group (see Figure 6.1).

Figure 6.1

Sarah began to draw; she struggled desperately to draw the kitten. The more she tried, the harder it became. The kitten in her drawing had one paw that appeared to be very swollen and the kitten looked very angry. Sarah too had a very swollen arm due to lymphodema. This was the same arm/paw as the kitten. When I gently pointed out to her the similarities, and asked how the kitten was feeling, Sarah began to cry. 'Is this what art therapy is?' she said.

Once we had talked for some time about her difficulties in drawing the kitten, she was able to acknowledge that she was feeling angry. Sarah was very sociable and never refused a visitor. There are many volunteers and students that visit the hospice and Sarah always appeared to welcome them when they stopped to talk to her. It emerged that a male volunteer whom she did not like had become a regular visitor. She felt as though she was being petted by him. Sarah did feel angry and upset about this, but had not been able to tell him or acknowledge her feelings. By the end of the session, Sarah realised that the kitten was herself. She did in fact want to growl at this man and tell him to go away, and to stop what she had experienced as him stroking her. With support she was able to do this. The kitten torn from a magazine acted as a bridge for Sarah that day. Sarah had discovered a voice through her images and was able to begin to express her feelings in a way that was new to her. This also affected how she was viewed within her family. Her brother and sister seemed to relish hearing about her drawings and they were held in great value by them.

Nearly two years after Sarah's death her brother came to visit the hospice. He still had all of her drawings and spoke at length about his feelings for his sister. He told me how she had been teased all of her life and had never been taken seriously. He then said, 'it is very sad to think that her time in the hospice was the happiest of her life.'

JANE

Jane was a lady with an abdominal carcinoma of unknown origin, possibly ovarian. She was 57. She was a single lady who was a primary school teacher. On her first admission she was feeling that she could not cope at home, she had major issues surrounding her body image, which manifested in her requiring a tremendous amount of reassurance when it came to any kind of physical examination. Some years previously Jane had done some voluntary work at the hospice and had run some art classes.

My first contact with Jane was following a referral from the nursing staff and she seemed understandably wary of me, questioning me at length about art therapy. She told me of art projects that she was working on which seemed to be very ambitious. But even so Jane said that she would like to come to the art therapy group. It took a number of weeks, however, for her to be able to come to the group. She had built this up as a big issue for herself, being very self-castigating about not having achieved what she had planned. I went to see her outside of the sessions and we talked through what it was that would allow her to be able to come and decided that coming to the group could act as a new beginning. She came to the next group. Jane needed to feel that she could come to the group unburdened from the weight of work that she felt she should have by now completed. She brought many drawings with her that she had made over the years, and said that she wished to turn one of them into a Christmas card design. Over the next few sessions she reworked many of her drawings and changed them into potential designs. Jane appeared to gain great pleasure from being able to do her own creative work again and her energy levels seemed to be on the rise.

The nursing staff had reported that she had seemed very irritable and angry on occasions, and because of this it had proved difficult to treat her. She would constantly question the medical staff, wanting to known how much time she had, a question that was almost impossible for them to answer. Doctors can give an opinion based on their experience about the state of a patient's health, but they can often not satisfy a patient's need for certainty. Jane was very frightened about her illness, but until now was reluctant to talk in any great depth about her feelings, with me or anyone else.

Jane made her decision about which design she wished to print. It was a landscape of a place that she had visited. She talked at length about the feeling of open space in the countryside. The print was to be a lino cut. She arranged for a friend to go and pick up or buy the tools that she required in preparation for her to begin this project. Jane missed a couple of sessions due to not feeling so well, and then became very frustrated about what she described as not 'getting on'. Once feeling stronger she was able to complete the lino cut, and was now planning her colour scheme. Jane was pleased with her design.

Her sister had now become a regular visitor and was often dispatched to collect or purchase materials. She was expressing her distress about Jane and although Jane and herself at times seemed to have a difficult relationship they were beginning to find an easier way to communicate.

Jane's health and strength was by now declining. She had been able to express some of her fears within the sessions, and had been feeling a little easier about the physical contact with the medical and nursing staff. However, she was becoming increasingly frustrated about her lack of speed in completing the task she had set herself. I suspect that she had always been a hard task master. It was becoming more apparent that she would be unable to complete the print run by herself. I decided to negotiate with her that in this circumstance I would act as a technician under her instruction so that the print run could be finished. We arranged a time and set up the print run in the day room of the ward. I did not act until I was given a specific instruction, and Jane seemed comfortable with this arrangement. By the end of the second session we had completed a print run of 100 cards. Jane was delighted. She did send a few, but the rest she sold in aid of the hospice.

As we worked together Jane clearly was feeling relieved that the task she had set herself was nearing completion. She seemed less burdened and more relaxed. Setting herself this goal and being able to see the project through to completion was of crucial significance to her. The way her sense of self-worth grew was almost tangible. As her feelings of deep frustration waned so did her outward appearance of being angry. Generally she seemed much more approachable.

It is a difficult issue to engage in work with the patients. I did not want to compound any feelings of me, the therapist, being able and well. By placing myself in the position of being under Jane's instruction, it seemed to enhance her own 'well' part and allow it to grow.

The nursing staff had expressed great interest in the cards and Jane took delight in explaining how the printing technique worked. This was part of a changing process in her relationship with the staff, who up until now had created a wary respect of Jane's need for individual space due to her often angry demeanour.

REFLECTIONS ON THE JOURNEY

The journey into art therapy as a process had allowed both of these women to move a long way. They had both made the process very individual to themselves and stretched and challenged myself as the therapist. Both women had also managed to shift how they were perceived by the wider service within the hospice. There had also been a subtle change for both of them in their family relationships.

The issue of personal control within the therapeutic relationship is of paramount importance. They both self-elected to begin an encounter with the creative process. Their experiences were very different, but both women were very clear about how they wished to use this opportunity once they had begun.

Sarah for a good number of months referred to the art therapy group as an art class. She felt that she was learning new skills, and indeed she was. Not only did she gain in personal confidence – it was as if she was learning to speak. For her the opportunity to voice her own thoughts and feelings was a very new experience. I think it felt as new as making the marks on a piece of paper. The relish with which she began to draw was a very exciting process to observe. For her it was engaging with the 'well' part of herself and allowed her to be viewed in a more rounded way. Sarah's standing within her family changed. She became the artist, not just the sister who was dying of cancer. For Sarah using the found images not only acted as a bridge to her own creativity, it allowed her to step over to a place where she was in touch with herself in a new way.

Jane's dialogue with the process of art therapy began from a different place. She was already familiar with her own creativity, but had to find a new way for it to work for her in this setting. Jane was very clear about what she wanted to do, how much she wanted to say and when. As she became more confident with our relationship, she was able to voice more of her own feelings. I was only too aware that she had run an art class at the hospice some years previously – it was important that I acknowledged this and gave due respect to her skills and experience.

For Jane, voicing her anger was partly a way of protecting herself, as she was feeling incredibly vulnerable and exposed. She was a very private person who had been very independent. I had to be very careful how I negotiated a collaborative approach to her printing. I was very clear that she had to direct me in every aspect of the process. Jane was to be in charge and in control. The importance for Jane of being able to complete a project that she had set herself was vital, it linked directly to the 'well' part of herself. Jane also felt a great sense of achievement, which for the dying patient is often hard to find.

It became apparent to me that both women through sharing their images with the staff at the hospice had changed how they were vi ed. Sarah at first was a highly anxious patient who at times could be perc being demanding. Now she was seen as a woman who was worki ing skills and was pleased to share her experiences. There was mmon ground that was nothing to do with disease and dyi en to hear how her latest drawing was developing, and wh nt work on next. One member of the nursing staff purcha es of her drawings for his wall at home.

For Jane the sharing of her work nifted her from at times being a lady who was difficult to , an accomplished artist in her own right. Staff had been f how to approach her; she had acted out huge amounts of en difficult to offer her treatment when she was so untouchable. not disappear but certainly eased as she got to know and trust staff. Aga aff were keen to hear of her latest developments and achievements.

The creative process is a well activity, the kind of thing we do in our own spare time, we choose to draw or paint, we might decide to join an evening class or rent a studio space. I know when I have done some of my own work I feel different. It is a life enhancing activity. Jane and Sarah were engaged in active living when they were making their images. It affected how they perceived themselves and at this point in their lives how they viewed the world.

Art therapy as a non-invasive treatment can work on so many levels and at the pace that the patient can deal with. Patients who are dying often dip in and out of denial about what is happening to them and this can give them periods of respite from confronting such difficult issues. As Kübler-Ross (1970: 35) states: 'Denial is usually a temporary defence and will soon be replaced by partial acceptance.' How and when this acceptance is reached is a very individual process. The subtleties that art therapy can offer at this time can be immeasurable.

I am keen that my contact with each individual is appropriate for that person. I attempt to join them at the point where they can begin to engage in this process. If this is calling the art therapy sessions an art class for a period of time, until they can embrace the process in a different way, then I am happy to meet them at this place.

I now no longer question patients bringing found images into a session. On so many occasions there has been a specific meaning that has evolved for each individual. I need to trust in their own sense of direction, in relation to their therapeutic journey. This very much links to the individual being able to take control, and feeling empowered within the session. For someone who is dying finding a sense of achievement has immense value. I was very moved by Dennis Potter's last interview with Melvyn Bragg when he spoke of the need to leave something behind that he was proud of, the need to 'go out with a fitting memorial'. The significance of making one's mark and leaving it was not lost on Sarah and Jane. Art therapy as a process was able to provide them with a vehicle and mode of travel for their own very individual journeys.

> What lies behind us and what lies before us are tiny matters compared to what lies within us.
>
> (Ralph Waldo Emerson 1994: 69)

BIBLIOGRAPHY

Cox, Murray (1997) *Mutative Metaphors in Psychotherapy*, London: Tavistock.
Levine, Stephen (1986) *Who Dies?*, Somerset: Gateway Books.
Uchida, Yoshiki (1973) *We Do Not Work Alone*, Kyoto: Nissha.
Kübler-Ross, Elisabeth (1970) *On Death and Dying*, London: Tavistock.
Elliott, Lesley (1994) *The Longest Journey*, Weymouth: The Dorset Respite and Hospice Trust (PO Box 42, Weymouth, Dorset DT4 8XQ).

Gill Thomas BA (Hons), DipAT, RATh, DipEH, P.NLP works as an Art Therapist for Marie Curie Cancer Care and for the oncology department at St Bartholomew's Hospital. Gill contributes to conferences, as well as in-service training courses for Marie Curie and at Trinity Hospice where she is employed as a Hypnotherapist. Her special interests include Visualisation and Hypnotherapy linked with Art Therapy in symptom control.

Chapter 7

The search for a model which opens

Open group at the Royal Marsden Hospital

Camilla Connell

> For neither doth he wholly know,
> And neither doth he all forget.
> But that high thing which once he saw,
> And still remembers, that he holds,
> And seeks to bring the truth forgot
> Again to that which he hath yet.
>
> (Boethius)[1]

> What then is our course, what the manner of our flight? This is not a journey for the feet; the feet bring us only from land to land; nor need you think of coach or ship to carry you away; all this order of things you must set aside and refuse to see; you must close the eyes and call instead upon another vision which is to be waked within you, a vision, the birth-right of all, which few turn to use.
>
> (Plotinus)[2]

After nearly a decade of work in a National Health Service cancer hospital, I now feel that it is probable that therapies involving the arts will assume an increasingly important place in the psychological treatment of people with cancer. In part this is due to the growing interest in so-called complementary therapies and recognition of the therapeutic aspects of engagement in the arts. Moreover if, even by default, as the costs of high-tech treatments and their efficacy are subject to constant re-evaluation, the arts therapies could be viewed as a valuable strategy in helping to cope with the later stages of illness.

The setting for the approach to art therapy which is described here is a specialist cancer hospital which functions as a research centre for cancer treatment, and offers specialised treatment for all cancers on both a local and national level. It caters for 12,000 in-patients per year. There are ten wards which include a gynaecological unit, a breast unit, a head and neck unit, a palliative care unit and a rehabilitation unit. The rehabilitation services came together as a unit in 1989 within a refurbished building. Art therapy is one of around twenty different services which are available in this unit; other include physiotherapy, occupational therapy, speech therapy, and so on. The official philosophy for rehabilitation begins: 'We believe that patients with cancer are first and foremost individuals with unique physical, psychological and spiritual needs who have the right to an optimum quality of life.'

Patients in a cancer hospital are there for the treatment of a physical illness, they are not looking for a psychological therapy in principle. Therefore art therapy may be the last thing they expect to find. Responses to the offer of art therapy can be very different, ranging from enthusiasm and curiosity, to indifference, even anxiety. It is something which is largely unknown and unfamiliar. It doesn't fall into the expected categories of tests and waiting for results of diagnosis, prognosis, surgery, chemotherapy, radiotherapy. The resilient and grateful patient is also facing shared accommodation, unfamiliar company and surroundings. Many identifiable professions enter the patient's life. Not only doctors and nurses, but many others including social workers, physiotherapists, occupational therapists and so on, all of whom are predictable and understandable. However, art therapy falls outside these categories and is not so easily comprehended. Because of this the therapist finds herself in a difficult but unique position regarding the patient. Her role is not so clear and requires a careful introduction. However, since art in therapy can help a person to access their inner world more quickly and deeply than many other means it may offer something quite unique for those who wish to embark on it. I have come to the simple conclusion that the most important aim of art therapy in this setting is to help the patient to access a deeper level of themselves, with the corresponding increase in understanding that this can bring. Many other outcomes may have therapeutic value but finally this would seem to be the prime purpose.

A patient may initially perceive art therapy as a way of passing the time and making a pleasing picture. For the therapist, among several questions is that of how to discern if an individual is wishing to open to a deeper experience of themselves or not, and, if so, whilst providing a safe space, materials, time and attention, is it possible to help them attain to this need. She has to help them see that they do not need to perform but that they can experiment and explore without fears over the outcome. After painting for a while anxiety subsides and a new freedom may appear for the novice painter. The therapist tries to maintain an atmosphere in which this can take place. Several therapeutic benefits may occur and all can combine in their effect. The physical contact with art materials, experiencing the energy of colour, the pleasure and achievement in making a painting, the appreciation of other viewers, release and relaxation and sharing of current concerns, all have their beneficial effects and can be part of a life-enhancing process. However, beyond this remains the search for understanding, which is where we are encouraged by the words of Plotinus and Boethius at the opening of this chapter. They can help us to look further if we are to respect the secret needs of every human being, and especially those with a life-threatening illness.

At the beginning with brush, crayon, collage or clay in hand suddenly there is found a tool, an instrument, a substance, that can be used to explore, discharge, attack, create, caress, comfort and communicate. A sheet of drawing paper becomes a recipient of all the sorrows, anger, pain, fear and frustrations that are being endured, as well as impulses of hope, courage and of questioning. For some patients at first it is difficult to allow the awareness to appear that can let the materials serve them in this way. Indeed often their foremost wish is to find out what the materials can do and how to use them to make images which will support the need to affirm a certain ability or something for the world to see.

The interface between patient and art materials can evoke strong feelings and unexpected energy, even at the end of life. This interaction seems possible because the psyche is intact and welcomes, even needs, an opportunity for creativity, although imprisoned within a declining body and influenced by the situation in varying ways. This need activates a deep impulse which is seldom realised. Having been locked into physical problems and deprivation the patient can turn towards another world from where these impulses can be released and actualised. The physical activity of using materials plays a part in this as well as the resulting images themselves. Moreover, the fresh impressions from this wordless activity, entering a maybe tired, sick body or anxious, overburdened mind, can generate enormous energy for the process that has been started. Interest and attention become engaged, which too brings energy despite modifying factors. However, it should be added that for some, too many concerns may hinder the attempt, the effort may seem too much and the experiment may end. For others it can be the beginning of a new source of meaning which can grow in importance or at least serve them for a while. For the therapist it is difficult to know in advance which way it will go, here lies the risk but also the possibility.

THE GROUP NOTEBOOK

From a practical point of view one of the most useful documents that has been developed over my years of introducing patients to art therapy has been a 'group notebook', this now occupies five volumes and continues to grow. The volumes consist of A4 two-ring binders. The sheets of work are inserted into clear plastic envelopes, back to back, with perforations for the rings. The envelopes protect and enhance the appearance of the work, enabling it to be handled frequently without damage. The title of C.G. Jung's autobiography, *Memories, Dreams, Reflections* seemed to describe what was envisaged as being the sort of material that might be generated for this group notebook, and as a title it has served very well. Indeed it now contains the artwork of a very large number of people. Successive patients through the hospital have contributed their art or written work to the notebook. Many themes are depicted related to the situation of being in a cancer hospital. It is available to be perused by patients, who usually find some correspondence with their own feelings and perceptions, thus helping them to feel less alone with their difficult experiences. Moreover, they may then consider that they have something to add through a contribution of their own.

In the setting of a cancer hospital and in developing a model of art therapy which is relevant to the situation of the patients, the value of shared experience becomes evident. This group notebook offers some of the benefits derived from cancer support groups. In a short-stay hospital regular on-going groups with a closed membership are not a practical possibility. Yet at the critical periods of hospitalisation and treatment a recognition that they are not alone can be of comfort to some patients. In comparing themselves with others through the artwork in the book, patients can gain a perspective about their own emotional reactions. Just as in being part of a group, self-worth can be enhanced in the giving and receiving of support through art and written work. Much poetry and prose is written or quoted, so that hope and understanding can be shared even when the worst fears and losses are depicted.

The notebook serves a valuable purpose as the focus of an opening conversation, because at the outset it is impossible to judge from appearances whether or not art therapy would be of value to a particular person. So patient and therapist look through the book together. Sometimes three or four people will gather round looking and exchanging comments. Remarks made by the artists will be recalled by the therapist where it seems appropriate to amplify what is on the page. Often responses are readily forthcoming from the patient who identifies with or reacts to the picture in front of them. Many people are very apprehensive initially about drawing or painting, so this viewing serves to reassure that most people are not 'talented' and that it is quite acceptable to make very simple renderings of anything they wish, even to doodle. If the patient is encouraged by what they have seen and feel able to try something themselves, A4 pads and materials of their choice are offered for them to use during their stay as an in-patient. If they are confined to bed the therapist promises to visit them again if possible in order to share their experience with them. If they wish to contribute to the book it is remarked that anything they care to offer will be much valued and seen by many people. Indeed this is so, and in looking through it over and over again with patients it can be seen what an extraordinary human testimony it is.

A WAY OF WORKING

In trying to formulate the way of working that has been developed in response to the needs of the patient group in this hospital, it has become clear that most people are not looking for 'therapy' as such. They find themselves diagnosed with a life-threatening illness and their primary concern is with treatment and cure of cancer. Most people are psychologically intact although the impact of a diagnosis of cancer and subsequent events quite naturally produces an emotional disturbance in many. The duration or severity of this disturbance varies. For some it is merely a hiccup in their pattern of life, for others it has a far greater disabling effect which may take time to settle, only to reappear if there is a recurrence of illness with ongoing problems. So it is not a corrective form of treatment that needs to be offered since the patient is not fundamentally maladjusted. Here it can be added that this is the reason why the mode of working is not deeply analytical but more of a holding and facilitating process in order to support a development of the patient's own understanding. The therapist approaches the patient with respect for their circumstances, allowing attitudes and defences to exist which may be very important for them. Obviously it is their right to choose their own degree of involvement with what is offered. In due course, as the patient begins to know and trust the therapist and the art process itself they may begin to open to greater self-scrutiny. On the other hand, when the need is great, a sudden and rapid plunge may be taken into the unknown at a very early stage of art making, in order to obtain release from emotions that have been exerting pressure for too long. However, the course may yet be different again, the patient simply being happy to experience pleasure, relaxation and a sense of achievement in picture making – recalling time past, bringing their hope into the pictures, making something to give another person, enjoying the processes involved in the use of colour. All these have a therapeutic aspect and are not to be belittled. It has been necessary to develop an inner position where the therapist's subjective need for 'success' in inspiring patients to engage deeply in art therapy is kept to a minimum, having found that it all happens when and where it is needed. All this poses quite searching questions since the therapist has not lived through some of the experiences to which patients are being unavoidably subjected.

I have found that a certain focused quality of energy is required to approach a patient sensitively and creatively. It has been useful to repeatedly discover this. With a distracted manner an important element of the interaction would be missing, that is one's own presence. This influences the opening conversations and the way that art materials and time and space will be perceived should the patient recognise a potential in the offer. As the therapist I should not even covertly dictate. It may appear that I have but little authority compared with other professionals, but this is misleading. It is not necessary to suffer from feelings of disappointment when the uptake is slow because a great deal is learned from seeming lack of success in finding how to become more sensitive to the patient and to the way one's energy is deployed. This becomes a very interesting study. An aspect which should not pass unnoticed is that art therapy is inviting a response from the patient which requires *them* to be active. Everything in hospital life encourages passivity, indeed it is sometimes desirable in such an institution that it should be so, but people get used to this mode of living. So who is this unusual person requiring an effort to be made by the patient themselves, especially in the face of all their current difficulties? I have found that a minimum of understanding is conceded to art therapy from other disciplines at this stage of its development in cancer care. But with continual efforts to inform and engage people something has been possible, as patient accounts have testified.

EXHIBITIONS

It has been my experience that it is useful to give the practice of art therapy a wider base by including elements that may seem strange in another context. For example it has been possible to mount exhibitions of patients' artwork, as much for the sake of the patients as that of the viewers.

Exhibitions serve several purposes. First they make patients' artwork available for all to see, in order to raise awareness of the art therapy service in the hospital, including an indication of the benefits it may have. Second, such a venture gains the interest and support of other members of staff wishing to enhance the appearance of their corridor with meaningful pictures. This helps to bring to fruition a yet further purpose which is to recognise a therapeutic value in stimulating and increasing feelings of self-worth in patients whose lives have been seriously reduced by the impact and ongoing effects of an illness such as cancer. A need for this has been demonstrated by patients demanding to be identified with their artwork. All ethics surrounding confidentiality are contradicted here. Very often they feel a wish to inspire others to try their hand at art therapy, as well as to be seen exhibiting themselves. In the words of some patients, 'never in their wildest dreams had they imagined they would ever see their work hanging in an exhibition'! Excitement can be intense and the sense of achievement is tremendous thus contributing meaning to the lives of people who have been and continue to be sorely tried by illness.

POETRY READING

Pursuing the evolution of this model whose aim is really to bring people in a specialist cancer hospital to a greater openness towards themselves and to a better understanding of their situation, a broad interpretation of the word 'art' can be used. Concerning literature, writing and, in particular, poetry it has been asked whether it has a place within the discipline. Would it combine, in the sense that good poetry, like art, speaks so directly to the soul that it could be an additional means of finding understanding in a muddled and disturbing situation? As I recall those patients with whom I have read poetry, it seems undeniable that the event is nearly always a source of psychological nourishment for both the patient and, incidentally, myself. As I reflect on what it is I wish to offer someone whose life has been narrowed to the point where they are seemingly denied everything that had made that life worth living, it is clear that influences such as are transmitted by art, literature and music can be of profound help. It is the patient's own capacity for responding to an innate and finer area of perceptions within themselves that is often aroused by these means, so that they can touch a deeper understanding of the direction their life is taking. I recall vividly listening at length to a patient while she spoke of her despair and incomprehension of the situation she was in, and trying with her to find a way through it, but to no avail. I then offered her the anthology of poems that I always carry with the art materials and, opening it at the sonnets of Shakespeare, this perplexed lady began to read aloud. She wept as she read two or three and finally said with great feeling, 'Perhaps that is what I needed to understand.' It was obvious that no amount of conversation could have brought her to the realisation that had appeared in her while reading those sonnets. It may be that suffering can render people much more sensitive to the inner content of works of art or literature, particularly it seems if they are shared with another. In this instance there was no doubt that those words of Shakespeare, as she voiced them, had released this woman from the torment of that moment.

It now seems quite natural to move towards this art form if and when an individual no longer wishes or is able to draw and paint. A genuine relationship has usually been established between therapist and patient, and poetry reading can offer another path, not unrelated, for exploration and expression of feeling within the security of the relationship.

Michael was from the Caribbean and in his fifties. Physically he was very incapacitated, confined to a wheelchair and unable to co-ordinate his hand movements, so drawing and painting were not easy, but neither was his interest in that direction. He had been educated in his home country in the traditional colonial style and was well versed in history and English literature. Sitting in the ward week after week he was desperate for a quality of interest that he could not find in the daily routine and he had become increasingly silent and uncommunicative. Here an occupational therapist and I began to find ourselves in close collaboration. She visited Michael frequently, taking him out of the ward in his wheelchair, addressing his OT needs and sharing long conversations with him. I responded to his literary interests by offering him the same Oxford Anthology of English Verse that I had used previously. He seized upon the book and read, recalling all the poetry he knew. We read aloud to each other in turn, his voice often shaking with emotion as he read. I saw him over several weeks and after a visit or two he began to choose and read aloud poems on the subject of death. Taking my cue from this I introduced him also to the poems of D.H. Lawrence, including 'The Ship of Death'. Michael never actually spoke about dying, but this was an inspiring way of exploring his deep feelings about it. For the therapist too this is challenging, yet of great help to be reminded of our impermanence and to try to understand what it means to face the unknown. So this sort of opportunity is to be welcomed rather than avoided, or for what other reason is one involved in this type of work?

At a late stage when painting no longer was possible for her, I continued to visit a young Malaysian woman, lying in bed with barely the strength to talk. Nevertheless, on producing the anthology, she recalled to mind herself a 'tiger' and 'daffodils', so I read Blake and Wordsworth to her, and then she remembered 'water, water everywhere', but instead of 'The Ancient Mariner' in its entirety I chose D.H. Lawrence's 'The Snake'. I find that this poem has a very strong visual quality and also expresses a certain sense of scale, something I search for in poems when choosing myself what to read to a patient. For many, maybe, this sense of scale is always forgotten when difficulties seem insurmountable. When I had read 'The Snake' the woman opened her eyes and whispered: 'It's not often that poets write about egoism.' This remark, so unexpected, was evidence that there was a quality of awareness and sensitivity very much at work, able and maybe needing to respond to communication at a level offered by that poem.

With the experiences I have described behind me, I sat with a woman suddenly no longer able to speak due to metastatic spread of illness to her brain. Previously she had found drawing a great help during sleepless hours at night, and we had had some lively conversations. Now she could only make intermittent eye contact and occasionally squeeze my hand – I wasn't sure how much she was understanding. Recalling from our conversation what had amounted to a spiritual quest on her part, I read some of the metaphysical poets to her, feeling it was appropriate to do so. She responded by smiling and meeting my eyes from time to time so that I felt my presence was welcome and not an imposition. What benefit she derived I will never know, but remembering the Malaysian woman I did not want to underestimate the powers of receptivity and awareness that could be there and the possibility of something in her being fed.

Poetry can communicate directly and visually, in the sense of word pictures, and can be a great ally in stimulating imagery which can then be translated on to paper with paint and crayon. Hence it can enable painting to start where previously the process was blocked. This occurs both with 'artists' and 'non-artists'. Of special interest are 'Haiku', a traditional form of Japanese poetry, very short and descriptive in quality. So at many levels poetry transmits specific qualities to awaken corresponding energies in an individual, from sacred verse to funny rhymes. It can offer another dimension to the quality of a life which is seeking resolution.

ART THERAPY IN A GROUP SETTING

I will now give an account of an open group which takes place once a week in the hospital.

Silence. A silence filled with energy which arises through attentiveness. For nearly an hour a group of people, most of them with cancer, were sitting together around a table painting, and none had spoken. One was using wax crayons, another felt tip pens; all were involved in a public but intimate process of image making. It is interesting that quietness in the presence of others can conduct such an intangible yet potent quality. This has been remarked on many times by people who come to the group, which is seen as a refuge from a busy ward externally, or internally from the clamour of anxious thoughts. The group, which meets for two hours once a week, has both regular members and a constantly changing number of patients who may only be able to attend once, or for six weeks in the case of those undergoing a course of radiotherapy. There are also those who return for treatment such as chemotherapy who may come intermittently, so each member is always meeting new faces. It may well be a first encounter with art materials for many years, probably since childhood when they labelled themselves or were labelled 'hopeless'. On arrival names are exchanged and news shared amongst those familiar with each other. Most people arrive at the beginning of the session but frequently newcomers to the group appear at any time during the two hour period. They have usually been detained by treatment or doctors' appointments, but not wanting to miss the session they still come.

So for this and other reasons, flexibility is a key note. However, such is the power of the creative process that in spite of a fragmented start a form does appear and a silence which has been described ensues.

Patients who have been attending for a while, some now for two or three years, through all the vicissitudes of illness or remission, are able to resume work at the start of a session. They have found ways of using the art therapy for their own purposes, relatively free from fear at their perceived inability, self-judgements and the judgement of others. The fear of appearing childish or foolish is very real in the public setting of a group. The older members have also discovered how they can use the materials that are available with confidence. So for them the process has often begun before they arrive in the room; the anticipation of furthering work which is already in progress, the imaging of some concern which is troubling them, to the security of knowing that as soon as paint or crayons are before them an internal state or event will give rise to an image. A trust has developed and so now when faced with a blank sheet of paper it no longer holds any terrors, rather it becomes a moment for reflection.

For the newcomer is it a different story. A woman, a few days post-surgery, arrived complete with drip stand and drip. Exactly why she came still feeling maybe tired, weak, or in pain, I could not tell. Curiosity, boredom, the need for a change of scene, a wish for something different from all the medical input she had received, a memory of childhood when she was allowed to play, make a mess . . . wondering if this thing called art therapy would help to relieve her inner emotional tensions? But she made the effort, and many do, in the midst of their varying circumstances.

So the newcomer is welcomed and seated as comfortably as possible at the table. Expectations may be voiced or concealed. 'What am I meant to do?',

'I haven't any imagination', 'I can't draw a straight line', 'All these other people here are so good', looking round at the longer-term members busily engaged in their own work. 'Don't worry, we were like you when we started' is the ready response. However, some newcomers are full time, part time, leisure time or would-be artists and they will have their own manner of conditioning, objectives, expectations. Art therapy can lead to outcomes on many levels. Whether patients come with apprehension or with confidence in an established skill, what will it take for an individual to work through either if the process is to lend itself to a genuine search? It could be immediately, it could be never within the duration of the therapeutic contact.

There are many ways to start the journey. With a clean and challenging sheet of paper in front, a tray of paint pots beside, and a brush in hand, the diffident newcomer to art is encouraged to plunge the brush deep into the pot containing the colour which attracts them most and without pausing for too much anxious thought, carry it straight to the paper and make a mark as bold as they dare, then a second colour to join the first accompanied by whatever encouraging words seem appropriate from the therapist who is in supportive attendance. Unexpectedly and almost miraculously the painter is painting and the therapist withdraws to let what has begun be continued. With stops and starts the paper will be filled, ideas will feed back from the work to its maker who is encouraged to be sensitive to them thus realising that the image can give birth to the idea as well as the other way round.

Not all beginnings are like this; there are a variety of approaches. Some people are helped by pictures on cards or by poetic words. Although there can be enormous joy in making drawings or paintings of closely observed subjects, this is not usually proposed, but neither is it discouraged if it occurs. Some seize on a simple jar of flowers placed at the side of the room.

So the group settles down, the satisfaction derived from using art materials is evident. Not only in the dab dab dab of colour upon colour, but in the mixing of different hues, the sweep of a big brush or the detailed touch of a fine one. Dry paint, thick paint, watery paint, waxy crayons, soft charcoal crayons, tearing coloured tissue paper. Smearing, rubbing, scratching, there is a sensual delight in all these processes, especially for someone rendered inactive, frustrated and seemingly ineffectual due to illness. Sight, sound, smell, sensation, not least sensation. A young woman found her crayon produced a screaming sound when she used it with furious energy. Pressing with all her might with zigzag strokes, the crayon screamed and screeched. 'That is me screaming,' she announced, 'this is the first time I have been able to give vent to my anger.' Later she told me that if it had not been for the presence of an elderly lady in the room she would have screamed out loud. Then later, with her fingers gently softening, smoothing and blurring the violent marks, she remarked: 'It's like talcum powder.' It seemed that much had been released in that experience with the crayons. Over and over again the materials lend themselves to angry slashing and stabbing, to detailed painstaking work, to tender loving touches, to gaiety and carefree abandon, to gloom and despair, and through it all the appearance of a new and astonishing energy in even the most debilitated people.

After an hour or so, with general agreement, the work is displayed on a wall and tea and talk intervene. By this time patients are relaxed and usually animated, some a little dazed after what they have just been through, surprising as it can be. Others are quieter, finding a need for reflection. However, people now feel related through the shared experience of working with art materials and earlier constraints have disappeared, together with fears of being artistically inadequate. A conversation begins. For some the experience has been so unexpected and rich they cannot wait to unburden themselves of what it has revealed and what it means to them. Others are faintly bemused, a landscape is simply a landscape, no more, and they may wish to find a focus on the artistic qualities of the work. For those members of the group who are familiar with the process, an agenda has often been present from the beginning and they feel enabled to talk about their concerns with reference to their painting and how it reflects their situation. For some, the experience has been on a level which as yet is too profound for words. There is no pressure for anyone to speak if they do not wish to do so. Laughter, tears, compassion and mutual understanding are shared. Conversation becomes animated and the group comment freely on each other's work, offering their own interpretations, but usually with extraordinary sensitivity towards the feelings of the artist. The session usually has to close before all has been said that might be said. This is to be expected as it is often the first time patients have been able to plumb their own feelings in company with others in comparable circumstances, particularly under the relaxing, revealing, animating influence of art making in a therapeutic setting. But every effort is made by the therapist to ensure that all feel comfortable with the way that things are left – careful closure is important. The possibility of further sessions is offered.

What of the artwork, what happens to it? This is an interesting question. In spite of feelings of artistic inadequacy very few people destroy their efforts, at least not in the presence of the therapist. It seems that the work can acquire some of the attributes of an icon, holding a significance for its maker. So frequently it accompanies them back to the ward, room or home, to be showed to others or kept as evidence of their plunge into the unknown on that particular afternoon. Others appear to find their achievement of little significance and leave the room seemingly indifferent to the future of any of their work. If difficult feelings have been discharged in the painting, some patients definitely prefer to leave the work with the therapist. Thus they walk away somewhat freer from the burden with which they entered the room two hours previously. Patients who attend the art therapy groups regularly, name, date and store their work carefully in individual folders made for them. These folders are left with the therapist for safe-keeping. She is entrusted to take care of that part of their lives and takes her responsibility seriously. On later occasions the pictures will be taken out and reviewed, becoming an important element to the patient's raison d'être, constituting something which affirms the life of that individual.

The multi-levelled possibilities of an art therapy group make it a very useful option for cancer sufferers whether in or out of hospital. It can be engaged with on whatever level the individual chooses. There are no expectations or judgements made by others. Ideally it can be a very free and enabling setting for patients to involve themselves with as far as they feel able and wish to do so. For any who engage deeply, the search is never ending and the potential for discovery of meaning is great.

> If the doors of perception were cleansed, every thing would appear to man as it is, infinite.
>
> For man has closed himself up, till he sees all things thro' narrow chinks of his cavern.
>
> (William Blake)[3]

CONCLUSION

'Quality of life' is a frequently used phrase in oncology and by multidisciplinary care teams. However, when all the skills have been provided on a physical, social and even psychological level, a patient can still be left bored and in a vacuum, starved of the sort of impressions which can feed a deep psychological need for meaning and provide material for thought. Energy may be very low and capacities reduced, but below the surface the desire for some sort of fulfilment may still be there. Is it enough to leave a patient with pain under control and physical and social needs addressed? How also to help rather than hinder that voyage of exploration that may urgently need to be continued, or even begun, when a patient recognises that they have a life-threatening illness?

In this chapter I have chosen to write more about processes than about outcomes because I think that the approach to art therapy in oncology is very specific in nature. At the beginning I have tried to understand the viewpoint of a patient when encountering art therapy, both before, during and after recognising that their problems are far more than just physical ones, although these may predominate. Several elements of the broad model of art therapy that has evolved have been described: the group notebook, the value of poetry reading, the purpose of exhibitions and the functioning of a very open group.

It has seemed important to show how the situations encountered in a cancer hospital radically influence the therapist's approach. She works with what she finds, people who are enormously challenged by a life-threatening illness. Her role is constantly being rediscovered as she spends time with each individual, and the aims of treatment revealed in their many aspects seem to lead to but one aim: that for the patient, amidst all the fears, muddles and incomprehension, at least something might be understood.

In life-threatening illnesses, where medical science has reached its limits, recognised or unrecognised, disciplines such as art therapy can offer patients a new sort of hope, one that leads in the direction of meaning. In time these therapies will be given the place they deserve alongside medical science.

REFERENCES

1   Boethius, from *Mediaeval Latin Lyrics*, translated by Helen Waddell, Harmondsworth: Penguin, 1952, p. 59.
2   Plotinus, *The Enneads*, translated by Stephen Mackenna, London: Faber and Faber, 1969, p. 63.
3. William Blake, 'The Marriage of Heaven and Hell', *The Prophetic Writings of William Blake*, vol. 1, Oxford: Oxford University Press, 1926, p. 19.

Camilla Connell BA(Hons), DipAT, RATh works as a Head IV art therapist at the Royal Marsden Hospital, London, where she has pioneered the use of art therapy with cancer patients since 1987. Her special interests include combining poetry reading and writing with art therapy and the creation of a 'group notebook' to which patients contribute their work for sharing with others.

Chapter 8

Will the kitchen table do?

Art therapy in the community

Simon Bell

Passing through the living room David leaned over his father's shoulder, and peering at the picture in front of him, said, in a broad Yorkshire accent, 'When tha's finished that, tha can paint side o' my van!'. Being unprepared for this interruption to the art therapy session taking place, I was left feeling that some of my nice neat boundaries had somehow been a little ruffled. This incident, in these early days, was really only a taste of some of the unpredictable peculiarities of spending time as an art therapist with people in their own home.

For me to have arrived at the above situation was the culmination of many months of a gradual process of exploration, trial and error. I secured the post as domiciliary art therapist with the Sheffield Macmillan support team based at St Luke's Hospice in April 1992. The task of providing a domiciliary service was at this time an unknown quantity and, not unlike many art therapists in other areas of care, I found myself embarking on a pioneering endeavour with a degree of uncertainty as to how such a project would unfold.

St Luke's Hospice was established in 1971, and 1996 celebrated the unit's Silver Jubilee year marking twenty-five years of service to the people of Sheffield. It is exciting that art therapy has become an established part of the domiciliary, day and in-patient care of the hospice and is amongst the wide range of disciplines and departments that celebrated this point in the life of the hospice. St Luke's has been at the forefront of many developments within the hospice movement and palliative care, and has become a national training and resource centre. The unit is joint funded by the Sheffield Health Authority and, as a registered charity, by the financial support of local people.

Domiciliary support for the dying and their families has been a long-established part of the services provided by St Luke's and I became part of the Macmillan team at a time of further expansion. The aim of the Macmillan team is to provide the best possible support for people living with a life-threatening illness where curative treatment is no longer appropriate or desirable. The Macmillan nurses provide access to a range of domiciliary services, such as physiotherapy, social workers and art therapy, and they also make referrals to St Luke's in-patient and day care units.

Figure 8.1 'When tha's finished that, tha can paint side o' my van!'

I began my hospice career by encouraging discussion with my colleagues about the relationship between medicine and art therapy. During this time I found it helpful to make comparisons between my discipline and the physical and emotional support provided by other members of the team. An example of this is the sensitive and intimate care involved in bathing someone during the pre-terminal stage of their illness. Nurses will speak about the vulnerability of such a situation for the patient. Yet, as the patient relaxes and places their trust in the care of the nurse, it can become an opportunity for sharing thoughts and feelings of a personal nature; a few tears may even be disguised beneath the drips of the sponge. The same tenderness and preservation of dignity is required when responding to the emotional needs of the patient in art therapy. Unfortunately further counselling cannot always be facilitated around the bath tub. The art therapist however, can provide the continuity of psychological care needed to allow further communication of emotional needs to take place.

Apart from family and friends, our homes are often entered by an assortment of visitors from the meter-reader to the minister. The home can become a thoroughfare for so many callers. In recent times the art therapist has become one of those people who may also be invited into the home at a particular time for a specific purpose. In the case of people with a diagnosis of cancer or other life-threatening illness, art therapists working in the homes of their clients is still a relatively new practice.

TEA AND THERAPY: AN ENCOUNTER WITH TOM

I would like to return to my opening vignette. The referral from the Macmillan nurse informed me that Tom was 50 years old and experiencing panic attacks and depression. He had known of his diagnosis of mesothelioma (cancer of the bronchus) a year before he was referred to the Macmillan team. Until this point the family had been coping with his ill health fairly independently, requesting extra support from their general practitioner and district nurse when needed.

During my initial assessment interview with Tom and his wife, at the family home, I gained sufficient information and understanding of their circumstances to recommend that Tom may find art therapy helpful. Tom and his wife had both reached a point of exhaustion and felt helpless and forlorn. Tom was initially withdrawn and only able to describe in a limited and faltering way his sense of despair. He was intrigued by the opportunity of doing art therapy and acknowledged that he needed something that might enable him to work through some of his experiences; some way of being able to communicate his needs. He was also wanting to change, in a very practical way, his fairly mundane and unstimulating routine at home. Once Tom, with the agreement of his wife, had decided to use art therapy I returned a week later to provide our first session.

I would begin our sessions by putting out a small range of materials on the table and positioning myself to one side looking out across the back garden with a mug of tea in front of me. Early on in the development of my role I was given a hand-made wooden box designed to carry art materials. This enables me to transport a range of acrylic paints, pencils, pastels and ink from home to home. It has become a characteristic of the art therapy sessions and is often opened out on the kitchen table, pushed under a chair or tucked up against the patient laid in bed, with paint, brushes and paper immediately to hand. By the time of our third meeting Tom had overcome some of his initial reservations about using the art materials and uncertainty about drawing and painting. He had also become accustomed to my clearing the table to make room for my art box.

During this session Tom was quiet and sorrowful, with a worried expression in his eyes. He was feeling very weak yet was determined to go ahead with the session. He soon became involved with his drawing and began to create a picture of a large farmhouse in the countryside (see Figure 8.2). He had been a farm labourer in his youth and dreamt of becoming a successful farmer himself. Tom often drifted into such deep concentration in his artwork that at times it often startled him when I reminded him of my presence; such was his need to cast his thoughts far away from his current circumstances. It was at just such a moment when Tom was quietly focusing on his artwork that his son appeared from the kitchen and remarked on his picture.

Figure 8.2

I discovered during the first few weeks of my contact with Tom that there was much unhappiness within the family relationships adding to the stress incurred through a long period of physical ill health. The long-standing family problems were a significant influence impeding Tom's overall ability to cope. He expressed a great sense of isolation within his family and disappointment with how his family life had turned out. To me the image of the farmhouse that Tom created embodied many of the conflicts that he was experiencing in his home and family life. Tom, however, regarded his painting as representing an unrealised dream of achieving a more fulfilling and happier conclusion to his life. I regarded the interruption by Tom's son as being very poignant given the theme in Tom's picture and the issues we were discussing.

A TIMELY INTERRUPTION OR ATTEMPTED SABOTAGE?

To enable a patient like Tom to use art therapy in an effective and helpful way whilst coping with such interruptions as that made by his son has involved much adjustment in my practice as an art therapist. I remember finding this interruption difficult to accommodate and recall faltering in my response. My anxiety was softened by the wry smile on Tom's face. Throughout I was desperately trying to accommodate what had just happened. Thinking on the one hand that this might have disastrous consequences for our therapeutic relationship, and on the other making a strained attempt to be vaguely amused in the hope that the incident would soon pass and I could re-establish the therapeutic work being undertaken.

This kind of interruption is less frequent now that I have become more proficient at negotiating with the family members for uninterruptable time with the patient in the home. I now feel better equipped to respond spontaneously to such an event and may even incorporate it into the therapeutic work. This event may have been an opportunity to involve Tom's son in the care of his father in a more positive way. It could have been an opportunity to improve communication and understanding. The son's remarks were a normal attempt to engage in conversation. Due to his unfamiliarity with the concept of boundaries in therapy he could not have appreciated my concerns. I now realise that most of my anxiety was unnecessary, as the therapeutic process was not at risk and the dynamics were not rendered more confused and potentially harmful.

Some weeks after this incident Tom began attending St Luke's day unit, and because of some of the pressures caused by the conflicts within the family home it became more appropriate to meet with him at the hospice. This, however, did not always solve the problem of interruptions. Whilst meeting with Tom in a seemingly secluded part of the day unit, we would often be disturbed by volunteers or other staff who would unknowingly interrupt a session taking place. Over the past four years it has taken time for colleagues to appreciate that the time a patient spends doing art therapy is confidential and requires privacy. More recently a room within the hospice has been designated specifically for art therapy so that meetings can be conducted with potentially fewer interruptions.

Having worked in the homes of many patients, I have had the privilege of being with families at a level of intimacy that is unique to home life. Inevitably the domestic environment influences, sometimes very strongly, the way in which the therapeutic relationship develops. As the home environment has many unpredictable hazards, such as unexpected callers and occasional interruptions by family members, the therapeutic process could potentially be undermined, or certainly momentarily hindered. This can happen when the family routine is too unpredictable and busy to accommodate the confidential space and time required for art therapy to take place. If there are family difficulties and conflicts that prevent the continuation of art therapy within the home then I have found it appropriate to review the domiciliary arrangements with the patient and other professionals involved. This may result in the art therapy being provisionally put on hold and reconvened when the other family needs have been addressed and resolved, or another venue may have to be arranged.

OFFERING SOMETHING THAT IS DIFFERENT

The situation I have described is an example of the art therapy service that I now provide. I was to gradually discover, like many a district nurse or health visitor, that the home life of patients is complex and unpredictable. I learned to respond and adapt creatively to a multitude of domestic situations and find ways of becoming an accepted part of the family routine. Joint home visits with Macmillan nurses certainly helped me to gain much insight into the skills required for sensitively negotiating with family members. To be supportive by demonstrating a willingness to adapt to the pace and routine of the patient and family's domestic life has become a necessary pre-requisite to any later discussion about art therapy. I have found, for example, that it can be helpful to look through family photographs and to take a stroll around the garden as part of building a relationship with the patient and their family. Being flexible in an appropriate way to the uniqueness of each home environment, and the life styles of those people living together under the same roof, is an essential part of being able to respond therapeutically to the circumstances and needs of patients being cared for at home.

I have evolved referral criteria for the nurses to follow which emphasise that art therapy is for those patients who require emotional and psychological support. It has been essential to establish a clear distinction between art therapy, the counselling role of the social worker and others who facilitate art and craft activities within the hospice. My priority is to those patients who are perhaps going through a more intense period of distress and difficulty as a result of specific, identifiable worries and concerns. Some of these are adjusting to bad news regarding prognosis, accumulated loss, fear, depression and so on. The patient may wish to address issues relating to specific experiences such as coping with a course of palliative radiotherapy, but also less easily defined needs relating to the all encompassing effect of anticipating death. Coping in the present and the anticipation of the future for the dying can evoke a time for reviewing life. Art therapy can become the means for exploring changes in personal values and priorities, matters of faith and belief and the need to either creatively engage in life or creatively withdraw and let go.

The initial assessment interview for the patient who is considering art therapy can be an intensely sensitive and difficult event. They may choose to use art therapy in order to reflect on and grapple with the distress caused by the reality of their illness and the impact this has had on their immediate circumstances. I have developed a check list of issues that I try to cover throughout this kind of meeting. I begin by asking for a brief account and history of the period of time since diagnosis and more recent experiences are discussed. I will also encourage the patient to share what they can about their perception and understanding of the current status of their physical health. My primary aim is to discover more about the emotional and psychological well being of the individual. This meeting also provides me with the opportunity to explain more fully what art therapy is and how I would facilitate this at the family home. During this part of the conversation with family members, there are often a few bemused expressions and a degree of puzzlement. However, once I begin my explanation it is not unusual for the patient and family to become animated by the idea of painting and drawing. I will encourage some debate about the relationship between feelings and expression through art in these initial interviews and it is not too long before an adequate understanding of art therapy is achieved.

ADAPTIVE AND THEME-FOCUSED ART THERAPY

Over the past four years I have developed an approach to my work which I define as adaptive and theme-focused art therapy. The experience of entering the home environment and responding to the needs of the terminally ill and dying has involved adapting my practice as an art therapist in order to provide the most effective therapeutic help I can. The theories of adjustment which explain the different kinds of experiences that the dying and bereaved can pass through (Parkes 1972; Kübler-Ross 1969) have contributed to my practice. I have observed that the images created by the terminally ill reflect many of the responses experienced during the period between diagnosis and death or at points that can be described as the living-dying phase (Pattison 1977; Stedeford 1994), when the emotional responses such as denial, depression and acceptance may be experienced, often at different times and in no particular order. The process of adapting to significant change is regularly communicated and explored in art therapy. The artwork can become the means for reducing the distress caused and can enable emotional and cognitive adjustments to be made alongside planning practical strategies.

The imagery created in art therapy by the terminally ill can be a description and exploration of specific issues such as accumulated loss or the anxieties relating to treatment and physical symptoms. In many other ways the imagery that emerges in the artwork can contain significant themes that are different from the aforementioned needs – the thematic content of an image is both its pictorial configuration (that is, the arrangement and expressive qualities of every mark on the paper), and the analogies made in relationship to the patient's life experience. This kind of image making can reflect many aspects of life and is interwoven with the contemplation of the creative process and profound emotional and psychological ruminations, such as the desire to survive, worry work, and how to be reconciled with one's own mortality. Such themes may only partly be explained yet as the dialogue sustained within the three way relationship between myself, the patient and their artwork unfolds, some meaning is slowly and tentatively uncovered.

During these times of theme-focused image making I may be acting as a questioning companion (Connell 1992) or as a witness to the patient's painful struggle to cope and maintain hope (Learmonth 1994). The relationship I develop in this context will be to enable the patient to contemplate and perhaps make intelligible their suffering. I aim to facilitate an opportunity for the patient to express and communicate their inner personal struggle, intuitively, experimentally and imaginatively through the non-verbal process of making visual images in the form of drawings and paintings. I hope to enable the patient to feel confident and safe enough to articulate difficult thoughts and feelings and become attuned to their inner needs. Most of us have a daily diet of visual experience which comprises of many facets: dreams, visual memory, fantasy, the 'media', and all that we consciously and not so consciously absorb as we look around us. The significance and influences of these inner images cannot be contained within finite explanations, their meanings can be infinitely varied. The image we have of self and others, our roles and responsibilities in public and private life, are complex and in constant interaction. Art therapy in the context of my work with the dying and the bereaved is a way of making visible something of the nature and qualities of these inner images.

The images of ill health, pain, suffering, ageing, death and dying are some of the most poignant we retain and probably the most easily distorted. Encouraging someone to explore making images is a way of opening and engaging the imagination and enabling pictorial language and communication. This can become a code of understanding belonging only to the person who has created the image in front of them. The art therapist as an enquiring companion may then become privileged to enter into this pictorial language. The verbal dialogue that may then follow can be metaphorical. It is not always essential to be descriptive in a literal sense, as inference may be as close as one comes to identifying the truth of someone's experience. The created image has the potential to symbolise the anticipation of death. For example, a finely painted, glowing peacock-feather-like pattern of colour, for one woman, contained many heartfelt responses to living in the face of untimely and impending death.

Art therapy can be a catalyst for the expression of some of the more distressing aspects of illness, pain and suffering. I have discovered that one of the first things a patient may need help with is to acknowledge the often unspeakable feelings of bewilderment and isolation experienced when coping with serious physical illness. The non-verbal intuitive nature of image-making can be the way in which a patient communicates to the world feelings of what may seem like unfathomable despair and uncertainty. The dynamic communication that then takes place between the creator and their image can soothe, nourish and contribute towards their reaching a more tolerable place in relationship to ill health and impending death.

Art therapy sessions in the home regularly take place around the kitchen table, on the living room floor, coffee tables, bedside cabinets and the laps of wheelchair users. This is an indication that responding to the circumstances of each person can involve some imaginative manoeuvring of household furniture, fixtures and fittings by the therapist. On one particular occasion I worked with a man who only had the movement of his right arm and hand. He was positioned on his left side in bed, and whilst I patiently held the paper above him he dabbed and splattered paint onto it with painstaking determination, becoming increasingly excited with each strike of the paintbrush.

The approach I have developed takes into consideration the dynamics of life at home, the specific emotional and psychological needs of the patient and the different ways in which the patients wish to engage in the process of art therapy. I now consider the boundaries within which I work to be the garden fence surrounding the home I am about to enter. The therapeutic focus of my work can be sustained quite securely within the parameters of the home by responding appropriately and imaginatively to the needs of those who dwell there, and by securing a provisional status as an accepted and welcome guest.

THE HOME ENVIRONMENT AND THE APPLICATION OF MY APPROACH

Jack and the brick wall

The home can consist of a multitude of different kinds of relationships and circumstances and no two domestic situations are the same. For example, Jack, in his early fifties with a diagnosis of cancer of the colon and the liver, was referred for art therapy as he was experiencing an increase in anxiety and expressed some fear about how the disease would progress and how he would cope with his general situation. At the time of our meeting him he had been informed that the disease was progressing and that his prognosis was poor. During the period of time that I worked with him he approached our meetings with an air of bravado and solid determination to fight his illness and to over-come the obstacles that presented themselves, which he illustrated in a drawing as a solid brick wall that he believed he was continually having to surmount (see Figure 8.3).

Jack was able to discuss many issues to do with dying and to share his thoughts about the anticipation of his own death. He was a stout, tall man, making me feel somewhat meek as I sat alongside him in the dining room. He was a man who favoured straight talking, and when I met his sons, who visited regularly, their towering size and 'macho' jocularity suggested to me that he might have needed to be quite tough as a father. We would often work quietly whilst clocks ticked, the dog itched and he tearfully worked through his grief at the loss of dignity he felt due to his increasing physical limitations. The brick wall also represented Jack's working life as a builder. He was used to being outdoors, engaging in strenuous physical labour. So his confinement at home imposed because of increasing ill health was frustrating and humiliating. Jack found his image helpful in that it became an aid to communicating this expe-rience and enabled him to release some of his accumulated stress. It also, paradoxically, embodied some of his remaining strengths and resilience, giving him a sense of reassurance and comfort. I was to have one final and brief contact with Jack, four months after beginning my visits, before he died at the family home.

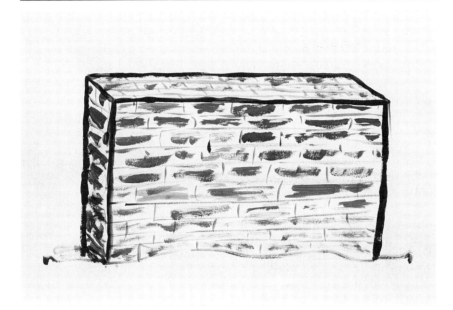

Figure 8.3

Lisa and the family do art therapy

Lisa was in her forties and married with two daughters who were still at school. Lisa learned of her diagnosis of cancer in her lung shortly before she was referred to the Macmillan team and then for art therapy. My visits often involved a preamble with her husband and lively banter with the children prior to her setting up the drop-leaf table in the kitchen and providing me with an orange drink from the refrigerator. Lisa was always firm about this period of time being exclusively hers and would often organise her husband to go and do some shopping. During school holidays the children would be asked to go and play quietly in their rooms or visit neighbours. On occasions the meetings would be delayed if her father popped round to visit her just after my arrival. At this stage in her illness, Lisa was experiencing an increased level of anxiety and at times an intense fear concerning her ill health.

Lisa worked through many painful needs during our meetings and found her artwork an effective way of addressing some of her deeper concerns. Her images were often an expression of confusion, doubt and uncertainty. Her pictures would be a thickly painted array of colour and unformed shapes. She would describe her paintings as her search for hope, interwoven with a trepidation about dying and a search for reassurance about her belief in life after death. A significant image emerged which became the focus of her attention for some weeks. This cell-like image we agreed had the appearance of an amoeba. The image evoked troubling feelings for Lisa and she responded to this by saying that it conveyed previously unexpressed thoughts and feelings that she had been trying to communicate. She developed a fondness for this image despite those elements about it that were unsettling and regarded it as a symbol of disease, pain, love and hope.

A significant concern at this time was the future welfare of her children. After a period during which she explored these worries, Lisa requested a family art therapy session. She had begun to feel a little distant from her family and wanted to meet together in order to increase her sense of togetherness with her husband and children, and to give her confidence to begin discussing with them the subject of her anticipated physical deterioration and issues to do with her death. I agreed to this idea and we met together around the kitchen table that had somehow grown to accommodate five of us.

This turned into a time of sharing and fun with much splattering of paint. The family were relaxed with only a little hesitation about painting a picture. Each person was issued with their own set of materials. As the family were unfamiliar with this way of working to make it a little easier to get started I asked each person to paint a picture that would feature a tree, an animal and a bridge. There was much giggling from the girls as their father boldly began his picture. However, not to be outdone by his demonstration of confidence, they soon enthusiastically began their own paintings. Between drinks each person invented a story to go with their picture and the theme of change emerged and became the focus of our discussion. This meeting helped Lisa to feel that she and her family were ready to begin dealing with the difficult and painful issues relating to her future ill health and death.

Arthur vents his rage

I met Arthur, who was in his sixties, on only one occasion. He had become very ill during the period in which his diagnosis of adenocarcinoma of the gastro-intestinal tract was made and he continued to be poorly throughout the following weeks prior to his death. When I met him, he was still in a state of shock and acknowledged that he was disturbed and profoundly distressed by all that had happened. He explained as we sat together on the old family sofa, that he needed to find a way of comprehending what was happening. He knew he was dying, but felt unprepared for such a sudden deterioration. Arthur was determined to have a go at doing some artwork and with much effort, briefly overcoming his fatigue and, with paper pinned to a tray balanced on his knees, angrily painted an image of his stomach where the cancer was located and venomously attempted to slice it in two with an energetic strike of the brush (see Figure 8.4). He explained that it was helpful to acknowledge his despair and to communicate his hatred for the disease which had so rapidly robbed him of his health. He died a few days later.

Figure 8.4

CONCLUSION

The pictures on the walls, photographs of relatives on the mantlepiece, the effect of changes in the designated domestic areas (when it is necessary to move the patient's bed from the privacy of the bedroom to the downstairs living room and to introduce the use of a commode in a space previously occupied by a familiar piece of much loved family furniture), can stimulate and aid the therapeutic process. The loss of mobility, along with the loss of independent management of personal care and other increasing limitations so often result in many ambivalent thoughts and feelings about being confined to one or two rooms within the home. The organisation of this confined living area can, at best, provide a sense of compact security or, at worst, create a frustration leading to resentment, anger and helplessness at the sense of living in a restricted space.

In this situation the patient can experience a loss of choice over personal routine and has to adapt to being dependent on others. This can mean that daily life becomes planned and ordered. A rigid routine takes the place of the more unpredictable drama of everyday life resulting in the elimination of spontaneity and a poverty of creativity. The inner life of a person is full of imaginative possibilities and the opportunity to be creative through the making of images in art therapy can be deeply nourishing, bringing relief to those inhibited responses, such as physical affection, sustained conversation and the free expression of thoughts, feelings and opinions, that are accumulated during such a time of adjustment and endurance.

My experience has shown that a purposeful and successful therapeutic relationship can be formed in these situations. Art therapy is appropriately placed in this context as part of the palliative care services available to people living with a life-threatening illness who are being cared for at home. Many of the people I have worked with would not have considered the need for therapy or any kind of counselling support or advice before the advent of their illness. Art therapy is able to offer people something that bridges this unfamiliar gap because of its practical focus. Despite the puzzlement that often greets me on my first visit to the family home, art therapy is a very accessible means for people to communicate their profound emotional needs. The lack of familiarity with art therapy is soon overcome once the patient has experimented with the process of creating an image and grasps the connection between the content of the picture and their interests, memories, ideas, opinions, experiences of ill health and the implications for them of a life-threatening disease.

The skill of the domiciliary art therapist lies in maximising the opportunities that the home can offer. If this means involving, to a greater or lesser degree, the patient's loved ones, and this may include the family pet, then we must be encouraged to feel confident in widening our approach. I have found the experiences of the district nurse and social worker a rich source for understanding the practical and social difficulties in meeting the patient's needs and those of their loved ones. I have also gained much from the principles of family therapy and the different approaches to understanding family dynamics and the complex social structure of the home environment and the relationships sustained there. To ensure that art therapy can be provided within the home safely and with integrity, procedures that provide adequate means for accurate assessment, careful monitoring of the therapist's interventions through supervision and appropriate management will contribute to this exciting development within palliative care.

REFERENCES

Connell, C. (1992) 'Art therapy as part of a palliative care programme', *Palliative Medicine* 6: 18–25.

Kübler-Ross, E. (1969) *On Death and Dying*, New York: Macmillan.

Learmouth, M. (1994) 'Witnessing in art therapy', *Inscape* 4: 19–22.

Parkes, C.M. (1972) *Bereavement. Studies of Grief in Adult Life*, London: Tavistock.

Pattison, E.M. (1977) *The Experience of Dying*, London: Prentice-Hall.

Stedeford, A. (1994) *Facing Death – Patients, Families and Professionals,* Oxford: Sobell Publications for Sir Michael Sobell House, Churchill Hospital. Second edn. Previously published by Heinemann Medical Books.

Simon Bell BA(Hons), DipAT, DipFA, RATh works as an art therapist at St Luke's Hospice, Sheffield, providing a domiciliary art therapy service for patients and their families as part of the community Macmillan nurse support team. He also runs support groups for bereaved children. In addition he has a research post with Trent Palliative Care Centre.

Chapter 9

The story board
Reflections on group art therapy

Sheila Mayo

Four people are the subject of this chapter. They, with their companions, are seated round a table. On the table will be a piece of white paper, perhaps 65cm × 130cm, large brushes, paints and pastels, water and mixing bowls. In my capacity as art therapist I may encourage the telling of a story, perhaps one I have already heard from a participant before. Sometimes I will tell one which I guess will resonate with the life experience of one or more members of this group. We begin with a silence during which images and symbols may arise in our minds. First one, then another, will begin to paint. From the moment we begin we also begin a journey full of wonder and surprise, lament and hope.

Our first character is Grace, one of ten children, five boys and five girls. She was 27 years old, married, and a mother. Now, an alien, a stranger exiled from her native land of Uganda, she remembered the death of her husband, and a little later on the death of her baby son. HIV/AIDS had taken them, now she too is living with AIDS.

She had been invited to group art therapy. What is it? In her country art was the clothes you wore, how your hair was dressed, how your house and door lintel were decorated. She told this to the half-comprehending group. She, born in the Acholi district of Uganda, told the group that her favourite English poet is T.S. Eliot. Not everyone had heard of him. Not everyone understands the poem –

> be still, and wait without hope,
> for hope would be hope for the wrong thing,
> wait without love for love would be love of the wrong thing
> wait without thought for you are not ready for thought . . . [1]

The blank incomprehension on the faces of most of her companions, only serves to alienate her further. She is very afraid. She likes the sunny studio, plants and trees are everywhere. But the table with its large expanse of empty, white paper and its rows of colours and brushes frightens her. She feels dependent and hates the feeling.

Our second character is Edgar. He is an active, impatient character. He has had a stroke, followed by an extraordinary sequence of dreams. He is now receiving treatment for cancer. As I tried to understand the dynamics of the psychological process operating within him he seemed to me to represent the dilemmas of a man accustomed to responsibility and reflection in a society which now provided him with little opportunity for either.

His behaviour in the group and the presentation of his paintings oscillated between an attempt to lead and control the group and a retreat into private coded messages which he made no attempt to explain. Six months after he joined the story board he began to resolve some of his personal dilemmas through painting. As his own immune system broke down, he represented not only his own fears and hopes, but a society in which we see the breakdown of old traditions and the fragmentation caused by sporadic wars and violence. But it is in the story of Pangma-la by Alison Fell, *The Shining Mountain,* in which he began to come to terms with his ambivalent relationships to women, power and failure, helping him to paint, helping him to change.

When Edgar stood on the threshold of the studio he was clearly in the grip of two contrary emotions, to withdraw and escape; or to move into this new situation with panache and some of his old combative spirit. The physical result of this emotional turmoil was to show itself in a sudden attack of vomiting. Undeterred he made his way into the room, and eventually to the story board, the open space where he found it possible to join his story to the story of others.

Figure 9.1

He would entertain the group for hours with stories from his travels but it was not until the story of Pangma-la that he found a land which matched his interior landscape. He painted the mountain; he painted tiny figures lost, bowed beneath their rucksacks advancing inch by inch in the teeth of the storm.

Here is the beginning of the story –

Once there was a Scottish girl with a strange name, and a father who was always on television. The girl was called Pangma-la, and of course she was teased about it. At first she cried but her father scolded her. 'Pangma-la' he said, 'I called you after a shining mountain so that you could stand tall and be proud. Pangma-la, one day you will climb this mountain with me.' So Pangma-la dried her tears and vowed never to be ordinary and disappoint her father. He taught her as the years passed to balance finely on the high tops of walls and shin up sheer rocks by toe and finger holes. Her mother shook her head and fussed. 'Pangma-la, you will tear your good jumper.' 'Pangma-la, you will fall and hurt yourself.' But her father only laughed and said 'Let her be, she is as tough as nails.' And Pangma-la was proud.

At last it was time to set out for the shining mountain. She fell asleep and dreamt a bad dream. She was a white swan flying high above the shining mountain with no father or mother anywhere. She was tired and she wanted to land on the top of the mountain and rest her wings, but the mountain turned its back on her and said 'You can't land here and you can't rest; you must fly on until your white wings freeze and you tumble down to the ground.' She woke up frightened, wanting her mother, but she said nothing for she was afraid her father would be disappointed in her. When the plane landed they set out for the mountain. The villagers sang and danced for them and gave them sherbet and figs, but when the Sherpa men crowded round offering to carry their loads, Pangma-la's father said 'My daughter and I do not need porters, we are strong, we will climb the mountain alone.' The Sherpa men were angry. 'The mountain Goddess will send winds to tear at you' they said, 'and spindly snow to sting your face and avalanches to toss and tumble you.' But Pangma-la's father turned away and laughed. 'Only weak men believe in Old Wives' Tales' he said after that.

The mountain rose like a tall white tower before them. At first Pangma-la climbed happily, smelling the clean air, while up ahead her father's feet made deep blue prints in the snow. But soon she began to grow weary. Just then an old Sherpa woman appeared in a ragged brown cloak. 'Let me carry your heavy sack, daughter' said the woman. But Pangma-la shook her head, she was afraid her father would be disappointed in her. On the second day they set out boldly and well, but she began to feel weak and ill under the weight of the rucksack, and the Sherpa woman appeared once again and pulled a handful of swan's feathers from under her ragged cloak. 'Take out your heavy things from the sack, daughter, and fill it with this swan's down, then you will get to the top of the mountain and your father will never tell the difference.' At sunset the woman gave back her heavy things and Pangma-la lay down to sleep. On the third day she set off with a weary feeling already in her bones. The snow blew up to sting her face and once again the Sherpa woman appeared. 'Take off your heavy, heavy clothes, daughter, and I will cover you with swan's feathers and you will get to the top of the mountain.' And so, once again, Pangma-la did. And once again as the sun went down the woman gave her back the heavy clothes and her father never told the difference. On the fourth day the roar of an avalanche thundered past and Pangma-la cried out to her father. 'Oh father, I want to go home to my mother more than anything in the world. I am so tired.'

'Pangma-la', her father scolded, 'look at the mountain I named you for, is it not beautiful?' She felt so ill she could hardly bear to look up at it, and her father climbed on and on and she tried hard to keep up with him. Soon her legs would not go another step and a dizziness took her and she fell down in the snow. Just then the Sherpa woman appeared, kneeling over her. 'Give me your heavy, heavy heart, daughter' she said 'and I will fill you with swan's down.' So Pangma-la gave up her heart, and the lungs which panted and hurt, and the bones which weighed like iron, and flew easily to the top of the mountain in all her light swan's feathers. But this time when it came to sunset the Sherpa woman did not give back Pangma-la's heavy, heavy heart, and Pangma-la's father stood at the top of the shining mountain calling wildly for his daughter.

Then the Sherpa woman appeared in her ragged cloak. 'Here is your Pangma-la' she said, pointing to the white swan which fluttered beside her, 'but now she is my daughter for ever and always.' Pangma-la's father cried out in anger. He raised his ice axe to strike the woman down, but just then a peal of thunder shook the mountain and threw him to the ground, and there in front of him stood no hag but the mountain Goddess herself. Tall and straight with skin of darkest gleaming gold and eyes yellow and far-seeing as a snow leopard. She wore a cloak of swan's feathers and blue lightning fire danced at her finger ends. 'You wanted your daughter to get to the top of the mountain' said the Goddess, 'and I have given you your heart's desire. You named your daughter after me to be strong and light as the Gods and feel no human pain and weep no human tears, and I have given you your heart's desire.' Then Pangma-la's father saw that his daughter had given her life away just to please him, and he cursed himself and his heart's desire and ran to the edge of the mountain to cast himself off. But the Goddess barred his way easily with a bolt of blue lightning. 'Not so hasty to make an end of it, brave hero' she said. She brought Pangma-la's heavy sack and heavy clothes from under her cloak. 'First you must feel the weight of your heavy, heavy burden' she said. Then she brought out Pangma-la's heart and gave it to him. 'And now you must feel the weight of your heavy, heavy heart' she said. At this the father fell on his knees and for the first time wept tears like any human. The mountain Goddess, seeing this, was satisfied. 'You have learned your lesson' she said, and was gone in a swirl of swan's feathers. Pangma-la's father looked down to see his daughter alive and heavy and human in his arms. Feeling the wet drops on her face, Pangma-la opened her eyes. When she saw that her father the hero was crying, she was no longer ashamed and a great weight lifted from her. She jumped up and pulled him strongly to his feet, then skidding and sliding Pangma-la and her father ran all the way to the bottom of the shining mountain while the snow flew up behind them like sherbet, or swan's feathers, and never again was Pangma-la afraid that her father would be disappointed in her.[2]

Margaret was born in April 1916. She had worked for the MOD during the war and had breast cancer. She smoked incessantly and painted incessantly. Three husbands, numerous children and grandchildren emerged onto the paper; together with memories of her mam, spiritualism; chapel going; toffee making; shoe mending; baby minding; unemployment; life in the Welsh valleys and the market at Pontypridd less accessible, but to be revealed dramatically on the story board, the death of siblings, stillbirths and suicides were to be recorded. She wrote these words to accompany an exhibition of her paintings.

I've always drawn since I was a child, but I started painting when my first husband was dying. He was a lovely man.

I brought up five children, got a job in the Drawing Office of MOD. My third son is gifted, his work's been on show; also he makes good pottery.

Unless you try something, you never know, do you?
   Some of my pictures come out of memories of the War and how life was then. We lived between Worcester and Birmingham.
   My daughter said to me yesterday 'You're supposed to be dead Mam', but here I am.

I don't really want to copy things. My paintings come from real life and how I'm feeling at the moment.

True life is superior to fiction. If you knew the stories I could tell. I've tried to draw some of them; not all of them on the bright side, I can tell you. But, if you dwell on all the bad things, it shows in your face.

If I have to describe my paintings, I'd say 'You just put it down to experience.'

(6 May 1994)

Much of her rich life was to be remembered with a developing sense of self-knowledge and wonder in a series of paintings done in 1994 during which she was calm and absorbed.

Apart from these hours of exploration, she presented herself as a disappointed, resentful person, taking (and refusing) fourteen different drugs; chain smoking when she got the chance; complaining of loneliness and neglect, apart from the faithful, daily visits of one daughter. She had, of course, far more support from her husband and children, from friends and hospice staff than she would admit to.

But her life at the centre of a quarrelsome, energetic, normal family for sixty years had shrunk to a solitary and embittered old age; only to flower again as she reached the age of 79 in a series of exciting, retrospective and beautiful paintings. Her first painting was anecdotal, one in which she recalled past experiences and significant events in her life. Then there came the day when, in the middle of a group painting, she stood up and said 'No, that's not true!', walked to the other end of the table and started again. Sombre colours, a closed door and tears, but no explanation followed. Later she said that it was her grandson's birthday, and that he had committed suicide in his twenties.

When expressive material like this emerges it often signals a radical change, not only of style but of content. The painter may or may not want to share the coded message this work contains, but if it is brought to consciousness, it can help to deal with unspoken fears, regrets and longings.

After this painting, Margaret's work became more abstract and more profound. Vital images of tree, cave/womb, doorway, water, sun, moon followed. A tape recorded conversation with her, a year before she died, illustrated these themes, as she recalled her life experience with humour and grief.

Margaret died in the summer of 1995.

Albert had been an engineer. He had 'networked' across Africa and Europe and had vivid memories of war, communications and cables which appeared frequently in his work. But chiefly, as he painted, he remembered the Sussex villages, churches and pubs of his childhood. He was born in 1908.

When Albert came in to the hospice in 1993, his wife D. and their three children had prepared themselves for his death. He was referred for art therapy because he declared his interest in drawing and painting and for some time he drew and painted on his own, often giving his work away at the end of the day. He was, however, curious about the work of the group and finally joined in. Although a genial and friendly character, any invasion of 'his' space on the paper was resisted and resented, and his neighbours came to recognise the invisible boundaries which existed around his work on the story board.

He met Margaret on 19 May 1993. Each seemed to mirror the shadow, or unconscious side, of the other, and this set up a dynamic in the group which was to last until his death, three months later.

John Spearman wrote in the *Guardian*:

to conquer a blank page with a paintbrush for most people entails the risk of humiliation; it is a venture that threatens exposure of our childish selves, with match stick men and pill box houses cocking a snoop at our adult persons. We learnt at school that art was for artists and have long since buried our sadness at being denied free and easy access to such a natural form of self expression.[3]

Albert was never 'free and easy'. His first paintings, like Margaret's, were anecdotal. Then came one that set his feet on an interior journey; his last painting was water pouring down between two gigantic cliffs. All he could say about this was 'I couldn't stand her tears.' Nor could he stand his own. He remained to the end a quiet, private man, with anger and panic not far away.

He and Margaret were 'King and Queen' of the story board. Usually sitting opposite each other, they painted, quarrelled, co-operated with others when they felt like it, and asserted themselves with equal energy. They were consorts, rivals, friends and enemies, which often threatened to obliterate the work of more timid mortals.

Albert – 27 May 1994:

I've got a lot of landscapes in mind because as a lad I travelled a lot. I was in the British Isles during the war, working through the bombing. I was lucky to get through.

All my working life I've been laying high tension cables and setting up telephone exchanges. I was six months in Colombo, back to British Rail, then in the Sudan for three and a half years, two hundred and fifty miles from Khartoum.

Y'know it's work, whether it's in the desert, across the fields, under rivers, overground, overhead. . . . Then we packed up home and went to Australia for three and a half years, but my younger son didn't like it so we came home – back to British Rail.

I've always been in work. When I first came here I couldn't settle. So I started painting, or rather drawing. I'm a local man and I draw the house where I was born over and over again, with me and my wife, Doris, walking up the path together. My daughter is over from Australia. That is some country. She is doing a tapestry of John Cobb who used to be postmaster in Sydney. Art therapy has made me some good friends here and its given me a lot of understanding.

I was very upset about leaving Australia. I loved it there – the great spaces. But my son didn't like it so we came home. After Australia I was sent to the Isle of Man, Port St Mary and Ramsey. That's when I came to love rocks and the sea.

The cable I was laying was experimental at the time. But most of all I remember Egypt – the sand, and the beautiful sunsets over the Nile.

I don't want to paint my mother's tears any more, or my father's death, and my brother's death – I was only 20 at the time. . . . I want to paint the happy things . . . the golden things.

As an art therapist I need to observe and ask certain questions. What evolving flow of signals persuades certain women and men to move from their comfortable chairs, and face each other around the expanse of paper? How do we trust each other enough to continue to participate in the process for one and a half hours; and in that process allow 'frozen' parts of a larger experiential pattern to be transformed into line and colour, light and shade, sometimes of amazing complexity, sometimes of surprising simplicity?

At first conversation and tentative 'graffiti' may appear chaotic. One person may present some ordinary or extraordinary event; some memory, hope, dream or reflection which will prove to be the catalyst for the whole process. In it the others will recognise inherent patterns of creativity which, if assisted to unfold, will contain the seeds of new creativity for themselves.

In the years immediately after the Second World War and later at the Tavistock Clinic, W.R. Bion's psychoanalytical study of group behaviour described the intense emotional activity he shared in various groups as therapist/observer.[4] He records how the completion of a group's task is often obstructed, even thwarted, by emotions of anxiety, fear, love and hate. He names these emotions 'basic assumptions', unconscious responses to early life relationships, and divides them into three categories:

dependency
fight/flight
pairing

Bion demonstrated how these assumptions influence a group's choice of leadership; its orientation to events and its capacity to deal effectively with the task to which it is ostensibly addressed.

DEPENDENCY

We all have the experience of dependency, in childhood, in old age, in sickness or emotional crisis, when one person in the relationship depends on the other for physical care or emotional support. We can find distorted examples of group dependence in the political activities of dictators, in the pyramidal structure of some big companies (now changing fast), and in religious rituals which aim to help the worshippers pass from a state of 'extra-dependence' (reliance upon a strength outside themselves) to a state of 'intra-dependence' where the virtues shown during the ritual are internalised and subsequently demonstrated in the lives both of the individuals and of their communities.

To regress to dependency is a pointless act so long as it remains extra-dependency. Individuals who are competent in their own professions and optimistic when facing the future, may regress to a state of infantile dependency and expect other members of the group to take over decision making and responsibility for the tasks of the group. It is my opinion that art therapy should be based on a view of reality that is critical of narrow instrumental rationality, and which involves a search for meanings and symbols which offer possibilities for nurturing a diversity of human wellbeing. My four clients sought for such a meaning not by avoiding the pain of disclosure but by embracing it.

It is tempting to regard the care of illness (even the palliative care of illness) as a linear process of problem solving in which objectives are identified and overcome by rational means. However, people are not wholly rational nor is life wholly susceptible to solutions.

The group round the story board, in exploring these three basic assumptions, allowed themselves to regress, and then to rearrange attitudes/prejudices which had hitherto kept them in what Dr Michael Kearney calls a wasteland of meaningless and helplessness.[5] Grace at first expressed basic assumption dependency in her work with this group. HIV infection does mean a reduction in life's choices. My task in the group was to help her towards a process of empowerment in which she was enabled to determine her own identity; to define her own boundaries; to acknowledge her own emotions and to organise her own relationships. I shall describe later how I came to recognise that not only Grace but her whole culture and society, British and Ugandan, were constellated in our infrequent but powerful conversations in word, song, paint and silence in the studio. Figure 9.2 is a painting where she at last recognised her love and grief for her baby son, whose grave she had not visited for two years. 'I shall lift thee up and you will never fall again' she wrote beneath it.

Despite the fact that initially she found her companions frightening, eventually they became an empowering group of friends. When she subsequently met situations which caused her anxiety (including housing as well as health) she learnt to share it at once, either in line and colour, or in words or actions. Grace may have, in her own time and in her own culture, grappled with questions of self-identity, maturation and autonomy, but unknown events from her early years still had the power to impact upon her present situation. Dependency acknowledged, its need appropriately met, benefited not only Grace but the whole group. She now had few choices left, but those that she had, she made with confidence and courage.

Figure 9.2

FIGHT/FLIGHT

The second basic assumption, fight/flight, becomes evident when as an individual I face an issue which awakes strong feelings of fear and antagonism within me. A choice has to be made – do I oppose the suggestion vigorously and 'fight' to see it defeated, or do I decide the fight is not worth it, and that flight is the option likely to cause me least pain?

The story of Pangma-la represented for Edgar the challenge to 'climb the mountain', associated as this was for him with the control of his pain, with achievement, and the keeping up of appearances, and he struggled on the story board to represent the 'heroic' qualities he so much admired and associated with masculinity. But his final painting, in a series on 'The Shining Mountain' represented by the Sherpa woman now turned goddess, returned his loved daughter to him.

PAIRING

Pairing is another basic assumption described by Bion. This comes about when the group appears to elect two of its members to act as 'parents', king and queen; or even sometimes as opposites to good and bad.

In the course of a story board, Margaret and Albert would often take up a position which they obviously considered Dad and Mum at the family table. Without a word they would attempt to map out the area, often selecting a theme without listening to others' contributions. What surprised me, and what I would point out at the end of the exercise, was how otherwise independent participants could allow this to happen, sometimes keeping their painting carefully within bounds, at other times showing covert aggression by 'intruding' upon the pair's chosen areas. It was clear, too, that the rest of the group unconsciously relied on 'the pair' to produce something positive for the whole group.

Just as the beginning of the group is silent and questioning, so the end is often silent and astonished, at the sheer size and mystery of the finished painting. This small group has projected hope, fear, anger, love, a lot of strong emotions onto this exercise in group art therapy.

Here we need to consider the nature of 'myth'. This word is used in this chapter to mean 'the essential meaning of something' not, as in common usage, untruth or fantasy. I believe it is essential that the art therapist refrains from diagnostic comments but enables the participants to recognise their own truth, and to return to the world of consciousness often to make significant changes in their life before it is ended.

Myths are public dreams; dreams are private myths. The images of myth and religion serve positive, life furthering ends. These inner myths and the natural symbols of our bodies need to be related to our outward-oriented consciousness – the inner myths supporting the outer actions. They tell us, in picture language, of powers of the psyche to be recognised and integrated into our lives, powers that have always been common to the human spirit. They have not been, nor can ever be, displaced by the findings of science, which relates rather to the outside world than to depths into which we enter during sleep.

Yet there is a danger of being drawn by our dreams and inherited myths away from the world of consciousness and the world of necessary social action; that is, to be forever fixed in patterns of archaic feeling and thought inappropriate to contemporary life. What is required therefore is a dialogue by way of symbolic forms put forth by the unconscious mind and recognised by the conscious in continuous interaction. This process might be called magnifying the projection and is a group analytic way of working. It may perhaps describe the moment when group emotion is condensed and seen, as through a prism, formed by the differing perceptions of each person, and accepted and recognised by the group.

Peter Brook, writing about 'living theatre', describes a Polish company led by Zergy Grotawski: 'small means, intense work . . . discipline, precision.' 'His actors', he writes, 'have given up everything except their own bodies, they have the human instrument and limitless time – no wonder they feel the richest theatre in the world.'[6] Group painting proved to be 'the richest theatre in the world' for these four people.

What all the people round the table had in common was the knowledge that they were moving towards their own death, a knowledge which stripped away pretension. Of course, these people were not alone. They were members of families, clubs, churches, social networks of many kinds; in opting for palliative care in a hospice they became part of another network, therapeutic, medical, a world of strangers who had one task in common, to care for them, and accompany them, living and dying.

Margaret Morris describes our society as militating against any large-scale acceptance of a socially mature interdependence because of the continuing global shift to the political and religious right. She writes:

> Bion describes the three institutional specialised work groups which our society uses as containers for the three basic assumptions [which we have already noted in connection with our case studies]: the church, the army, and the aristocracy. Religion fosters dependency on deities; the army deals with our fight/flight responses; the aristocracy provide or fails to provide the structures and dynasties to keep alive our hope for survival. Today, all these institutions are under threat.[7]

What has all this to do with a little group of cancer patients gathered around a story board? The disintegration of their situations was reflected in their personal stories, for example Grace had to face the collapse of the infrastructure of her own country, as well as the collapse of her own immune system. Each was able to use the story board as a theatre, a stage, not only for themselves but for the whole company. What Peter Brook calls 'The Empty Space' holds not only the drama of individual lives, but perhaps the healing of the nations. It was theatre and therapy for my clients at that time.

REFERENCES

1   Eliot, T.S. (1974) *Collected Poems 1909-1962*, London: Faber & Faber.
2   Fell, A. (1988) *Close Company*, London: Virago.
3   Spearman, J. (1994) *Guardian*, 24 July.
4   Bion, W.R. (1961) *Experiences in Groups and Other Papers*, London: Routledge.
5   Kearney, M. (1996) *Mortally Wounded*, Dublin: Marino.
6   Brook, P. (1968) *The Empty Space*, Harmondsworth: Penguin.
7   Morris, M. (1994) 'What hope for survival when bishop, general and duke all have AIDS?', *Contact* 113, pp. 20–26.

Sheila Mayo ATD, DA Manc, NDD, RATh Previous to her retirement in 1995 Sheila worked as art therapist at St Catherine's Hospice, Crawley, which included running weekly open groups for patients and working in day care. Prior to this she worked in various educational settings. She is currently working with women and children with HIV/AIDS and undertaking an MA at the University of Hertfordshire.

Chapter 10

A narrow ledge

Art therapy at the London Lighthouse

Ann Bartholomew

Midway life's journey I was made aware
That I had strayed into a dark forest,
And the right path appeared not anywhere.

(Dante, *The Divine Comedy*)

London Lighthouse is the world's largest residential and support centre for people facing the challenge of AIDS. It opened in London in November 1988 and its aim has been to provide an integrated model of care and a wide range of support groups and services for anyone living with the diagnosis of AIDS or a positive HIV test result. Its focus is to use the crisis of this life-threatening virus to design a new and holistic model of healthcare. Christopher Spence, the founder and director, writes:

> The pretence that death is not the natural and healthy conclusion to life places limits on our ability to live life to the full and to devise workable solutions to the complexity of survival issues facing us. This socialised denial of death, with the grief and fear it masks, inflicts great individual and collective damage. I believe true empowerment lies along a narrow ledge, one which each of us must find in our own way and at our own pace, perched somewhere between these giant shibboleths, the medicalisation of health and the denial of death.[1]

When I first heard about the Lighthouse project it seemed that here was a challenge to use art therapy with a new client group. These were people who were not psychologically impaired but looking for a new evaluation of the time they had left – a way to negotiate this 'narrow ledge'.

A complementary health team was forming, and art and music therapy were seen as part of this service. Initially I was not sure that we belonged in this group whose treatment involved the body directly, but came to realise that we were all working in our individual ways with the body in transition.

The Lighthouse had emphasised the need to 'meet the challenge of AIDS', an idea which reflected the work of Elizabeth Kübler-Ross. Her remarkable seminars on death and dying in the early 1970s challenged conventional attitudes and helped the terminally ill explore beyond the boundaries of their suffering. AIDS has a greater stigma than any other contemporary disease and those people contracting the virus are likely already to have felt the most hostile of society's attitudes. I was not sure that I knew my own attitude well enough to offer impartial support so I decided to take the AIDS awareness course offered to Lighthouse volunteers. This indeed challenged many of my attitudes, but at the end of three months I felt I could make plans to form a group.

I saw no need to rely on art therapy theory, but rather let the needs of its members, for the most part, determine the character of the group. The common denominator would be a struggle to come to terms with a feared diagnosis, to extract some meaning from it, and find a new evaluation of the time which was left. If this could start to happen I would be shown the way by the group, not the other way around. I decided to offer an 'open group' which meant that anyone with, or related to, HIV/AIDS could attend. The first group met in September 1989.

When the groups began I was aware that we were all breaking new ground. There was no defined model for the work which would take place, and the people who came to the sessions did not have a clear idea of why they were there except to 'find out more about painting'. I decided that the best way to begin was to try and create a safe space in which each person could explore the materials as freely as possible without any idea of the end product.

After a few weeks several people left because this was not the 'art class' they were looking for, but those who stayed said they liked the freedom to work as they wished. Groups varied from one to eight people and the work was done individually, in pairs, or as a group. Supplies included pencils, crayons, paint, clay, and a variety of mark-making tools such as combs, sponges, textured objects and an assortment of odds and ends for collage. Sessions lasted about three hours, with plenty of time for reflection afterwards. Often the image and the experience of making it lasted long after a session was over, and sometimes a second and third picture was made in response to an earlier one. Several people said that this was the first time during the week when they had been away from their flat, and they spent time talking to the others in the group. The friendships which began to form through a sharing of images and feelings had a quality which is hard to describe, but a recurring area of exploration had to do with changes in the body. The preoccupation of one person often triggered a similar search in others.

As time went by and the group became more cohesive, less time was spent talking and some interesting work began to emerge. Several people had recently lost their jobs or had to give up work, and their sense of isolation was verging on depression. Fear, anger and guilt as well as stories of concern and support were exchanged. Those who had been recently diagnosed were encouraged to express the depth of their feelings.

Two men in particular had recently received an HIV+ diagnosis and were frightened by the strength of their fantasies about the virus. Others spoke of the circumstances in which they were given their diagnosis and how terrified it had made them. When people are first diagnosed they may have no physical symptoms, but there is a lot of fear connected with the future. The positive label of HIV is ironic to them as they see it as entirely negative.

Much of the early work depicted this fear in collective imagery. There were empty or unfinished areas on the paper, bleak landscapes and roads going nowhere. Two men made a series of pictures in a narrative style, with drawings of 'being invaded' or 'taken over'. One of them told the group: 'Living with the virus makes me feel very alone. I often think that people are looking at me and wondering what is wrong. I don't think they see *me* any more – only someone they believe to be me.'

A number of pictures began to explore the nature of the virus; what it might look like, its location in the body, its colour and shape . . . a transformation of the mysterious to the tangible. The virus pictures were the first important images to come from the early groups (see Figure 10.1). They reminded me of Jung's mandala pictures. Jung felt the mandala to be symbol of the centre goal, or the self, and during one period of his life he sketched each day in a notebook a small circular drawing which seemed to correspond to his inner situation at the time. He wrote:

> My mandalas were cryptograms concerning the state of the self which were presented to me anew each day. In them I saw the self – that is, my whole being – actively at work. At first I could only dimly understand them but they seemed to me highly significant and I guarded them like precious pearls.[2]

Figure 10.1 'Inside the virus'

In the art therapy groups at the Lighthouse we all share the same experience. We are all living and all of us will die. But for those who have been diagnosed HIV+ there is a new evaluation of the time they have left. Time is now of the essence. For some people the idea of death is so ever-present that they lose sight of the fact that they are still alive. 'Death isn't about after I've gone', one man said to me. 'It feels like I'm dead now and closed in by fear, anger and aloneness.'

Sometimes when they look at their work people say they don't know what the images mean. I remember a picture made several years ago by a man who was still well but facing the first symptoms of full-blown AIDS. He painted a stage with red curtains drawn closed. In front of the curtains was the simple silhouette of a man – waiting. He told me that this picture had been in his mind for some time and indeed he painted it quite quickly without stopping until he had finished. 'This stage is like the world, but I'm not in the play any more. Somehow I have the idea that there's no role for me to play, but I can't quite believe it. I'm still someone, but I don't know who that is. It's quite mysterious, isn't it?' he said, and I agreed. It seemed that in allowing the mystery to be there without interpretation he had begun to let something go. The experience of creating images can break through the walls which separate our real selves from the artificial parts we play. Staying with these images often begins the search in ourselves for what is genuine.

KAREN

When Karen joined the group she told us that she had spent most of her working life in the theatre, as a costume designer. The HIV+ diagnosis made no sense to her until she remembered having a blood transfusion which her doctor told her had almost certainly passed on the virus. From several years of counselling she had begun to come to terms with her deteriorating health. In all of her paintings she used strong, bright colours, merging and blending them into streams which flowed across the paper. They were painted quickly, with large brushes on very wet paper and they presented all sorts of ambivalent imagery. In one picture which she called 'The Whirlpool' all the colours spiralled around a big blue hole. Karen wrote a poem about this picture.

> Spinning
> Circling
> Gathered all together
> And losing my edges
> I float
> Surrounded by other circles
> Hidden in that blue space
> I will maybe come home.

We spent time with these paintings, not discussing them very much, just welcoming them. Karen told me that she was trying to paint the acceptance of her life's end in the hope that there would be a merging into something larger and unknown.

THE CREATIVE PROCESS

Creativity has to do with making connections. Before the connections can be understood, however, there is often a period of discomfort where experience seems fragmented and things do not hang together. There is a phase of uneasiness, of sensing that something wants to happen, and if we find a way to use our creativity at this time we are almost flooded with what wants to come out, what wants to be expressed. We *see* what we had not seen before. There seems to be something within each of us which, if given the chance and the materials to work with, we can start to explore. When we let go of our efforts a process begins which is full of surprises and the influence of the creative field begins to intensify. The same thing happens in our group that happens in most life situations. We come together to share an experience, and we have a choice – we can stay in our familiar roles and leave the group without having given anything much away about our real selves, or we can take chances and open up to something new, trusting that reaching out can be a healing process in itself.

Many people who come to the art therapy groups do so initially from a sense of isolation, wanting to find a safe place where they can make new friends and find acceptance. For each one the experience is different and the materials are used in ways which relate to individual development and growth. I notice that when someone enters a periodic return to health the group is not so important for them, but it draws people back when difficulties arise again.

CARLOS

When Carlos began coming to the groups he used to spend the first ten minutes of each session staring at the paper – 'facing the blankness' he called it. His HIV + diagnosis and failing health had forced him into early retirement and in his anger at the situation he withdrew from friends and community and spent most of his time within the four walls of his flat. Blankness. Gradually he allowed himself to feel this isolation and began to link it with the conditions of his life. In one of his first paintings a road stretched from the bottom left hand side of the page and seemed to disappear in the middle. At the horizon line a sun was rising. He painted variations of this picture for several weeks and others in the group asked him about the road and where it was leading. Encouraged by this interest Carlos linked his pictures with the idea of a journey and from that time until his death a year later he came to the group each week to explore this theme. His friends found the following among his papers. He had intended it for publication in the *Lighthouse News*:

> I have been part of the art therapy group for over three years since it was first offered at the Lighthouse. Over this time I have learned to be in touch with that part of myself which loves to express itself, using colour and shape. The group has been a joy to me right from the beginning and I'm sure has helped me to maintain my health. The nature of the group changes with the people who take part. During the discussion time about our work I have gained great insight into the nature of colour and how it relates to how I'm feeling.
>
> Carlos

THE SINGLE SESSION

One afternoon Andrew was the only person who attended the session, but seemed glad to have the space to himself. He told me he was in his final placement in psychiatric nursing and had been HIV+ for several years. He had one afternoon off each week and decided to spend some of this time at the Lighthouse art therapy group. He seemed rather relieved that there was no 'group' this week as he didn't want, at the moment, to share his feelings with other people.

He seemed confident about starting his picture, chose a large sheet of paper and rubbed into it a soft yellow tone with a pastel crayon. He worked with quite a fierce concentration, dividing the paper in half with a thick black line and drawing an expressionless face on the left hand side. The face looked as blank and lifeless as a store mannequin, but Andrew worked on every detail of the features and hair with great care. He stopped for several minutes and told me that it felt good to be using his hands – he had chosen the pastels because he could rub them strongly into the paper. He then took several bottles of paint, stood up, and poured thin streams of pigment all over the right half of the picture until the surface was thickly covered by a network of overlapping lines. While the picture dried, he talked.

> 'I feel that I'm living with a secret and have to hide behind a mask. I must give nothing away, particularly about my health. Because of the job I'm in, I feel it would be impossible to tell people I am HIV+ so I pretend I'm OK and present a good face to the world. But behind that face there is chaos. I wanted to make a picture of these two sides of me.'

We talked about what feelings lay behind the bland face, and Andrew said they were all buried under the web of paint.

'This thick paint is covering up all the symptoms and pain which are lying in wait for me. My head is full of images of the virus, all floating around, and I wanted to put them into the picture. Then I couldn't bear to look at what I had drawn and I covered it up. I'd like to find a way of removing that line in the middle of the picture. I wish I it would just melt away.'

He said he had thought of these two images for several months and was glad to be able to put them down on paper.

Andrew came back for three more sessions, but although he painted other versions of this divided picture I felt that the more important work had been done with that first image.

From time to time the Day Centre at the Lighthouse sent people to the art therapy group. These were often people who had developed AIDS-related dementia. They were accompanied by a volunteer helper. Dementia is characterised by deteriorating symptoms of confusion, memory loss and intellectual impairment, and the people who joined us often looked bewildered at finding themselves among strangers. People making pictures – what were they doing, and what was expected of them, the newcomers? The others in the group were always welcoming and I sensed that there was genuine respect and compassion for those on the threshold of a world which they might also one day inhabit. The response to art therapy from those struggling with dementia usually took one of two forms.

PAUL

Paul, a man in his mid-forties, had been a successful solicitor before the onset of AIDS and from his conversation was a man of artistic and literary interests. At this stage of his illness he had few inhibitions and told us that he was a fine painter with years of training behind him. He poured large pools of paint into a plate, took a brush in each hand and began to cover a large sheet of paper with generous circular strokes. As he worked I was reminded of the first paintings of a child who has just learned to hold a brush and focus on the paper. Lines are visible on the paper which are not related to objects. Sometimes they flow quickly. Big loops, ribbon-like patterns, repetitive whorls often go further than the paper or start beyond the edge of the page.

As Paul made these marks he gave only a casual glance to see how the various lines came together to make a picture. What appeared to interest him most, while painting, was the physical activity. Standing or sitting, his whole body was involved. In this respect, too, the whole process was like the child. Although his physical body was deteriorating rapidly, Paul used much of his energy and perhaps other capacities we don't know much about to make a series of paintings which recorded the feelings he could no longer express in words.

He took only a few minutes to make each picture and the effort usually exhausted him. For several more months he came to the group and always painted with the same vigour and enthusiasm.

JOHN

John's response to the group was quite different as his stage of the illness had almost erased his memory and along with it his interest in life. A small man in his mid-fifties, he showed very little response to any of the materials in front of him, but after about half-an-hour he picked up a pencil and made a dot in the middle of the paper. The suspense in the room was palpable, but no one spoke for fear of disturbing this fragile concentration. John seemed aware that designs and pictures were taking shape around him and slowly he began to move the pencil up, across and down. It took him almost five minutes to complete the square and another ten to place a triangle on top of it. He had drawn a little house. For the rest of the session he sat quietly, looking at what he had made, and from time to time went over the lines, making them darker and darker until the paper was almost worn through. He never spoke while he was with us, but smiled when he left, and the men in the group wished him well and said they hoped he would come back. He never did. His helper told me a few weeks later that John used to be the art master in a comprehensive school.

It's hard to know whether the experience of painting or making pictures is of any real benefit to people with AIDS-related-dementia, but in the case of Paul and John I felt that, in different ways, they had responded positively to being part of a group. I don't think they would have stayed to do work on a one-to-one basis. Their dramatic loss of memory and ability to communicate seemed to invite a non-verbal response. We may not have a clear idea of the individual relationship to the images made, but in each case there was an attempt to symbolise something from their inner world and maybe this represented reality, briefly restored.

DESTROYING THE IMAGE

From time to time in the group someone is dissatisfied or angry with their picture and tears it up. I have always felt that this decision is a valid one, but it seemed important to look at whether there might be another way of 'using the image'. Every image which is made is unique and as the shapes and forms appear we can see a pictorial record of how we are. We can connect with this or not, as we choose. We can dismiss our work with 'that's a mess', or 'it's no good' but the marks we make *are* an expression of ourselves, and are influenced by the events which make up our lives. Even the way we use the space on the paper says a great deal about our place in the larger world.

I began to explore with the whole group the (often very early) responses to the images they made and whether they remembered their childhood pictures being ridiculed or dismissed. One man remembered being told that his sister was always 'better at art'. I suggested the Gestalt idea of leaving such labels as 'better' or 'worse' outside the door of the art room as if they were baggage which could be reclaimed at the end of the session. For some this concept was interesting, for others not helpful, but it served to question evaluations about the work – even negative ones.

One man didn't want to keep his work but didn't want to get rid of it either, so we kept it in the cupboard for several weeks at the end of which time I suggested that he have another look at it, with the idea of tearing it up for a large collage. This seemed a way to recycle the 'bad' and come to terms with the destruction process. The collage took several sessions to build up and subsequently became a work of interest for the whole group. People did not always return to the rejected images but I felt that where a sense of 'play' was involved in the art making, the less it was likely to be destroyed.

The sessions are often a time for clearing away old self-images, and a lot of unfinished business begins to surface. Early family relationships appear in the pictures and whether it was safe to be open about being gay. When pictures like these arrive in the group there is an immediate response from the others, and a sense of relief that difficulties can be shared. There is a wish to look for 'meanings' or 'reasons why'. 'Why me?' and 'Why this disease which no one understands and no one can cure?' Faced with social issues which don't burden the cancer patient, the person with AIDS struggles with anger and resentment as well as the fear of dying.

An important aspect of working in a group is that people have an instant audience which responds! They are aware of each other while working – 'I notice you tore up the first picture and made the second one bigger', or 'You made a scraping noise with the chalk as if you were angry with someone'. While people on the whole are respectful of privacy and the right to silence, there is a genuine curiosity within the group to hear the story behind the marks on the paper. These questions can cause some clashes, but often clarify themes which were only partly perceived while the work was going on. I try to encourage the group to spend some of the time working quietly while the art making is developing. This attentiveness seems necessary if we are to be in the moment and contact ourselves through our senses.

One theme which the group explored was to go back to a time in childhood when they lived through an experience of disapproval. Memories seemed to flood in fast and I encouraged people to work quickly and spontaneously, making several pictures and welcoming mess and disorder Some people felt free enough to work with their hands and most of the images were simple and childlike. Seeing others work in this way helped a young solicitor who had recently joined the group. His work was usually small and neat, but he too came to enjoy these 'loud noises' as he called them. People began to talk as they painted.

'Whatever that painting is, it's really messy. Our house was always so neat and I never had anything fun to draw with, only those hard waxy crayons which don't make much of a mark. I got into real trouble if my clothes were torn or dirty.'

'My picture doesn't really show what I felt. Those drips of paint are my tears which I always tried to hold back, because only girls cry.'

'All the colours have run together to make a big black hole. I didn't realise what it meant but that's how I felt when I was 10 – trapped! That's what I fear most now, being put into a black hole.'

The experience allowed some people to talk more about their childhood. Their sexual identity was confusing, they didn't seem to fit into accepted patterns of behaviour and there was no one who wanted to hear about all this. Patterns of lying were established early.

DEATH AND DYING

When a member of the group becomes very ill and is close to death, this naturally affects everyone else, even though some may be new to the group and may have not known the person for very long. We're sad that there is now a space in the group instead of a person who was 'making their mark' in so many different ways. But while they are still alive there is often a wish to include this person, somehow, in the painting process. We get out some of their work and look at it, talk about it, and remember struggles they may have had while working on it. We put some of the pictures on the wall, which seems to satisfy a concrete need, and a friend usually writes or phones the person during the week to describe the way they remained a part of the group.

The Lighthouse has very special ways of celebrating someone's life after they have died. If they choose to design their own funeral before they die, and have been working with us, it is often their wish to decorate the space with some of their paintings. This gives other group members a chance to set the scene and work with the family, who often see for the first time the creativity which has taken place. 'Why all this beautiful work when he had so little time left?' one woman said of her brother. We had no ready answer.

After the death of a friend or partner it is not unusual for a member of the group to spend many sessions on a gift or special image for the one who has died. At these times there can be a pulling away from the others, and this need is accepted without question. One man decided to design the inside of his partner's coffin. The decorated sarcophagi in the Egyptian wing of the British Museum had made a strong impression on him and he wanted to bury his friend surrounded by similar images of life and vibrancy. Those who saw it said that it was a real celebration in pictures.

SHOWING THE WORK

I had thought of the work produced by the group as intensely private, and followed Lighthouse policy that strict confidentiality is maintained at all times. I had never let interested observers into the group, nor even for the first few years offered a placement to art therapy students. One summer several people from the group said they had shown their work to friends, and the response had been good. They felt that the work needed to be seen by a larger audience and we decided to show some of the pictures in the reception area at the Lighthouse. Names were withheld but short pieces of writing were attached to the images, which explained something about the process. The paintings and drawings were mounted in simple clip frames and one member of the group helped me decide how the work should be hung. This small exhibition was the beginning of several similar events which took place when appropriate work was available.

The response was gratifying. People who came were able to see that a picture becomes a screen onto which difficulties can be projected – anger, confusion, hope. Art, it seemed, could provide firm ground when everything around is changing. One visitor said, 'These pictures are like journeys. I had no idea that having AIDS could give people a direction.' The group was pleased – so there began a journey from the private to the public.

I was approached in 1994 by a fellow art therapist who suggested that we produce a joint exhibition in Germany, and the group agreed. Uwe Herrmann planned to show the work of a women's group who had been meeting with him in Hanover. Both of our groups live with the HIV+ diagnosis and both use the art-making process to get in touch with what is going on in their lives.

Twenty-five works on paper were shown, and a special feature of the exhibition was the 'visitors books' in which the public could express their feelings about what they saw. When the exhibition finished these books became a kind of bridge between the two groups who were involved in the project. In his introduction to the catalogue, Uwe Herrmann summed up our objectives when he said, 'This exhibition meant exchanging the safe, undisturbed and totally private frame of art therapy sessions for a gallery space. It is a big step for both groups to leave this safety behind and expose their work.'

Can we deal creatively with loss? This question has been at the heart of all the painting groups, large or small, from the most private mark to the public statement. It has given form to many different journeys. All of our learned theories and methods are meaningless unless we are open to knowing and being known. The art materials and group experiences are forms in which we can be available to each other in whatever way is possible, in the present moment. The 'narrow ledge' is that moment.

REFERENCES

1   C. Spence, *On Watch*, London: Cassell, 1996, p. 71.
2   C.G. Jung, *Memories, Dreams and Reflections*, London: Fontana, 1995, p. 221.

BIBLIOGRAPHY

Adamson, E. (1984) *Art as Healing*, London: Coventure.
Dante, *The Divine Comedy: Inferno*, The Portable Dante, trans. Laurence Binyon; ed. Paulo Milana, Harmondsworth, London: Penguin.
Gott, T. (1994) *Don't Leave Me This Way: Art in the Age of AIDS*, Canberra, Australia: National Gallery of Australia.
Jung, C.G. (1995) *Memories, Dreams and Reflections*, London: Fontana.
Kübler-Ross, E. (1972) *On Death and Dying*, London: Routledge.
Levine, S. (1988) *Who Dies?*, Bath: Gateway Books.
Rhyne, J (1973) *The Gestalt Art Experience*, Belmont, CA: Wadsworth.
Spence, C. (1996) *On Watch*, London: Cassell.

Ann Bartholomew studied painting in the USA and took the Diploma in Art Therapy at the Hertfordshire College of Art and Design in 1982. Since then she has worked in a residential psychiatric clinic and in 1989 formed the first art therapy groups at the London Lighthouse.

Ann has mounted several exhibitions of the work of her group, including a joint exhibition in Hanover with the collaboration of a German colleague. She is interested in exploring the connection between music and visual images and finds this important also in her own work. Ann also works with people with eating disorders.

Chapter 11

The butterfly garden
Art therapy with HIV/AIDS prisoners

Val Beaver

INTRODUCTION

Over an eighteen month period art therapy was part of a programme devised to help prisoners diagnosed as HIV seropositive and those who had already developed AIDS. Drawing on the theoretical framework of D.W. Winnicott and Wilfred Bion, I attempted to provide a facilitating and containing space for a small group of long-term prisoners. Thoughts and feelings, whether concerning HIV status or concerning prison life and confinement, found expression through the medium of paint, clay and other art materials. Fears and phantasies about death and dying were explored, sometimes privately, sometimes shared within the group. In this chapter I have opened a window giving the reader a glimpse of the group in progress, with particular focus on the imagery and work of one man. Some of the difficulties of working as a therapist within the prison system are addressed and the importance of support and supervision is emphasised.

BACKGROUND TO SCOTLAND'S HIV PROBLEM

The extent of Scotland's HIV problem was identified in 1985. Prior to this, in the early 1980s, the police in Edinburgh, in an attempt to clamp down on drugs, had made it difficult for young people to obtain injecting equipment. Needles and syringes were confiscated and a chemist's shop selling the equipment was closed down. 'Shooting galleries' where people gathered together to share whatever needles and syringes they had was the unfortunate consequence of this policy. The HIV virus therefore spread rapidly through the drug-using community in Edinburgh, affecting both men and women. Growing numbers of people became infected through heterosexual intercourse with the result that children were born into HIV families (*The Scotsman*, 25 November 1995: 5–8). After 1985 there was a change of policy. Needle exchanges were set up in parts of the city where drug abuse was a problem. A much needed programme of health education was gradually introduced, both in the community and within Edinburgh Prison.

Prisoners are already a subgroup, segregated from and to a large extent ostracised by society. Within prison the HIV prisoner may become further marginalised and ostracised. Some men will already know their status, some will volunteer for HIV testing, others prefer ignorance, frightened in case the test proves positive. Already serving a sentence as punishment for an offence, their 'deviant' lifestyle (whether homosexual or drug abusing) may be seen by prison staff and society at large to have brought them further just punishment.

> There may be a feeling that AIDS is a punishment for anti-social or deviant activity. Confining AIDS to particular groups of people, who are then to be avoided, is an attempt to deal with the fear of death, and of disease which is part of the process of dying. The person with AIDS is ostracised by a society that cannot tolerate the pain of its own mortality. Unlike cancer AIDS is transmittable through body fluids, and the person with AIDS has become a potential source of pollution, heightening fears of contact further.
> (Wood 1990: 32)

Within the closed community of prisons there are inevitable conflict points and tensions between prisoners and staff, and between the men themselves. When the extent of the known numbers of HIV positive drug abusing prisoners became clear there was cause for some anxiety and concern in the Scottish Prison Service. Whilst the task of the Prison Service is first of all custodial with a priority being security there has nevertheless been some change and slow move-ment towards establishing smaller, more humane regimes (Scottish Prison Service 1990). The idea of a respite unit for prisoners who were HIV positive and for those who had AIDS was therefore an imaginative as well as pragmatic response by the Scottish Prison Service in 1990 to the crisis posed by the growing AIDS epidemic. Rather than segregating the men, it was considered preferable to keep the men within their own 'halls' – residential units – and to offer respite by means of a day programme at first, with a view to residential respite later on. A small group of prison officers, who had had some training in AIDS counselling, volunteered to work in the unit, and a programme of counselling, health education and discussion groups was started in 1991. The art therapy groups started in October of that year, after considerable discussion, after an art therapy workshop was held for the staff involved in the programme and after regular liaison meetings had been agreed upon. Karen Camp, another art therapist, led a group for men serving short-term sentences whilst I led the group for long-term prisoners.

THE CONTEXT – WORKING IN A PRISON

To create a safe and accepting environment within the formal and rigid struc-ture of a penal institution was for us the most important ongoing task. To enable creativity and healing to take place there had to be a facilitating environment, a potential space where there was opportunity for reflection and reverie, and where the men could be protected from the harsh reality of prison routine, boredom and brutality – their own and others – at least for a while. The physical and psychological boundaries of this space needed constant attention, for the concept of therapy, and all that it entails, was new. It was important, for example, always to remember to put the sign 'Group in Progress – Please Do Not Disturb' on the door – which is normal practice anywhere – but it was also important to remind officers and senior staff that this applied to everyone. Subtle and insidious inroads were sometimes made, which were, I think, largely unconscious attempts to wear down something so different, so alien to the familiar prison system.

In addition to providing respite another aim of the unit was to facilitate communication between officers and prisoners, to break down barriers and to offer counselling, relaxation and therapeutic activities. One or two of the officers were keen to become involved in the art therapy groups. At first the unit governor considered it obligatory that a prison officer be present in the group room each week. After discussion it was thought preferable that a designated officer take part in each group to become, as it were, a group member rather than have an officer sitting by, watching and waiting in case of trouble. This did not always feel a comfortable solution – the men regarding the officers as 'them' even if they did take their hats off, and the role of the officers inevitably remaining a custodial one first and foremost. However, as the groups became established, and the art therapists were seen to be reliable and responsible people, trust began to grow. There were times when the officer was on holiday or engaged in other duties and the group took place without him. There were occasionally times when a group member would choose to talk to an officer after the group rather than disclose or share intensely personal or painful material with the whole group.

The officers who volunteered for work in the respite unit were unusual and stood out from their colleagues, at first having to cope with jibes and sometimes ridicule. There were, however, significant differences between their approach and ours. It was difficult for them working in the prison with a different training and background to think of the art therapy group as something other than 'the art (therapy) class', which they sometimes slipped back into calling it – sometimes teasing, sometimes unthinkingly. One officer used to refer to me as the 'space woman', not unkindly, in fact we developed a friendly and good-humoured relationship, but this encapsulated the feeling of someone alien from out there coming in to their 'space' to do something unfamiliar.

There were days when I felt helpless, small and vulnerable – days when I was exasperated and demoralised by the enormity and crushing weight of the institutional machine. There were the times of waiting at the gate, for hours it seemed, without explanation, before being collected and taken across to the unit so that the group time would be cut short. There was the dismay and the anger when staff changes occurred without warning, when the valuable liaison meetings were cancelled, when prisoners were not allowed to attend the afternoon group because they had reported sick in the morning. It was easy at times to over-identify with the prisoners, and to feel oneself drawn into a collusive projection against the punitive 'authorities'. Later, and on reflection, it was possible to see that the officers were caught in the same trap. And it was important to remember that the prisoners were there because of committing serious and sometimes violent offences.

It was at these difficult times that supervision was essential. Menzies Lyth (1985) has written cogently about routines and systems which develop within institutions as defences against anxiety, and the need for constant vigilance if they are to be sustained at a mature and adaptive level. It was a source of great comfort and strength to be able to share feelings and frustrations with Karen, the other art therapist. We were fortunate to have supervision from Joyce Laing, who had pioneered art therapy at Barlinnie Special Unit and who had years of experience of working within the Scottish Prison Service.

THE ART THERAPY GROUP FOR LONG-TERM PRISONERS

This group ran for eighteen months. Five men joined the group, one leaving after a few months, a sixth joining the group later. Their ages ranged from early twenties to mid-forties, all but one saying they contracted the virus through intravenous drug abuse, the sixth through heterosexual intercourse.

There was the opportunity for expression of emotions, whether concerning HIV status or concerning prison life and confinement. Through the medium of paint, clay and other art materials, fears, feelings and fantasies about death and dying were tentatively explored and expressed, sometimes privately and silently, sometimes shared verbally. There were difficult periods in the life of the group and painful times for group members and the art therapist.

There were days when I came away exhilarated, in awe, or humbled by the experience of working in the respite unit. On warm and sunny days in the summer it was occasionally possible to work on tables outside in the garden, 'the butterfly garden'. It was after a BBC2 documentary filmed in the unit, entitled 'The Butterfly Garden' and shown on World AIDS Day, that the unit acquired this name, the butterfly symbolising the soul ('psyche' in Greek means soul, spirit and butterfly). To be part of a programme in the prison where flexibility was allowed, to see the men enjoying the warmth of the sun, and yet still to be engrossed in their painting, was especially rewarding.

I will also not forget the first group session. I was apprehensive, wondering if the men would be able to engage in artwork and image making or whether they would see it as childish. After I had introduced myself and talked a little about art therapy and the purpose of the group I invited the men to try out the art materials which I had put out for them. They responded immediately, squeezing out the paint into the palettes, using brushes, sponges and rollers, pastels and charcoal. Only one of the five men in that first group acknowledged that he had done any artwork since school. It seemed like food to starving children, and indeed given their current experience and situation, and for some their childhood deprivation, it must have seemed a feast. One man said excitedly in a later group when I had brought clay that he loved the feel of it, 'I could eat it' he said. Another man commented 'it was good to use all the colours, especially as the prison is such a drab, dark place'. I was amazed at the involvement and the intensity of that first session.

The symbolic nature of the art materials representing food – and what I as 'mother/therapist' could, or could not, provide – continued as an underlying theme. I had to pay attention to transference and counter transference issues – my need to be a good mother for instance. There was also the issue of powerful sibling rivalry, and my not always managing to be 'fair' in a primitive society where unfairness and injustice were often felt to prevail. It was not always possible to recognise at the time, and not always appropriate to interpret, the psycho-dynamics of the group. One young man, who was disliked by the officers, and who managed to get himself scapegoated and excluded from almost every group activity in the prison, was particularly needy and emotionally deprived. In one group when I was giving attention to another member he picked up the tin of varnish and began using it in a greedy and wasteful way, spilling the sticky substance and waving the brush about. I had to confront him. This resulted in an angry outburst and he flung the brush on the floor 'You said we could do anything, use any of the art materials! You said . . . ! I'm leaving and I'm never coming back to this . . . group.' But he didn't leave, he just walked round and round the room. The other men were on their feet, one saying he was leaving too. The officer in the group, I could see, was on the edge of his chair itching to get up and march this young man outside, but he didn't. I forget what I said exactly, but I made some comment about it being hard when things didn't go right and I would be sad if he left. There were some more expletives and then he sat down, saying himself 'Let's sit down'. This was a crisis point and a turning point for the group – a potentially violent episode but one where anger and hate and jealousy were contained. This prisoner sat in smouldering silence for a while, but he later picked up a lump of clay I had put near him and began making a face with angry, violent features. Several sessions later, when I referred back to this incident, he again talked of his liking for clay and said 'you can say things in clay, you wouldn't get away with in words'. We both knew the head represented his anger and hate at that moment, but also represented me as the frustrating mother or parent figure and what he would have liked to do to me.

The group went through several phases during the eighteen months. For the first few sessions I suggested a theme which was optional – the men could take it up or work on their own ideas. Four of the men became used to working naturally with art materials, letting the paint or clay suggest ideas, thoughts and feelings. The other two, both younger men, needed more direction, more input from me. Sometimes I think this was because of their need for attention from me; at other times I felt they were not ready to face the emptiness, the loneliness and despair that being left with a blank sheet of paper might suggest. In their own way and at their own pace they were working at the same fundamental issues. One of them was very good at calligraphy and enjoyed copying out texts. He asked me to bring in selections and chose one, 'What is Dying?' (see Figure 11.1):

What is dying?
A ship sails and I stand watching till she fades
on the horizon and someone at my side says,
'she is gone'. Gone where? Gone from my sight,

Figure 11.1

that is all; she is just as large as when I saw her.
The diminished size, and total loss of sight is in me,
not in her, and just at the moment when someone at
my side says 'She is gone', there are others who
are watching her coming, and other voices take up a
glad shout, 'There she comes!' and that is dying.

This young man completed the text with care, illustrating it with a ship on the horizon silhouetted against the sun.

Occasionally the men worked together on a group painting – notably, and near the beginning of the group, one to commemorate World Aids Day '91. There was little discussion – they were keen to get going. We taped large sheets of paper together and onto the wall. The two younger men took the lead and began drawing out a design, the older man carefully adding the buildings and the boat. Another was hesitant but, encouraged by the others, he joined in, adding the sky and later the butterflies. The fifth, always on the fringe of the group, worked on his own painting but joined in with comments. In some ways a dark and angry image, nevertheless it was an expression of their reality – containing elements of hope and humour as well as death and destruction.

There was considerable anger in the group due to policy changes in the unit three months after it had started. The men had been told that the unit could not be used as a residential facility until electrical work had been completed. In early 1992 several men serving sentences for sex offences who were housed in the hospital wing were moved into the unit while the hospital wing was being refurbished. For a time there was a boycott of the whole unit by the HIV/AIDS group, who felt outraged. They were aware of all the publicity HMP Saughton had received for providing a 'special' facility for HIV/AIDS prisoners. They felt let down, powerless, and in some way 'used', angry with the authorities for making decisions without any reference to themselves. In fact the unit continued to offer a programme of activities, relaxation and counselling during the day, but never became a residential respite facility for HIV/AIDS prisoners.

This was the sort of issue which affected the men in the group and also affected the officers in the unit, who were caught in a difficult position. There were occasions when the men would arrive in a state of barely suppressed fury, the art therapy group serving as a safety valve, receiving and containing raw emotions. Then words would pour out as they talked – often I could not catch or hear all that they were saying, but I understood well enough the feeling content. Gradually they would quieten and turn to the paint or clay, losing themselves in the work. For a period of ten weeks, attendance was almost 100 per cent, apart from one or two instances of illness or 'bed down'. The four men were working in clay a lot of the time, producing a variety of images, sculpted heads, hands, figures. They would work in silence much of the time, totally absorbed, lost in their own worlds, appreciative of the safe containing space.

ILLNESS, DEATH AND FEAR OF DYING

Because of illness there were sometimes only two or three in the group and on two or three occasions I arrived to find no group. I was not allowed to see the men in the halls, so would talk with the officers, listening to them and hearing their story. I would ask them to tell the men I was thinking of them and would then leave the prison feeling heavy hearted and rather useless. Once again supervision and talking with Karen helped me to see the value of just being there, of waiting, and the value in talking with the officers. One man whom I shall call Tom had frequent chest infections. Aged 36, he had been transferred to HMP Saughton because he had recently been diagnosed HIV positive and was finding it hard to accept. He was well built, impulsive and excitable, serving an eight year sentence. In his first group session Tom was self-conscious and found it harder than the others to use the art materials. He drew and painted a tree, and then scribbled and scratched across it with charcoal. When we came to talk about the images Tom began laughing, ridiculing another man's picture of a boat: 'Is it a boat in yer bath then?' It was a somewhat naive picture but it had a freshness and charm of its own. The young man who had painted it looked uncomfortable. Tom went on laughing. I knew I had to intervene. I turned to Tom's picture commenting that it seemed he had found painting difficult. He said he hadn't done anything like this since school. I said his tree looked as if it were in a wind-swept storm. He almost visibly subsided, saying nervously that he had had a stormy time recently and then began to talk about himself, apologising saying he had not meant to laugh. Tom said later he had not been at school much anyway. From hesitant beginnings Tom began to enjoy experimenting and playing with paint. He loved colour, mixing the paint, swirling it about, getting different effects (Figure 11.2), using acrylic and inks, taking prints off the original. Sometimes he would work quickly and with excitement, often producing three, four, five images in a group session. At other times he would sit moodily, glowering, unsure what to do. Of all the men he was the most vocal and articulate in the group. 'Are we really all going to die then?' he asked.

Tom had lost contact with family and friends – his only visits were from an elderly lady, a prison visitor. He was the most socially isolated member of the group. In one difficult session, when Tom and another man seemed excitable and quite aggressive, he began asking me personal questions, wanting to find out if I was married, if I had a family and making occasional provocative remarks. Acknowledging his loneliness did not seem to help. He channelled his anger and energy into making clay figures, stabbing the clay to make holes for mouths and eyes. He laughed, saying these people were his family. The next week he made a larger figure saying this was the chief, the head of the clan. I felt an immense sadness, unable to reach him in his angry loneliness. The following week he continued to work on these figures, making more of them and greeting them as old friends when he came back (Figure 11.3).

Figure 11.2

Figure 11.3

One day when he had finished painting before the others he sat looking at a picture on the wall drawn by a child who was dying, given to the unit by Elizabeth Kübler-Ross. He then talked quietly about an experience he had had when he was 18 in London. He had been drinking and was knocked unconscious in a fight. He had landed up in hospital with a burst pancreas and remained in a coma for five days. He awoke remembering a curved tunnel with light at the end and voices saying 'Here's Tom, it's Tom' and another voice saying 'He's not ready yet'. The priest who gave him the last rites didn't believe him. The only other person he had told was his mother. He said people would have laughed at him, and he added in a hushed voice that people would laugh at him here. But having had that experience he said he would not be so frightened of dying now. The next week Tom painted a series of concentric circles, a tunnel with a light in the centre. Elizabeth Kübler-Ross in her book *On Death and Dying* describes similar near death experiences.

In some of the group sessions the men talked together about their images quite freely, at other times the feelings aroused by the images were too intense, too painful to share in words. The younger men sometimes used laughter and denial as a defence against their anxiety – still too frightened to face openly the reality of their situation. This made the others wary of exposing their vulnerability in the group. Words are sometimes superfluous – even intrusive. One afternoon when everyone was working quietly I noticed Tom concentrating hard, mixing colours, pouring paint onto the paper. 'I am going to put a crucifix' he murmured. It looked so much like a crematorium chapel, deep green and purple hangings or curtains, with a cross, strong and bold in the centre, and each side deep red and purple. Tom was totally engrossed, totally absorbed in creating his image – in every sense an 'embodied image' (Schaverien 1992). A moment or two later he had brushed the paint into a muddy smudge and was bending over it. 'It was too much,' he said. I stood near him, repeating gently 'Too much'. It was a moving experience to witness in silence his struggle in trying to come to terms with and face his own death. Malcolm Learmonth describes the special quality of the three-way conversation between artist, image and therapist in which 'we resonate rather than react'. 'In this triangle therapist and client can, if they're lucky, form some sort of joint witness to a previously inarticulate experience' (Learmonth 1994: 22).

Tom was asthmatic and was ill with a chest infection for the next two weeks, perhaps not surprisingly. When he returned he said he was glad to be back and continued to paint, this time creating more diagrammatic pictures of an imagined journey to the after life (Figure 11.4). Birds, symbols of the spirit, frequently entered his paintings (Figure 11.5). He was clearly on a spiritual journey, now more able to talk about plans for the future and what he wanted. He decided to take education classes, hoping to be transferred to an open prison and to make contact with his sister.

Figure 11.4

Figure 11.5

CONCLUSION

The art therapy group ended in March 1993 as further funding was not forth-coming. Anger at this decision and apathy due to a sense of powerlessness combined so that attendance dwindled over the last few sessions. Endings are often difficult and in this situation it was particularly poignant. We had discussed how to manage the ending earlier in the group, the men deciding they would like to have an exhibition. The prison governor, the unit staff, education and social work staff and Joyce Laing were invited. (The Barlinnie Special Unit was renowned for its exhibitions of sculpture and art work.) Refreshments were provided. All but one of the men attended, pleased and proud to see their work on the walls – Tom the proudest of all perhaps. It was a modest but signifi-cant occasion, the men experiencing a sense of achievement, a sense of identity, feelings of self-worth. I also felt proud and privileged to have had the experi-ence of travelling alongside these men for part of their journey – confident that the group had given them a safe place, a place for reflection and creative encounter, a place where fears and phantasies could at least to some extent, be expressed, explored and contained. Writing about her work in Perth prison, Julie Murphy describes the prison building as containing the body whilst art therapy can contain fears and feelings and at the same time can liberate the mind through image making (Murphy 1994: 37).

The sadness and anger at the group ending were expressed by the absence of the group member who did not attend. And it was, indeed, hard to accept that this vulnerable group of prisoners would no longer have the benefit of art therapy. With a change of number one governor, as well as a change of unit governor there was a change of priorities. A much needed drugs reduction programme was introduced. In addition the numbers of HIV/AIDS prisoners were not as great as had originally been feared. However, considering the plight of these men the question has to be asked – what lay behind the change of policy vis-à-vis the respite unit? On the surface it was change of priorities and lack of funding. Could it also be, at some level, a manifestation of denial inherent in the system – denial of the pain and horror experienced by these men as they faced illness and death in prison, and also a more universal denial, a denial of our own mortality?

At the time of writing I understand that all but one of the group members have since died, one being given early release by the parole board and returning home, most being transferred to hospital or the hospice in the last stages of illness. Tom was transferred to an open prison where he died.

To date there has been no further art therapy sessional work within the unit although recently two artists employed by SOLAS, the HIV/AIDS Resource Centre in Edinburgh, have led workshops there, a sculptor at one time and a stained glass artist making a window at another. Involving prisoners in creative artwork is important and undoubtedly beneficial, but it is different from the exploration of self through personal imagery within the context of a therapeutic relationship. Surely there is room for both artist and art therapist within a prison community?

REFERENCES

Bion, W. (1962) *Learning from Experience*, London: Heinemann.

Christie, B. (1995) 'AIDS ten years on', *The Scotsman: Weekend*, 25 November, pp. 5–8.

Coyle, A. (1991) *Inside: Rethinking Scotland's Prisons,* Edinburgh: Scottish Child.

Davis, M. and Wallbridge, D. (1983) *Boundary and Space, An Introduction to the Work of D.W. Winnicott*, Harmondsworth: Penguin.

Kübler-Ross, E. (1970) *On Death and Dying*, London: Tavistock.

Laing, J. and Carrell, C. (ed.) (1982) *The Special Unit: Barlinnie Prison*, Glasgow: Third Eye Centre.

Learmonth, M. (1994) 'Witness and witnessing in art therapy', *Inscape* vol. 1, pp. 19–22.

Menzies Lyth, I. (1985) 'The development of the self in children in institutions', *Journal of Child Psychotherapy*, vol. 11, no. 2, p. 61.

Murphy, J. (1994) 'Mists in the darkness', in M. Liebmann (ed.) *Art Therapy with Offenders*, London: Jessica Kingsley.

Schaverien, J. (1992) *The Revealing Image*, London: Tavistock/Routledge.

Scottish Prison Service (1988) *Assessment and Control*, London: HMSO.

Scottish Prison Service (1990) *Opportunity and Responsibility*, London: HMSO.

Winnicott, D.W. (1974) *Playing and Reality*, Harmondsworth: Penguin.

Wood, M. (1990) 'Art therapy in one session: working with people with AIDS', *Inscape* Winter, p. 32.

Val Beaver MA, CQSW, RATh has had wide clinical experience working with children and families in a variety of settings, both residential and community based. As a sessional art therapist Val worked in a respite unit within the Scottish Prison Service for men diagnosed HIV seropositive and those with AIDS. Since then she has developed an art therapy service within the Postnatal Depression Project funded by the Church of Scotland. For three years she was also a tutor on the postgraduate art therapy Diploma course based at Edinburgh University Settlement.

Chapter 12

The body as art

Individual session with a man with AIDS

Michèle J.M. Wood

INTRODUCTION

In this chapter I wish to present a detailed case study of a single art therapy session with a man who had AIDS and was close to death. This patient, who I will call 'Keith', used our time together in a most extraordinary way. In my seven years of working in this field Keith's particular use of art therapy remains unique and yet it illustrates some of the pertinent issues involved in working with people facing the final stages of their lives. I have chosen to describe this case not only because it portrays something of the patient's experience but also because it clearly highlights significant difficulties and struggles within the therapist. It also suggests a valuable role for art at a time when a person is close to death.

Working as an art therapist in a relatively new specialism of hospice care, and with a newly recognised client group (people with HIV/AIDS), I have had to adapt my previous clinical experience in mental health and psychiatry. There are few other art therapists working in this area and consequently very little literature from which to develop a working model. In the US Rosner David and Sageman's (1987) was the only article until Bussard and Dulhoefer (1991) and later Aldridge (1993), Edwards (1993) and Feldman (1993) in a special issue of *The Arts In Psychotherapy* devoted to arts therapies with people with AIDS. In the UK my article (Wood 1990) was the first to describe this type of work followed by a brief article in the *Guardian* by John Spearman (1992).

My therapeutic approach is informed by many sources and assumes that people have the capacity and potential to use their innate creativity to uncover and discover meaning in their lives. The role of the therapist is that of facilitator to this process. Aldridge (1993) takes a similar view in describing the value of the arts therapies to people living with AIDS. He suggests that the arts therapies provide a patient with the capacity to transcend seemingly hopeless situations in order to gain new perspectives on life and their sense of themselves.

The most testing adaptation of practice I have needed to make is in relation to the issue of time. Time permeates all aspects of the work with people with

HIV/AIDS. The diagnosis of HIV is accompanied by an unpredictably fore-shortened future. This unpredictability is replicated in the arena of contact time with professionals. The uncertain course of ill health and eventual death of the patient provides an extremely fragile framework for establishing a therapeutic contract. In the hospice where I work patients are re-admitted every few months depending on their physical or emotional needs and those of their carers, who require times of respite from caring for the patient. Since admissions to the hospice are for an average of two weeks it is usually only possible to see a patient for three sessions given all the other activities they are involved with (such as resting and seeing their visitors and other professionals).

Given such limits to the patient's time, I have come to view the initial session as a complete contract in itself. This first session functions rather like a one-off introductory workshop in which the patient can experience a 'taste' of art therapy. I also use it as a way of assessing the patient and his/her needs, partic-ularly if the patient decides to continue working with me for the duration of their admission or as an out-patient. It also allows patients to find out whether art therapy is a relevant and appropriate way of addressing their needs. Sometimes patients use the single session to explore an issue which they will develop further with a counsellor at the hospice or another professional outside the hospice. Sometimes the single session is a timely and profound experience which challenges, builds on or confirms something in the patient, becoming a milestone in their life. In this respect the single session does not differ from general aims of therapy where, to quote Van Deurzen-Smith (1990: 157), 'the process of change is initiated in the sessions, not accomplished in them.'

THE SESSION

'Keith'

Keith was a 36-year-old man who had been admitted to the hospice for terminal care with an expectation that he would soon die. He had suffered three bouts of PCP (pneumocystis pneumonia) and had KS (Karposi's Sarcoma), both AIDS-defining illnesses. His family and partner had gathered at his bedside when he was very ill and almost unconscious in the belief that he was dying. However, to everyone's complete surprise, he recovered. Following this, and with his agreement, Keith was referred to me for art therapy. My referral form had been completed by his nurse who gave as the reason for referral: 'Keith is poor at communicating verbally although he has improved dramatically over the last few days.' It was also pointed out that he used homoeopathic medicine and was not taking the standard conventional drugs.

Keith was a tall and extremely emaciated man. When he came for the session he was in his pyjamas and dressing gown. His nurse felt that he was too weak to walk down to the room in which we were meeting and offered a wheelchair, but Keith insisted. He spoke very quietly, almost inaudibly, and in addition to noticing how extremely thin he was, I saw from his urine bag that he had a catheter in place. We met in the ward's day room, which was spacious with large windows at one end, and contained a sofa, chairs, a large dining table, sink and drainer.

The conversation I have with patients at the beginning of sessions is the way in which we define the parameters of our time together. It enables the patient to establish how much I am going to do to, with or for them, and enables me to find out what their key issues or concerns may be. Keith had one question: Did I feel it was worthwhile analysing the artwork? I responded by being clear that I could not analyse his work and explained my role as a facilitator with whom he could look at and reflect upon his own work and art-making process. I picked up on the word 'worthwhile' and asked him to say a little more about this. Keith said that he was not sure how much he could do today, and that he would have to finish off next week. I told him that this time was all we had, since I was going to be away for the next three weeks. Keith decided to start working.

The art-making process was a joint venture. Keith requested a much larger sheet of paper than the A3 sheets I had. We assembled a large sheet (approximately five feet by two-and-a-half feet) of white paper by sellotaping several pieces together. I kept checking the size with him, and the paper got larger and larger. When Keith was satisfied with its size he asked me to put it on the floor.

He then got up from his chair, climbed onto the paper and lay down. The paper was too small for him to stretch out, and I asked him if he would like me to add another piece; he said yes. Keith lay down on his side as though in bed. I sat down on the floor next to him and we remained like this for between twenty and twenty-five minutes, the silence broken only by my three questions.

'Is it painful lying on the floor?'
'No,' he said.
After a long time. . . . 'How are you feeling?'
Silence.
'Does the paper represent anything?'
Silence.

Eventually he raised himself slowly and sat up on the paper. He said he felt stupid to have lain so long on the paper. He disliked not being able to pay for things at the hospice. I asked him if he was concerned about what I felt – was he afraid I thought him stupid? He nodded. I said it seemed to me that what he had done must have been important to him. I also wondered if there was a link between this feeling 'stupid' and the sense of not being worthwhile that he mentioned at the beginning. He agreed. He got up and I helped him to the sofa. I asked what lying on the floor had been like. He replied that it had been 'comfortable', and he wondered if this was because he had been lying in bed for so long. I asked why he chose to lie on the paper, he said that he didn't know, he wasn't sure why. I wondered if he wanted to see how much space he took up, and asked if he felt invisible. He agreed, but added that he did not feel this within himself. He described in a few words a feeling of covering himself up – of hiding parts of himself and 'things' from others. I commented that this must take a lot of energy, and he seemed quite struck by this. He said that he felt isolated. I asked if this was due to feeling that others cannot share his experience (which was how I felt) or because something kept people away, or if there were other reasons.

At this point his convene started to leak and we had to call a nurse. We had a brief discussion about the nurse seeing his large sheet of paper and about confidentiality. We did not put the paper away. I left the room while the nurse attended to him.

When I returned to the room, we acknowledged that this experience of his convene leaking increased his sense of isolation. It was the end of our time, and I gave Keith the option to go on for longer if he wanted since we had lost time while his convene was being re-fitted. He decided to end, and we discussed who would keep the paper. Finally Keith asked me to keep it. He ended by saying that I had made an interesting point which he could understand, and could 'see the connection'. I wasn't sure what this meant, but took it to be a reference to my comment about using energy to cover things up. We ended with a vague allusion to meeting again when I returned to work.

My thoughts during the session

This session was characterised by a sense of the unexpected. Keith's question at the beginning took me by surprise: 'Is it worthwhile analysing the artwork?' This seemed to contain within it very many other questions, yet seemed so precise and gave the impression that he had clear expectations of me. He also appeared to already have an idea of what he wanted to do judging by his comment about finishing off next week. Unfortunately the fact that we only had that day seemed to sharpen the focus upon the reality of his uncertain future. Suddenly we were facing this. I half expected him to decide not to carry on with the session. It is not uncommon for patients to change their minds or decide art therapy is not what they want after all. Keith surprised me again and got started.

As I watched the sheet of paper grow I was amazed at the contrast between its size and the frail presence of this very thin, ill man. I speculated on what he would do with it and assumed, since it was now too large for the table, that he would want it on the wall. I was taken aback once more when he asked for it to be placed on the floor.

When Keith stepped onto the paper I was left alone at the table. I felt at a loss. What was I to do now? This had never happened before. My patients usually sit with me at the table. I realised that the table represented what I expected and knew of art therapy. Do I stay in my territory or follow Keith into his? I felt that I could not be useful to him if I remained at the table. His quietness and frailty demanded an intimacy that was unachievable if I allowed several feet of space to stand between us. I was too far away, with no reason to stay at the table except a fear of what might happen next. And so I got up and sat on the floor close to Keith's head so that we would be able to talk.

As I sat with him I wondered what he might want me to do. Should I draw around him with a felt pen? I decided not to as this reminded me of detective films where the victim's body is marked out on the floor, my thoughts inevitably leading me back to death. I wished that I had a polaroid camera so that I could show him what he looked like. I was aware that he was able to be quite directive with me and decided not to suggest anything; instead I waited.

I wondered what someone would make of us here on the floor should they unexpectedly come in. I might look as though I was doing nothing. I was aware that I was anxious about 'doing something'. I was aware of the very hard floor under my buttocks, and also that since Keith's eyes were closed perhaps he did not know that I was beside him. I asked my first question. My other two questions followed fairly closely; and then I realised that rather than communicating with Keith I was trying to alleviate my own anxiety.

As I sat on the floor next to Keith I was struck by the difference between us. In much of my work with people who have HIV or AIDS I rarely experience such an acute feeling of difference. As my patients share their concerns with me, I empathise with them. It is easier to identify with another person who is sitting on a chair like you, who wears day-time clothing, and talks your language. But as I sat next to this fragile, almost skeleton-of-a-man in his pyjamas, lying on a sheet of paper while I sat on carpet just 12 inches away from him, I was filled with a profound sense that here was someone who was dying while I was not, and the grief felt immense. And the difference between us felt immense. What could I know of this man's experience? What could I possibly have to offer him?

I felt extremely 'present' and very moved as I sat experiencing the silence and gravity of Keith's enactment. It was difficult to put my experience into words for Keith when he asked me (indirectly) how I viewed him. I wanted to acknowledge the power of what I was witnessing without sounding pretentious or patronising, and without superimposing my self-reflections upon him. But he did not elaborate upon his experience. It seemed as though he was unable to, and so I hoped that my presence as witness of his act would be enough. When Keith got up from the paper he had hardly left any trace upon it. The question 'what is left after I have gone?' went through my mind although I did not articulate it.

The communication between us felt intensified by the peculiar way in which he phrased things and by the strength of his stillness. It seemed important for me to 'see' him, to 'hear' him and I was guided by thoughts of invisibility, of his being 'lost' to the patient role and of his battle to preserve his identity. His presence on the paper seemed to convey the message 'here I am, see me'. I was aware of my own strong feelings of inadequacy, of difference and of not being able to fully share his experience. These feelings seemed to resonate with his sense of isolation.

DISCUSSION

In discussing this case I want first to look at the idea of a one-off session before going on to a more detailed exploration of its three key elements: the therapist, the client and the 'artwork'. I will examine my responses as the therapist by considering issues of motivation, silence and bodily responses to the patient, and I will argue that taken together these comprise and inform the therapist's role. In discussing Keith's experience of the session I shall explore the themes and questions that seemed to arise – his need to maintain control, the effects of his physiological state, and the manner in which his use of himself as the artwork illustrated his recent experiences of being so close to death. In discussing Keith's use of his body as the artwork I will explore possible meanings for his action, and I will refer to contemporary performance art.

The one-off session – an inappropriate intervention?

A crucial feature of this session was the fact that it had to be a 'one-off' and that Keith had expected more. There seemed to be an echo of this dynamic in relation to the paper: what I had available was too small. If the paper represented my limited resources then it also provided the possibility of transformation in the construction of a large sheet of paper. This is the 'magic' of art therapy whereby desires can become realised albeit temporarily. In creating his large sheet of paper Keith could have more space. By adding on another piece so that he could stretch out I perhaps unconsciously made amends and provided the extension needed to the session then and there. I repeated this offer again at the end of the session with the suggestion we extend our time in recognition of what Keith had lost while his convene was being re-fitted; however, he declined.

In attempting to understand this session with Keith it is necessary to establish a framework within which to examine what took place. I have described earlier my use of the single session within a broadly existential paradigm. However, it cannot be assumed that this perspective is the only one. Art therapy colleagues working outside the field of palliative care have questioned the appropriateness of a one-off session, pointing out that this does not allow for the development of the trust required for the therapeutic relationship and that it may violate the patient's emotional/psychological defences, leaving them vulnerable and exposed. However, in a setting where physical, emotional and social changes are rapid and continuous strict adherence to, for example, a minimum number of sessions would make therapy a non-starter. The patient cannot, and should not in my view, be seen as reliant upon professional expertise for permission and guidance in their own process of anticipatory grieving and preparation for dying. In my experience people who are living with a life-threatening illness are often actively threading together the 'helpers' they feel they need, and also actively avoiding those they do not want, even if professionals believe they are needed. The value of a single session is to be determined by those who choose to try art therapy in this form. Certainly my clinical experience suggests that a single session, set within the context of a palliative approach to patient care, can be useful (Wood 1990). What is important is that the therapist and patient are clear about the brevity of their initial encounter, and this was determined in the opening conversation with Keith.

The therapist's responses

An important question for a single session is that of the therapist's motivation in offering something so obviously limited. Does the therapist respond to the identifiable needs of the patient or to her own unconscious response in the face of needs that she cannot possibly hope to fulfil? Skaife (1993) reviews the American and British literature on art therapy with the physically ill, and suggests that an inevitable part of the relationship between therapist and patient must involve envy. Skaife proposes that patients must envy their therapist's good health, and that therapists unconsciously attempt to protect themselves from this unstated envy. Skaife identifies several forms of protection such as: (i) merging with the patient to avoid making explicit the difference between them; (ii) not addressing the patient's feelings about the therapist; (iii) forming an alliance with the patient against an identifiable enemy (such as the illness, death or handicap); and (iv) feeling guilty about being healthy. By identifying these different responses in the therapist, Skaife draws attention to factors which might motivate the therapist to avoid confronting issues that are painful for the patient. Skaife suggests that it might be more useful to the patient to acknowledge feelings of fear and envy in order for the patient to gain some control over them. It is questionable how appropriate such an exploration is in as brief a meeting as a single session. Nevertheless the therapist must surely consider their own responses to their patients and certainly Skaife's analysis reflects some of my thoughts during the session described here.

The actions of assembling the paper, following Keith onto the floor and later onto the sofa were negotiated by a communication between us that included both silence and words. We were two parts of a whole. This flow of communication, however stilted at times, highlights the role of the therapist as partner in a unique therapeutic event and perhaps elaborates the notion of therapist as 'container' with its passive and rather rigid associations. My responses to Keith were guided by unconscious exchanges between us through the processes of transference, countertransference and projection.

All psychotherapists work through an augmentation of expression, whether we call this interpretation, intervention or an activated imagination. This is accomplished within the forming of a relationship in which the therapist, so to speak, acts as an enquiring and responsive body for the other. This is how the transference comes to fit, how it is solicited. . . . It is not a matter of telepathy, nor of technology, or of operating on the patient, but a metaphysical relationship mediated through images, words and *bodily selves*.

(Henzell 1988: 25; emphasis mine)

My movement and responses to Keith during the session went beyond verbal exchanges; they involved my bodily self, thereby demonstrating that I saw him – I was a witness. Learmonth (1994) discusses the importance of this aspect of art therapy. As a witness the therapist receives the client's art as a testimony of their experience, and faces it with them. He points out that for the patient to be denied a witness to their suffering is ultimately destructive to the human spirit, and he emphasises the capacity of the client's artwork to be a witness for them. Learmonth suggests that the process of bearing witness to our own experience is the mechanism by which we can experience it as meaningful. This analysis highlights the value of my presence and Keith's enactment on the paper in our session. The importance to Keith of my view can also be seen in the material of the session. His opening question 'Do you think it is worthwhile analysing the artwork?' brings to mind a communication about how much I could or would see of him.

Another important aspect of this session was the presence and use of silence as a means of communication. Case (1995) draws attention to the value of recognising the richness of silence during sessions as a channel of communication. She highlights the value of the emotional experience that a period of silence can provide as well as the importance of noting what precedes and follows it. She suggests that when we are unable to verbalise a feeling, that feeling resides within the silence.

The silences of our patients then become available to be understood through the countertransference in a similar way that we might understand images for the quality they arouse in us.

(Case 1995: 26)

Keith's enactment not only confronted me with the reality of our difference, and of the painfulness of acknowledging death, but paradoxically it brought into focus the value of my aliveness. In psychiatry or other directly mental health settings the attentive presence of the therapist maintains the ground of reality in order for the patient to feel safe and supported enough to explore his/her 'madness'. In a similar way I feel that the therapeutic value of my aliveness, of which I was so painfully aware, lay in the possibility that I represented an anchor in life from which Keith could explore the experience of dying. My role as audience was not only to witness but perhaps provided a mooring from which he could launch himself into some form of re-working his 'death bed' experience and to which he could return.

Issues for Keith

Control

> Through the image suffering is allowed to be itself.
>
> (Learmonth 1994: 20)

Keith's limited verbal communications make it difficult to discuss with any certainty what he had intended in his presentation of himself on the white paper. Perhaps however, by exploring the themes and questions that were raised in our time together we may understand something of his experience.

Control was a central feature of Keith's manner and attitude. He had insisted on walking to the session, although his nurse had offered a wheelchair. He had helped me sellotape together the pieces of paper, and he had stepped on and got off the paper by himself, and folded it up at the end. These were strong statements of the importance to Keith of remaining in control and understandable given how much control is taken away in the process of illness. Self-respect is lost too and the displacement of his convene during the session was a vivid example of this. Keith's comment about wanting to pay his way expressed something of a desire to have some control over circumstances. When he did speak his speech was clear, but most of the time he mumbled and grunted. I wonder if his silence was one way he could remain in control, making me listen very hard. A half-awareness of his determination to retain control seemed evident in my ambiguous comment about his using a lot of energy to cover things up, and which seemed to strike a chord for him. Giving him the choice to decide what was to become of the paper during and after the session was another way of enabling him to maintain his sense of control.

Physical health

One factor that also needs to be considered is the effect of Keith's physiological state upon the session. His difficulty in communicating was similar to many people with AIDS who have HIV-related dementia. I went to see him on my return from leave and he told me that his memory was not so good now although he did remember our session. McKeogh (1995) points out that the onset of HIV dementia is insidious, often appearing as forgetfulness, slowed mental and motor abilities and social withdrawal. At the time of Keith's admission HIV dementia had not been mentioned, although with the expectation that he was very close to death it may not have seemed a relevant factor to consider. However, in retrospect, if HIV dementia was a factor then Keith's presentation can be seen in another light. Feldman (1993) describes her work as an expressive therapist with a patient with this condition. She states that patients are often angry and despairing at their diminishing cognitive capacities, and may resort to becoming mute or passive. She points out this can stir up feelings of helplessness and inadequacy in caregivers. Some of these features described by Feldman fit Keith, although I did not experience him as angry. However, if Keith was experiencing a gradual loss in his cognitive skills and his capacity for communication due to physical deterioration then his need for a non-verbal means of expression may be regarded as pressing. His particular use of the session is not invalidated as a therapeutic experience by this possibility, but perhaps shows how important it might have been for him to find a stillness and attentiveness in which to be seen and heard.

Literature detailing therapeutic work with people living with AIDS (PLWAs) highlights the special problems caused by physical deterioration and ill health upon the parameters of the work. Lee (1995) in fact chose to exclude from his doctoral research PLWAs who were close to death and who had difficulties with verbal expression, in order to minimise the effects of the therapist's subjectivity and to increase the reflexivity of his clients. Certainly the work of Rosner David and Sageman (1987) in the early days of HIV and AIDS in the United States show therapists needing to be incredibly flexible about the style and location of their sessions (for example at patients' bedsides, in clinic waiting areas or chemotherapy cubicles). They point out that 'the rapid pace of physical decline in AIDS patients may lend increasing importance to each art therapy session (1987: 120).

The artwork

Several contemporary artists have used their own body as their primary medium for expression (for example John Coplans, Orlan, Mona Hatoum, Gilbert and George) and Keith's use of his body lying on the paper falls within the tradition of live performance art. As art therapists we are concerned to understand the patient's choice of media and we view the choice as another form of communication. The body in Keith's case carries profound connotations. He is facing death because of body fluids and bodily actions, because of a virus which has laid open his body to attack from uncommon illnesses, through his body he bears witness to the totality of his persona. Keith's homoeopathic approach to his health adds another layer of meaning to his possible view of his body – one that includes a metaphysical rather than a purely materialist sense of body/self. However, the transient quality of life appears integral to his presentation, and the choice of body over paint or clay reinforces the presence of the vitality that is in his body – he was not yet a corpse. I was reminded of this when I saw Parker and Swinton's show at the Serpentine Gallery London in September 1995 entitled *The Maybe*. This consisted of a collection of objects belonging to various famous deceased people, for example a letter from Magritte, the rug from Sigmund Freud's consulting room and Lee Miller's camera. These ordinary objects were contrasted with the central exhibit of the show which was a living person – a sleeping woman (Tilda Swinton) – placed like all the other exhibits in a glass case, where she remained for eight hours a day. She was the Maybe – the representation of the potential for becoming something in the future. This show raised questions about the value placed upon objects over people in our western society and about the transience of life. Watching viewers of the sleeping woman, I saw how unsettling it is to be confronted with a living body who perhaps at any moment may awake and view the viewer (unlike objects over which even the most insecure audience has some power to control a dialogue with the work). I remembered a similar tense dynamic between myself and Keith.

My countertransference to Keith in the session is interesting to consider at this point: I had the desire to photograph him yet clearly this was my desire to hold onto the moment, and to impose my preferred art form upon his, thereby missing the meaning of the performance. My preference for keeping a record, and my urge to 'do something' surely also arose from a difficulty with accepting loss and death.

Inner drama

Keith's presentation of himself on the paper takes Schaverien's (1987) notion of the 'embodied' image into the realm of live art like *The Maybe*. It is an enactment of his inner experience rather than an anti-therapeutic 'acting out'. In this respect it is akin to drama. Gordon (1989) discusses the psychic roots of drama and the therapeutic value to the patient of externalising their inner drama. She maintains that drama can be the most direct means of self-communication as well as a communication to someone else. There seems an obvious link between the gathering of his friends and family around his bed to say 'goodbye' and what he chose to 'explore' with me. His comment about finding the floor comfortable because he had been in bed so long appears to make the connection. In true psychodynamic fashion Keith cast me in the position occupied by his family and partner, thereby re-presenting to me and to himself his inner dramatic world.

Dying is a social experience

The value of Keith's artistic/dramatic act could also be viewed as a form of communication which directs attention to the reality that dying is a social experience as well as a personal one. The drama of Keith's family and friends gathering at his bedside is a social event anticipating the final goodbye at the funeral. The fact that Keith had got better rather than died accentuates one facet of the experience of living with AIDS (or any other life-threatening condition)

– that of being caught between living and dying. It is as though Keith had failed to complete some rite of passage and was left at the threshold (or to use its anthropological name the 'limen') between two different states of being. Greenblatt (1995) describes dying in its broadest sense as a loss of a reference point from which an individual had gained a sense of coherence and meaning. He states that whether there has been a choice involved in such a loss or not (as in the case of someone with AIDS), with the disappearance of what constitutes identity for the individual they enter a 'liminal period' from which to emerge transformed. This process when imbued with social ritual and meaning is understood as a rite of passage. The time in which I met with Keith could be described as a liminal period, and the sense I had of Keith as isolated and invisible corresponds with Greenblatt's description. Keith's decision to use art therapy at such a time resonates with art making which accompanies rituals found in other cultures. Greenblatt (ibid.) points out that often ritual acts involve the body, such as marking, painting or tattooing the skin. In discussing art works recently exhibited in London at the Tate Gallery in a collection entitled 'Rites of Passage', Greenblatt considers the pieces shown to be an exploration of the limen which is:

> The place that is no-place, a mutilated fragment, the empty space in an unworn unwearable set of clothes. And that no-place-u-topia is the place at once of art and dying.
>
> (Greenblatt 1995: 29)

This is perhaps the place in which Keith found himself when he met with me and may be the place described by the blank sheet of paper left by him on the floor. When understood from this perspective art appears to function as an exposition of the transformative passage from one state of being to another.

REFERENCES

Aldridge, D. (1993) 'Hope, meaning and the creative arts therapies in the treatment of AIDS', *The Arts in Psychotherapy* vol. 20, pp. 285–297.

Bussard, A. and Dulhoefer, S. (1991) 'Art therapy with AIDS patients' in Landgarten, H. and Lubbers, D. (eds) *Adult Art Psychotherapy: Issues and Applications*, New York: Brunner/Mazel.

Case, C. (1995) 'Silence in progress', *Inscape* vol. 1, pp. 26–31.

Dryden, W. (ed.) (1990) *Individual Therapy*, Buckingham: Open University Press.

Edwards, G. (1993) 'Art therapy with HIV+ patients', *The Arts in Psychotherapy* vol. 20, pp. 325–333.

Feldman, E. (1993) 'HIV dementia and countertransference', *Arts in Psychotherapy* vol. 20, pp. 317–323.

Gilroy, A. and Dalley, T. (eds) (1989) *Pictures at an Exhibition*, London and New York: Routledge.

Gilroy, A. and Lee, C. (eds) (1995) *Art and Music: Therapy and Research*, London: Routledge.

Gordon, R. (1989) 'The psychic roots of drama' in Gilroy, A. and Dalley, T. (eds) *Pictures at an Exhibition,* London and New York: Routledge.

Greenblatt, S. (1995) 'Liminal states and transformations' in exhibition catalogue *'Rites of Passage: Art for the End of the Century'. Tate Gallery 15 June–3 Sept. 1995*, London: Tate Gallery.

Henzell, J. (1988) 'Body and Soul', *Inscape* Spring, pp. 23–25.

Landgarten, H. and Lubbers, D. (eds) (1991) *Adult Art Psychotherapy: Issues and Applications,* New York: Brunner/Mazel.

Learmonth, M. (1994) 'Witness and witnessing in art therapy', *Inscape* vol. 1, pp. 19–22.

Lee, C. (1995) 'The analysis of therapeutic improvisatory music' in Gilroy, A. and Lee, C. (eds) *Art and Music: Therapy and Research*, London: Routledge.

McKeogh, M. (1995) 'Dementia in HIV disease – A challenge for palliative care?', *Journal of Palliative Care* vol. 11, no. 2, pp. 30–33.

Rosner David, I. and Sageman, S. (1987) 'Psychological aspects of AIDS as seen in art therapy', *American Journal of Art Therapy* vol. 26, August, pp. 3–10.

Schaverien, J. (1987) 'The scapegoat and the talisman: transference in art therapy' in Dalley, T., Case, C., Schaverien, J., Weir, F., Halliday, D., Nowell Hall, P. and Waller, D. (eds) *Images of Art Therapy,* London and New York: Routledge.

Skaife, S. (1993) 'Sickness, health and the therapeutic relationship', *Inscape* Summer, pp. 24–28.

Spearman, J.(1992) 'Drawing out the fear on a journey into the unknown', *Guardian* 27 July.

Van Deurzen-Smith, E. (1990) 'Existential therapy' in Dryden, W. (ed.) *Individual Therapy*, Buckingham: Open University Press.

Wood, M.J.M. (1990) 'Art therapy in one session: working with people with AIDS', *Inscape*, Winter, pp. 27–33.

Michèle J.M. Wood BA (Hons) Psychology, DipAT, RATh has worked at Mildmay Mission Hospital, London since 1989 where she developed the art therapy service for men, women and children living with HIV and AIDS. She also has experience of working as an art therapist in mental health services and in education.

Chapter 13

The invisible injury
Adolescent griefwork group

Mandy Pratt

In this chapter I want to take the reader 'through the therapist's door', to de-mystify the process of art therapy in my work with groups of bereaved children. In recent years there have been a growing number and variety of griefwork groups organised for children of all ages throughout the world. In the UK the most well publicised include Winston's Wish and the Good Grief programme (Ward 1989). I want to explore the particular contribution art therapy has to offer such work. I shall describe in detail the art therapy component of an adolescent griefwork group that was organised by St Helena Hospice in Colchester. In doing so I hope to explore a variety of issues, both within the discipline of art therapy itself, and for my work as part of a multidisciplinary team.

ORIGINS OF THIS WORK AT ST HELENA HOSPICE

In my work with patients at the hospice I am totally non-directive, employing a psychodynamic model. In 1992, the Director of the Family Support Group (FSG), keen to respond to the needs of children who had lost a parent at the hospice, asked me to devise an art therapy programme specifically for them. The difficulties most likely to be encountered by children and adolescents in this situation were researched (see Appendix III). The work of Furman's team in Cleveland, USA (Furman 1974) proved invaluable in this as did Worden's concept of the tasks of mourning (Worden 1983). More recently some of the concepts from Walter's construction of a 'durable biography' have also been incorporated (Walter 1996). The activities I proposed were designed to engage with those difficulties peculiar to different ages to enable the children to work with their grief. We now run griefwork groups several times a year for children or adolescents. There are no more than twelve members in any group with five or six staff. The young people referred to the groups have lost a parent or sibling 6 to eighteen months previously. We now regard this as an optimal time for this work, any earlier and we might add to the trauma by challenging necessary psychological defences. It should be long enough after the death for problems with grieving to start to emerge but not so long as to allow them to become too entrenched. Referrals come from across the multidisciplinary team and are co-ordinated by FSG staff who work with the whole family from the patient's first contact with the hospice.

The adolescent groups start with a residential weekend away and are completed with four weekly sessions in the art therapy room at the hospice. The intensity of the experience is heightened by this initial change of setting, away from familiar surroundings and routines. An independence or rather a self-reliance is encouraged that might be hard to replicate on a sessional basis. The weekend art therapy sessions take place in the spacious and well used art room which has access to a fully equipped pottery. There are several large tables spread out at one end, a space in which we assemble a circle of chairs in the middle and an assortment of battered sofas.

THE GROUP MEMBERS

Katherine (12) was a lively outgoing character who had inherited her mother's slight build. Her sister Chloe (14) was also confident and friendly, but perhaps more reserved in expressing herself in front of others. I had worked with their mother both at the hospice and in the family home until her death from cervical cancer six months earlier. The group also had another pair of sisters, Emma (14) who was very shy and initially inseparable from Susanne (16). Susanne was very protective of Emma but, despite being the eldest in the group, lacked confidence in relating to the adults present. Their mother had died seven months previously from cancer of the colon, leaving them and an 8-year-old brother who later joined the younger group. The group was completed with Jonathan (also 14) who told us at the outset that we should call him John, 'not Johnny that's for wimps'. He had a sister of 5 who also joined the younger group. Their father had died from a brain tumour eight months earlier.

BEGINNING TO WORK WITH ART THERAPY

My observation of the group and its members starts as each individual enters the art room for the first time. What is their mood? Do they explore the space for themselves or wait to be invited? Do siblings stay together or seek their own space? Are they noisy, nervous, quiet, busy, anxious? How do they relate to each other, the space, the staff? These initial observations can provide an invaluable insight into how these young people have learned to deal with new situations, as well as their familiar patterns of relating to others of all ages. They may also indicate individual difficulties and suggest how best to work with them. The process at this stage is common to all psychotherapeutic group work, monitoring the emergence of multiple transference issues to encompass all those present (Bion 1968; Bloch and Crouch 1987; Foulkes 1983; McNeilly 1987; Waller 1993; Yalom 1975).

All staff are present for this first session, and will make their own assessments of the group according to their own discipline. Their contribution over the course of the programme in supportive and counselling roles will be considerable, and it is useful for everyone to observe this session as the participants' stories start to unfold. At the end of each session, the staff meet to discuss our observations of what has been happening in the art therapy sessions and at other times. Pre-group training ensures that staff understand both the objectives of the work and the requirements for staff in this setting. For example, they must resist the temptation to 'rescue' a participant struggling with a difficult issue (by perhaps offering a consoling word or a hug). They are aware that their own childhood or adolescent experiences of loss will affect their response to the situation. To give in to the urge to rescue the young person would effectively disempower them, confirming that it is unacceptable to express pain, fear, anger or other difficult emotions. It would also suggest that the answer to their difficulties lies not in devising their own solutions, but in finding an adult who will help them sustain their denial.

My role in the group is soon registered by the participants as I run through the ground rules that govern how we work, and outline the structure for this and all subsequent sessions. Setting these structural boundaries provides a reassuring element of predictability, and engenders any transference issues between group members and myself. I introduce the working space and materials and invite members to be as inventive as they please. This is to be their space and their equipment to use however they choose for the duration of the group. I explain that since the artwork they produce is not intended to be a demonstration of artistic skill but rather a reflection of their thoughts and feelings, they should not be judgemental of their own or others' work. It is also important to respect one another's working space (this point seems to require particular stress where there are siblings present) as it can be very distracting to be interrupted when engaged in something very absorbing.

Most of the young people who choose to attend the griefwork programme are understandably apprehensive at this stage. They may have had contact with some of the staff during their parents' admission to the hospice, but they seldom know any of us well. Over the course of the programme they will discover a great deal about themselves and each other. Most group members are still in full-time education and the model with which they are most familiar is the classroom (often staff are addressed as 'miss' or 'sir'). I find it helps to distinguish this therapeutic group from school groups, emphasising that the staff are not there to teach or direct but to facilitate and support.

As with any psychotherapeutic process, confidentiality is essential; it is vital that the participants develop confidence and trust in this way of working. I point out that while any individual is welcome to discuss their own work outside the group, it is essential that everything other group members say or do is kept in total confidence. I explain that the reason for this is that there may be many difficult or uncomfortable issues that emerge in the course of our work both as a result of the death and from other sources. That it is common, for example, to feel very strong emotions, anger or even hatred toward those close to us (including the person who has died) and that it is OK to be honest about that here. This provides the ideal opportunity to explore and express the full range of thoughts and feelings both around their loss and any other difficulties they may have. I have never yet encountered an example of disclosure, even from a sibling; this is the one rule that no one has any problem respecting!

Each session will have the same structure. We come together and there is an opportunity for anyone to share anything they choose (whether it concerns how they are feeling, an event that has taken place or even a dream that seemed particularly important). I then introduce the activity for that session. There will be a set time for work, during which participants are free to employ the art materials in whichever way they choose (the activities are not compulsory and often become secondary to the images that emerge unbidden as the individual starts to explore the process for themselves). Finally we will come back together to explore all the images produced. As with other psychotherapeutic groups, the pressure to engage with this part of the process comes from within. In art therapy, the image itself speaks. Where thoughts and feelings are too painful or complex to put into words, the image gives access in a way which may not need to be verbalised.

AIMS OF GRIEFWORK

The first activity is designed to encourage participants to explore the materials and the workspace – to relax and feel comfortable in this unfamiliar environment. Everyone (staff included) uses the materials to introduce themselves to the group, to tell us a bit about themselves and perhaps how they are feeling about what lies ahead. This relatively straightforward activity establishes that here the participants are the experts. We look to be informed by them, value their views and are interested in what matters to them.

In observing the group during this activity I begin to get a feel for their familiar ways of being, particularly when confronted with an albeit minor challenge. The griefwork groups have a number of objectives aimed at enabling children and young people to overcome some of the more crippling effects of the death of a parent. The long-term effects of parent loss in childhood have been well documented (Black 1978; Rutter 1972; Birtchnell 1970, 1972; Hill 1969). In the short term, children, like adults, will adopt a variety of coping strategies to prevent their being overwhelmed by this loss. For young people, grief presents a particular challenge. Whilst death is an inevitable part of everyone's experience, the loss of a parent in childhood is devastating, arguably more so than any adult bereavement. As Erna Furman puts it:

When his parent dies, a child finds himself in a unique situation because of the special nature of his ties to the deceased. An adult distributes his love among several meaningful relationships – his spouse, parents, children, friends, colleagues – as well as in his work and hobbies. The child by contrast invests almost all his feelings in his parents. Except in very unusual circumstances, this single relationship is therefore incomparably rich and intense, unlike any close adult relationship. Only in childhood can death deprive an individual of so much opportunity to love and be loved and face him with so difficult a task of adaptation.

(Furman 1974: 12)

Losing a parent in childhood is extremely isolating, particularly where the illness carries some social stigma as in AIDS. Those to whom the child would naturally turn may well be locked into their own grief, and friends are often unsure how best to help. Bringing children with similar experiences together can replace this isolation with a sense of belonging. Using art therapy to facilitate the process also offers each participant the possibility of drawing something positive from their experience which will benefit not just the individual but the whole group. In sharing their work, they consciously reflect on their creativity in devising ways of coping and find the ideal medium for telling their story. In the safety of the group, they can explore different ways of expressing themselves. Through the images, difficult thoughts and feelings become malleable, mutable, tolerable. Participants come to an awareness of their individual potential and ability to cope with the most difficult situations. In sharing this insight with one another they build self-esteem and confidence. The courage this takes earns them the respect peculiar to this unique group. Without an opportunity to work with these difficulties, young people may become stuck in their grieving, locked into damaging ways of behaving that can hamper their development (Bowlby 1963, 1979; Furman 1974; Pincus 1974).

OPENING SESSION

Each member of the group has been asked to bring with them a photograph of the person who died. In this way, they will already have started the process of reflection – looking back over holidays and celebrations to select the image that was important to them. They are asked to use the art materials to produce a mount or frame for the photo which will enable them to introduce their relative to the group. The staff do not participate in this activity although they will all be present as the group comes together to share the product. The group are asked to consider *all* facets of the person (good and bad) and to describe the particular relationship that has been lost. This helps distinguish the unique quality of each member's grief. It also puts firmly on the agenda our reason for being there. In my experience, sharing these self-conscious first efforts is the hardest thing imaginable, both for the young people themselves as they struggle with overwhelming emotions, in front of strangers and in an alien environment – and for the staff.

This session started for John with a search for sellotape and staples (fixing materials). No substitute would do, and several group members brought this feeling of things being inadequate, not right or even a failure into the discussion at the end. Searching and the sense of things never being 'good enough' or right any more are of course central to the grieving process, as indeed is the need to fix things (both in the sense of putting them right and of holding them firmly – exerting control). John's frame – red card with the photo central – was decorated in felt tip drawings, 'a fishing rod bending the wrong way', a speech bubble 'hello', one corner blocked in with black and another in blue glitter. He had been very restless during the work period asking each of us in turn 'what shall I do?'

He volunteered to go first with his introduction, saying 'the problem is, I don't really remember what he was like . . . so I can't introduce him to you'. John then gave a vivid account of how, towards the end of his father's illness, he had taken a friend home after school as he had often done in the past. His father's appearance had changed as a result of medication and radiotherapy to the head. His face was abnormally large and rounded and he had irregular bald patches in his otherwise thick dark hair. 'He looked like a freak or a monster really.' John's friend may have shown his shock at these changes, but something sparked the aggressive behaviour that was a feature of this phase of the illness. His father had struggled to his feet and pulled out a handful of his own hair before brandishing it at the boys and saying 'look at that, see it's all coming out now'. John has not taken a friend home since.

By the end of the story, John was crying and quite incoherent. I acknowledged to the group how hard it must have been for John both in telling us and at the time. It also seemed appropriate to suggest that maybe now would be the right time and place for 'it all to come out'. Many of their individual accounts would feature progressive illness, physical and mental deterioration. Through his introduction, John had as it were given permission to the group to cry, and also to grieve for themselves as witnesses to this appalling loss of their own carefree childhood. Over the sessions to come, John was often to act as facilitator, enabling the others to express the full range of their feelings by his courage and willingness to show his emotions.

Chloe seemed anxious to lift the mood of the group as she started to talk about the photo she had selected. It showed her (aged 9) with her parents and a Spanish au pair who had become a family friend. The mount used a variety of materials and styles to depict particularly happy associations from this period. This would have been the last summer before her mother's cancer was first diagnosed. It showed a beach hut and sailboat, 'happy holidays, party glitter and flowers'. Across the top she had printed ESPAGNOLE, commenting with some pride that she had learned to speak Spanish that summer.

One theme common to Chloe and Katherine was that their mother had taught them so much that they valued. The boat was painted with a palette knife – a technique shown her by her mother. As she described each detail of the mount, Chloe became progressively more subdued. Her yearning for that lost, carefree time was tangible. Her sister did not figure in the photo or its mount. It felt important that Chloe should have some opportunity to regress to this time of relative security in her life. Would it be possible with Katherine looking on?

Susanne was next to talk, although the tears started so swiftly that she was only able to mumble a few words before hiding behind her hair to cry 'unseen'. Her hair was long and parted in the middle, giving the effect of curtains behind which she had withdrawn – like the coffin discreetly disappearing at a crema-tion, a rather melodramatic interpretation, until you reflect on the audience in this instance. What Susanne had withdrawn from was actually a group of mourners.

Whilst she participated in all the tasks and activities, she found it easier to share her thoughts and feelings outside the group with the staff, effectively withdrawing from the group process. Her response to the set activities was to suggest that they were somewhat childish but that she could be cajoled into joining in rather than spoil our fun! It emerged that her way of coping with her mother's death had been to take on her role for the other family members. They in turn had welcomed this substitution, until it became impossible for her to relinquish. To do so would be to force each of them into facing the painful reality of their mother's death. The effect of this form of denial for Susanne was to make it impossible for her to acknowledge her own loss and start to grieve.

Brief therapy of this sort must always provide for the needs of those for whom the pace or timing of such work is inappropriate. In group art therapy, as in all psychotherapeutic groupwork, sensitivity to individual need reflects an awareness of the needs of the group as a whole. This group was especially needy of a mother. Susanne was unable to resist that need, just as she had been at home. Over the next few weeks, the staff were faced with the difficult task of containing Susanne's needs within the group process whilst not allowing that to disrupt the work of the group overall.

Emma seemed dramatically exposed by her sister's withdrawal. The two sisters had brought only one photograph, showing mum and grandad smiling together on the sofa at home. He had found the loss of his daughter so unbear-able that he was no longer in contact with the family and so represented both an additional loss and a model for avoiding this painful situation. Emma was clearly shocked to see Susanne cry and she hastily described the frame they had made together, 'Mum liked flowers, animals and beach holidays', to deflect the group's attention away from them both.

For her, Susanne's visible grief re-enacted the sadness her mother had shown at leaving them and effectively ended Emma's practice of mirroring Susanne's every move. Emma gradually detached herself from her childlike dependence on Susanne. Over the next few sessions she observed the other group members and was finally able to depict her true feelings and thus to genuinely own them for herself. Whilst she remained quiet throughout the span of the group, she was able to explore new ways of being, modelling herself on the other group members. This helpful outcome was the product of a particular group dynamic sparked by her search for an alternative mother substitute.

Initially Emma felt very isolated, finding it hard to relate to the other group members. She encountered a consistent refusal to adopt the parental role Susanne had withdrawn from, by staff and group members alike. She was encouraged to share her anxieties with the group and use the art materials to explore the reasons for her dependence on Susanne. She was eventually able to reflect on her parents' rather separate lives, their different interests and tendency to argue when they were together. Her way of dealing with the anxieties this produced had been to become so self-effacing as to be almost invisible. Her images during this period were equally indistinct, drawn in faint pencil lines. Support from the group enabled her to gain confidence in her capacity to state her own emotional needs.

At supper a staff member commented that it felt as though we had opened something up and left it open. Everyone nodded agreement at this, but the consensus was that it was OK – they were game to continue now that they had started. The rest of the evening was spent getting to know each other better with some group games but scope for some quiet chat too. Despite the exhausting day, group members seldom go to sleep before 1 or 2 o'clock in the morning which reflects their curiosity about each other and the process they are engaged with. Another boundary is tested as these young people explore some independence whilst taking responsibility for themselves.

I introduce the Saturday morning activity by telling the story of the New Guinea mudmen, where frightened, vulnerable villagers disguised themselves to hide from attack. Their makeshift masks enabled them to frighten away their attackers. The mask is a universal phenomenon, appearing in diverse cultures across the globe and throughout history into contemporary western culture. It can perform a variety of functions, principally concealing or transforming the wearer and enabling them to adopt an alternative (often superhuman) role. In many cultures, masks are used in transition rituals, specifically during coming of age rituals for adolescents and in funerary rites for the dead (Mack 1994). In both instances the mask enables the wearer to be literally transformed into and empowered as an ancestral spirit who will oversee the ritual and ensure a good outcome.

In selecting mask making for adolescent griefwork this creative, empowering capacity was significant as was the role of the mask in facilitating transitions. Many of the maladaptive behaviours associated with bereaved adolescents have their origin in the repression of 'unacceptable' thoughts or feelings. Providing an opportunity to reveal such feelings enables the participant to recognise that they are not unnatural or bad. At a later session, the hospice medical director answers questions put anonymously into a question box. These reveal a high incidence of fear about participants' own health: 'can you catch cancer?' They also suggest a real sense of vulnerability and anxiety about change: 'what would happen to me if Dad died too?' Such fears can be associated in our minds with retribution or punishment for 'wrong' thoughts or feelings.

The participants are asked to pair up (not with a sibling) and create their own individual mask from a base formed from their own face with plaster bandage. The materials available allow for an extraordinary variety of outcomes as the base is extended, trimmed, painted and decorated. Even when, as in Figure 13.1, two or more group members deliberately try to produce identical masks (possibly in an attempt to create a group motif or identity), the end products vary considerably. These three 'Phantom of the Opera' masks (a particularly popular variant, especially with adolescent boys) have dramatically different expressions, described as 'laughing/surprised, menacing/worried and tragic/sad' by their makers. The Phantom wears his mask because he is so deformed that people would be repelled if they saw his face. Beneath that superficial appearance of course lies the true phantom – loyal, loving and desperate to be loved in return.

The masks produced in these sessions often reflect contemporary culture – Emma's was from the movie *Silence of the Lambs*. The lower half of the face was covered 'so it couldn't talk . . . or eat'. Talking about Hannibal Lecter (the menacing psychopath who is the film's central character) allowed Emma to express her lost innocence and her sense of being expected to keep silent about

Figure 13.1

her grief (to avoid distressing their younger brother) despite the pain this caused. It also became clear that she feared having contributed to her mother's illness and death. Guilt is a common feature of grieving, related to the helplessness encountered in watching a loved one die. It is also a product of negative feelings around the deceased. Unless it can be expressed and acknowledged in an accepting, supportive setting, guilt can produce enormous self-contempt and loss of self-worth.

Susanne's mask, divided lengthways down the middle (like her hair the night before), 'started out half happy, half sad' – this felt like a conscious attempt at rationalisation on her part. 'But it wouldn't work and ended up like camouflage, it's a bit bright though.' In effect, despite her attempts to conceal her grief and suggest that 'everything is fine', her image emphasised that she could not succeed. The 'camouflage' in dayglo orange, yellow and black was paradoxically striking.

Katherine's mask 'started out as a clown' with a long chin and doll-like features that her sister commented 'made it look like grandma'. This was painted over in far stronger colours, yellow, black and red with 'crazy hair' added in cellophane, card and tissue until the end result was 'really quite frightening!'. Katherine still felt extremely vulnerable and frightened, with a need to have her fears recognised despite her seemingly carefree, 'clowning' behaviour.

For this group, masks have additional, fearful associations. John, for example, described accompanying his father for radiotherapy which involved dad wearing a protective perspex mask to cover the untreated parts of his head. This was clamped firmly so that he was immobilised during treatment. In an attempt to render this process less alarming to John, the nurses had invited him to try the mask on. In fact he had found the whole experience horrifying, and described the mask as 'monstrous, with a suffocating feel and an inhuman, featureless appearance'.

The mask he made in the group was 'like a carnival character' in dramatic colours with red cellophane over the eye holes. He said that it 'seemed like fun, but would be threatening up close'. He also said he disliked the effect when looking out through the cellophane and would not want to wear the mask or 'be seen like that by other people'. John's behaviour at home had become increasingly aggressive and his mother was seriously concerned about his angry response 'to the least little thing'. After the groups she wrote to us and asked: 'What have you done to him? It's like having the old John back, he is so relaxed.'

In creating their mask, the participants can face their worst fear and engage with it in the security of the group. In John's case, he was able to use his mask to reflect on his father's monstrous behaviour and to recall the nightmarish feel of being in his father's place. He was terrified of being in that state himself. Facing that fear made it no less dreadful, but demonstrated that he had survived it and could render the memory tolerable. Acknowledging the fear and horror made it possible for John to set aside the behaviour he had started to adopt at home to conceal his vulnerability.

Most members choose to leave eye and mouth holes but Chloe's mask was cast over the whole face and left smooth and almost featureless, like a death mask. Chloe said that she didn't care to see other people's reactions, or how she appeared. Instead she mounted the mask onto white paper, resembling a corpse laid out and covered with a sheet. In the free time after the session she used dayglo spray paints to give the image a dramatically stronger presence. It felt as though she had been able to leave her mother in this act of laying aside the mask, and had emerged herself metamorphosed. Young people are often excluded from death rituals. Chloe had attended her mother's funeral but here it felt as though she was devising her own ritual in which she could mourn her loss of self in the loss of her mother. The ritual marked a dual transition – her acceptance of adulthood, and her acceptance of her mother's death.

THE INVISIBLE INJURY 'HELD' IN THE GROUP

Later in the day, several of the group used the plaster bandage to make casts of their arms. Katherine had some of the others write on hers. The effect was so convincing that at a later session she told us she had worn the cast to school, and was 'excused a test . . . the teacher actually had someone carry my books for me!'. The story provoked much delighted laughter, but also a bitter recollection of other occasions at school. The unqualified sympathy evoked by this 'visible injury' would have been in stark contrast to the reserve or outright hostility many children experience when their parent's death comes to light. If the creative activities are confined to the formal sessions and rigid interpretation of set tasks, opportunities such as these which function for the whole group would be lost.

The isolation death had inflicted on each of them was both recognised and dismissed as no longer important through Katherine's practical joke. It served as an affirmation of the value of their new identity as members of this special set of young people. In reflecting to the group that Katherine's clowning behaviour had on this occasion served an extremely valuable purpose, contributing a mature insight, I was able to bolster her self-esteem and endorse her role as a valued member of the group. Finding a place with your peers is vital for adolescents in the transition to adulthood. The group can both acknowledge the pain felt by the child who has lost their parent and provide a peer group in which this form of transition to adulthood is respected.

My role is to respond to the particular needs of each group and its members. There is no set formula for my response to the images, process, individuals or the group. Each session is unique, and I see my role much as that described by Casement (1985), learning from the participants, tolerating uncertainty as they explore what emerges in their images. Whilst the set activities are designed to facilitate overcoming obstacles in the grieving process, there is no set agenda for what can emerge. The young people will use the sessions to their own ends which is as it should be.

In facilitating the emergence of unconscious material, I may encourage participants to engage with the symbolic or metaphoric content of their images. Masks for example, could be used to encourage dialogue with the character revealed. In a separate group, the 8-year-old who produced the bright red mask in Figure 13.2, for example, said it was 'screaming at everyone to fuck off and leave me alone'. Sometimes it can be helpful to compare the expression on the outside with that on the inside. Often the child is surprised at the differences they perceive. The same boy said in genuine amazement that from the inside his mask looked 'really frightened' (see Figure 13.3).

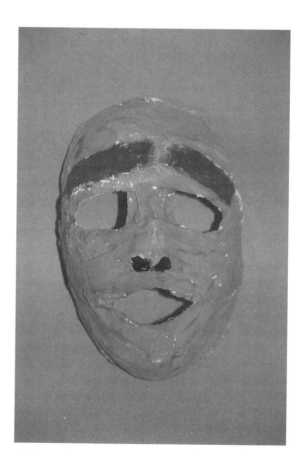

Figure 13.2

Figure 13.3

THE GROUP BECOMES THE SAFE CONTAINER

On Sunday morning the group are asked to make a container 'in which you might keep something precious to you'. We have access to clay and some are made on the potter's wheel with great determination in the struggle to gain mastery and keep the clay centred. Others are coiled or pressed into shape and most are painted or decorated with great concentration. The imagery of this task is evident to all – sometimes acknowledging their strength, frailty or openness, or their need to keep things private. We emphasise at this point that at least within the group it is safe to open up but that it also helps to explore supportive contacts outside the group.

The final activity for the weekend is to write or draw a message to the person who has died onto a small square of tissue. These messages are profoundly personal and are not shared in the group. The messages are tied to a helium balloon to be released in the garden as each individual feels ready. This ritual of 'letting go' is different for everyone. Sometimes pairs or small groups release their messages together, others may need considerable time alone before the right moment arrives. There is often unfinished business around the death, things left unsaid or that they wish they could retract. It can reflect a profound yearning to reconnect with their parent and is not intended to symbolise an emotional detachment but rather a letting go of negative thoughts and feelings that can prevent their being satisfactorily reintegrated into the memory.

The group continues to meet once a week for two hours over the next month. One session is run by a drama therapist, at another the images are of good and bad memories. This session provided John with the opportunity to reconnect with the father he had loved but had 'lost' in banishing more painful memories. He told us how his dad would bring him a takeaway meal on his lunch break from work whilst John fished the local river. A warm, nurturing memory in stark contrast to the 'monster' described in the first session. Katherine used this session to show her sense of achievement in being selected for the netball team at school despite her small stature: 'Mum used to help me practise, she really taught me how to play.' Another session is attended by a medical expert able to answer worrying questions with reassuringly detailed answers.

It was at the first of these follow-up groups that Katherine's practical joke with the plaster cast came to light. In reply to my comment that her clowning had achieved a far more serious purpose than usual on this occasion, she said 'It's really great at school now, everyone knows why I went on the weekend and some of them even envied me!!' This was greeted with much laughter, it was OK now to be different, the group had formed a special kind of bond. Each of them had been able to recognise and let go some unhelpful behaviours and start to rebuild their lives, drawing on their own inner strengths. Through restoring the loved one in their 'enduring biography' (Walter 1996) they can find personal meaning in their loss.

Using this form of intensive art therapy is based on the assumption that these young people are essentially psychologically sound, though experiencing difficulties in the natural processes of grieving and growing. The weekend and follow-up groups provide a crucible in which all superfluous activity is shed as the pace of therapeutic activity accelerates. The search for meaning that characterises the analytic process described by Jung involves the completion of four (non-sequential) stages summarised in Samuels, Shorter and Plaut (1986). I believe it is possible for all these stages to be experienced in this form of brief art therapy with bereaved children – to thereby render meaningful that which is otherwise brutally meaningless. The initial catharsis – as the youngsters unburden themselves to the group – breaks through personal defences and ends isolation, preparing the way for a new stage of growth and emergent adult status. As the therapeutic creative process develops there is a period in which unconscious processes emerge in the symbolic content of the images. The insights this produces must be worked through and integrated into the psyche to enable the conclusion of therapy as the young person undergoes a transformation of attitude and assimilates this new sense of meaning.

Occasionally individuals will be unable to resolve their needs within the span of this brief art therapy programme. Identifying these individuals and ensuring their needs are followed up (usually with one-to-one art therapy work) is essential. To encourage young people to re-open this wound and yet fail to provide adequate scope for healing would be to traumatise them irreparably and to nurture mental ill-health.

In the context of an art therapy group specifically designed to facilitate the expression of grief, young people can both end the crushing isolation of loss and find a way of telling their unique story. As a result they will have laid the basis for a resolution to their individual grief process. In struggling to make these images, they will also have discovered and devised creative new ways of dealing with difficult thoughts and feelings that will aid them throughout their lives.

REFERENCES

Bion, W.R. (1968) *Experiences in Groups and Other Papers*, London: Tavistock.

Birtchnell, J. (1970) 'The relationship between attempted suicide, depression and parent death', *British Journal of Psychiatry* 116, 307–313.

Birtchnell, J. (1972) 'Early parent death and psychiatric diagnosis', *Social Psychiatry* 7, 202–210.

Black, D. (1978) 'The bereaved child', *Journal of Child Psychology and Psychiatry* 19, 287–292.

Bloch, S. and Crouch, E. (1987) *Therapeutic Factors in Group Psychotherapy*, Oxford: Oxford University Press.

Bowlby, J. (1963) 'Pathological mourning and childhood mourning', *Journal of the American Psychoanalytic Association* 11, 500–541.

Bowlby, J. (1980) *Attachment and Loss, Volume 3: Loss,* London: Hogarth.

Casement, P. (1985) *On Learning From the Patient*, London: Tavistock.

Foulkes, S.H. (1983) *Group Analytic Psychotherapy*, London: Gordon and Breach.

Furman, E. (1974) *A Child's Parent Dies*, New Haven and London: Yale University Press.

Hill, O.W. (1969) 'The association of childhood bereavement with suicidal attempt in depressive illness', *British Journal of Psychiatry* 115, 301–304.

Laufer, P. (1966) 'Object loss and mourning in the adolescent', *Psychoanalytic Study of the Child*, vol. 21, New York: International University Press.

Mack, J. (1994) *Masks*, London: British Museum Press.

McNeilly, G. (1987) 'Further contributions to group analytic art therapy', *Inscape* Summer, 8–11.

Pincus, L. (1974) *Death and the Family*, New York: Pantheon.

Rutter, M. (1972) *Maternal Deprivation Reassessed,* London: Penguin.

Samuels, A., Shorter, B. and Plaut, F. (1986) *A Critical Dictionary of Jungian Analysis*, London: Routledge.

Sheldon, F. (1997) *Psychosocial Palliative Care. Good Practice in the Care of the Dying and Bereaved*, Cheltenham: Stanley Thornes.

Torrie, A. (1978) *When Children Grieve*, Richmond, Surrey: CRUSE.

Waller, D. (1993) *Group Interactive Art Therapy*, London: Routledge.

Walter, T. (1996) 'A new model of grief: bereavement and biography', *Mortality* 1(1), 7–25.

Ward, B. (1989) *Good Grief*, Uxbridge, Middlesex: Good Grief.

Worden, J.W. (1983) *Grief Counselling and Grief Therapy*, London: Tavistock.

Yalom, I. (1975) *The Theory and Practice of Group Psychotherapy*, New York: Basic Books.

Mandy Pratt BA, SRN, DipAT, RATh is founder member of The Creative Response and Senior I Art Therapist at St Helena Hospice, Colchester. Mandy works with in-patients, daycare groups and patients of all ages in the community. She provides art therapy for griefwork groups of all ages. She has also worked at St Francis Hospice, Romford and Farleigh Hospice, Chelmsford, Colchester Headway and Colchester Huntingtons Disease Association.

Chapter 14

From psychiatry to psycho-oncology

Personal reflections on the use of art therapy with cancer patients

Paola Luzzatto

INTRODUCTION

I have worked for about ten years as an art therapist in the area of mental health in London. Three years ago, I moved to New York, where I now work as an art therapist with patients with cancer at the Memorial Sloan Kettering Cancer Center. This chapter is about my personal reflections following this professional move to a different country and to a different patient population. It is also about how this experience led me to devise an art therapy intervention, which I have called The Creative Journey, which is quite different from the art therapy interventions I used to offer to psychiatric patients. Of course patients with cancer, although they share a similar traumatic experience, do not constitute a homogeneous population. Among them there may be patients with a psychiatric history, whose vulnerability has been revived; other patients may have developed a dysfunctional coping mechanism, like a substance abuse, in reaction to the stress of cancer diagnosis and treatment; others may go through a temporary stage of anxiety or depression, that will subside within an appropriate supportive environment; other patients seem to find the strength to cope in a mature way, without denial and without giving up, and they may ask for therapeutic help not because they are not coping, but because they know what they need, and they know how to ask for it.

Both in the UK and in the US the majority of the art therapists work in mental health settings, or in the field of education. Only recently have they started to work with medically ill patients (although we must not forget that Adrian Hill, one of the pioneers of art therapy, started work with patients affected by tuberculosis). This seems to be an area rich of potential for art therapy, but we need to reflect on whether we can apply the same kind of art therapy interventions which we have developed throughout the years in psychiatric settings, or whether we need to be innovative.

THE ENCOUNTER WITH THE BODY

Working in mental health, my objective has always been to establish a contact with the internal world of the patient. Even when the patient was complaining of physical pain or discomfort, my attention was still focused on the psychic reality of the patient. The bodily pain could be an expression of psychic pain, or vice versa the psychic pain could be an effect of physical pain suffered in the distant or more recent past. Still, my mind was directed towards the patient's mind, as an encounter between two minds, and I never felt that the presence of physical pain was an obstacle in the therapeutic relationship.

Suddenly, here I find myself taken into another realm: the physical realm of the suffering body. The patients with whom I work most of the time are out-patients, and cancer survivors, and therefore are not usually in pain. Nevertheless, often the memory of the pain is still very alive, or the effects are visible in their body. They may be suffering from side effects of surgery, or radiotherapy, or chemotherapy, or bone marrow transplant. They may suffer from fatigue, weakness, migraine, swollen arms, difficulties in walking, talking, eating, impairments in any area of functioning. The body becomes suddenly very important in the therapeutic relationship. As a therapist, this unavoidable fact at first shocked me. My feelings triggered all sort of self-reflections: do I wish to deny the existence of the body, or the existence of physical pain, or the existence of death? I felt pulled in two directions: either keeping my emphasis on the mind of the patient, as I used to do in working with psychiatric patients, or turning towards the body with my full attention, and accepting the physical need for relief, for relaxation, for soothing experiences that the patients were presenting. What is the role of the art therapist in facing the physical pain?

At present, I try to follow the patients in their different needs. This is easier if I see them individually. At times I use image-making as a form of relaxation, following the principles of self-hypnosis and visualisation (visualising a safe place; a beautiful landscape; a warm light enveloping the body, etc.), or as a form of cathartic expression (taking negative feelings out on the paper, making a mess, throwing out the paper, etc.). At other times we work with specific physical sensations, trying to find the right colours and the right shapes to express them, and produce 'images of pain'. In American art therapy, the circle (mandala) is often used as a healing container, to be filled with positive colours and shapes. Personally, I prefer to use the outline of a human body, or any symbolic shape chosen by the patient, or the shape of the paper itself, to express and contain the pain. Nevertheless, these approaches focusing on physical pain make me feel as if I am a hypnotherapist, or a recreational therapist, or a behavioural therapist, which I am not. When the body of the patient does not require full attention, I become more aware of myself as an art therapist. Then the dialogue may move towards the effect of physical pain on other aspects of life, and on the meaning given by the patient to the pain and to the illness itself, and to deeper connections between past and present, and self and others.

THE EMPHASIS ON CREATIVITY

Whether and how much to emphasise creativity, this is the second question I have often posed to myself since working with this population. There are many artists and writers who have had cancer, and who have used their art or their writing to record, to express, to heal themselves from their traumatic experience, and to keep the communication open with their families and friends. Art exhibitions by artists who are cancer survivors, and public lectures and encounters with journalists and writers who talk about their cancer experience are very common in the US. For some patients this has created a misunderstanding, based on the belief that one has to become visually and verbally 'creative' (artistic?) in order to cope with cancer, and even to prevent recurrences. Usually the word creativity does not reach such healing intensity for psychiatric patients. British art therapists are more cautious about the use of the word creativity in their profession than their American counterparts. I feel I have to remain cautious, maybe because of my training, or maybe because in my mind I am on the side of the patients who feel empty, blocked and unimaginative, and I do not want to make them feel they 'should' become visually creative. Nevertheless, I do realise that to feel creative is a very healing experience, and that many patients here expect and ask to be guided towards creativity. At the beginning I felt torn between offering 'art-psychotherapy', where the emphasis is on the understanding of the internal world, and offering 'creativity workshops', where the emphasis is on the special creative relationship between the patient and the artwork. Of course this is the old dilemma at the heart of art therapy itself, and each art therapist gives a different answer to this dilemma. In moving from psychiatry to psycho-oncology it was as though I had to start all over again, to ask the question from the beginning. I have not found a definite answer to this question. From a clinical point of view, The Creative Journey is a time-limited intervention where I attempt to integrate the two approaches. Throughout the ten weekly workshops we focus at one level on the development of the patient's visual style, and at another on the symbolic representation of the patient's internal world. What the patients wish to reveal is up to them, and the workshops become for some an opportunity to feel creative, and for others a time for self-discovery.

I find sometimes the concept of creativity too broad and vague to be used effectively with the patients; maybe it would benefit from being broken down into its components. There are factors which are part of creativity which may be isolated and focused upon. One is the feeling of control over the art material; another the contact with the unconscious; another one is the 'meaning-giving' factor. This third factor may be particularly important for cancer patients, who are going through an experience that challenges the usual meanings of their life. They need to be able to change perspective and give new meanings to a different body, or to a different mood, or to a different way of life, where the concepts of loss, vulnerability and mortality have become primary. From the general concept of creativity, I have moved my attention to this more restricted concept. My questions have become: 'What kind of art therapy techniques should I employ to facilitate the patients in giving meaning to what seems to be a meaningless image in front of them? And, how can this meaning-giving ability be used to give new meaning to one's life? And what is a meaning anyway?' Meanings emerge out of relationships between visual elements, and these relationships may correspond to similar relationships in the internal world of the patients. According to this approach, I first help the patients to make 'meaningless' pictures, then as a second step I encourage them to give 'meaning' to their picture. The so-called meaningless pictures may be facilitated through many techniques: the use of squiggles, drawing with eyes closed, drawing with the left (or right) hand, making a mess, etc. Patients then may be helped to give meanings to their pictures through the use of other techniques: looking at the picture and discovering small sections to be enlarged; using verbal or visual free associations to the picture; finding a title; creating a story. Any time there is a gap, a space between the external world and the patient, there is room for the development of free associations, alternative images, connections between conscious and unconscious material, new meanings. The issue of the use or abuse of the word creativity may be tackled by focusing on different elements of creativity, and devising appropriate art therapy interventions.

THE RESPECT FOR THE NEGATIVE

This is the third point that keeps coming up during my work with cancer patients. The culture of 'positive thinking' is very strong with some cancer patients, and many of them believe that the 'negative thought' may facilitate, if not directly cause, the cancer or a recurrence. The negative thought must be avoided then, and positive thinking becomes a must. In my work with psychiatric patients this dilemma was rare, although in another way one could say that denial, as a defence, is nothing other than a form of unconscious positive thinking. Art therapists are usually very good in respecting the defence of the patient and establishing a therapeutic alliance on the basis of this respect. But in the end any psychotherapist works on the assumption that it would beneficial for the patient to be able to resolve, sooner or later, an attitude of denial of psychic reality.

Working with the cancer patient I find myself in doubt. Positive thinking may be good for some patients and not for others. 'Nobody has to die in Freud's grace', a chaplain in the hospital said recently: self-awareness is a choice, not a duty. But is it possible for a psychotherapist to work without aiming towards increasing the patient's self-awareness?

The basic type of negative thought for a cancer patient is the thought of death. Often the thought of death is not a quantitative thought, like 'My life might be or will be shorter', but a qualitative jump from 'I am invincible' to

'I am not invincible any more'. Many patients describe it like a major loss: the loss of the feeling of 'being in control'. For other patients death is connected to fear, and the major fear appears to be the fear of abandonment, the final abandonment. But other feelings come to be connected to the thought of death: fears of being damaged, or persecuted; fears of being powerless and humiliated; fear of experiencing physical pain, fear of extreme loneliness.

In working with psychiatric patients I felt all thoughts and feelings had the right to be, and to be expressed. But here I often struggle with the cancer patient who says 'I should not have this thought, it is a negative thought, it is not good'. Is it true for that patient? Nevertheless, when we allow the negative thoughts to emerge and to be externalised, many patients say 'It was such a relief to be able to express them'. Cancer patients often feel they have to be positive not only for themselves, but also they have to show a brave face to their doctors and to their families, and to their colleagues at work. The art therapy space may become the only space where they can be true to themselves. When the open admission of the negative thought is too difficult, art therapy then can work at the level of symbolic expression, allowing the patients to talk about death without giving a name to it. The patients can draw symbols of loneliness, of powerlessness, of death, but other patients in the group may not know what the image is about. A patient recently said, after several months of group art therapy, 'I have always talked and made pictures of my illness here, but I have called it by another name: I have called it "stress".'

AN INNOVATIVE ART THERAPY INTERVENTION, SPECIFICALLY DESIGNED FOR CANCER PATIENTS: THE CREATIVE JOURNEY

The Creative Journey is an art therapy programme which has developed out of my personal reflections described above. It is a time-limited intervention: it consists of a series of ten weekly workshops, each lasting one and a half hours, for small groups of cancer patients who have completed treatment (surgery, radiotherapy, or chemotherapy). Each workshop has the same structure: a) a short guided concentration/meditation exercise; b) the introduction of an art therapy technique for image-making; c) time for patients to work according to that technique; d) time for looking at the pictures and for verbal feedback (which is optional).

This intervention is different from the group art therapy I used to provide to psychiatric patients:

1   *Guided concentration/meditation.* I have never offered a guided concentration or meditation, at the beginning of an art therapy group in psychiatry. From these patients' feedback, there is no doubt that they want it and seem to benefit from it.

2   *Development of personal imagery.* With psychiatric patients I used to offer basically two types of art therapy groups: either aimed at self-expression, without any given theme; or based on a theme-oriented approach, focusing on the patient's psychological issues (with more or less emphasis on group interaction in both cases). Here I offer groups where, on one level, the aim is self-expression, but the patients need guidance; on another level, I offer themes, but mainly they are not psychological themes, as these patients seem to be very ambivalent about self-revelation, and about group inter-action. (I must point out here that other patients benefit from the 'talking groups' offered by the social workers and ask for those groups; art therapy seems to attract the patients who would not otherwise attend any group.)

   The Creative Journey focuses on one simple concept: the development of personal imagery. I have identified three basic ways of allowing images to emerge: 'from outside' (from images in the outside world: it could be pictures from magazines, or a still life on the table); 'from inside' (from the patient's mind: thoughts and feelings); and 'from nowhere' (through the use of art materials). Each of the ten workshops offers the possibility of experimenting with one or the other of these modalities, and with the way these modalities interact with each other. The emphasis is on the image to reach a symbolic and meaningful level for the patient (which the patient does not have to talk about).

3   *Transformation of personal imagery.* Many patients struggle with their understandable ambivalence about the thoughts of 'illness', 'pain', 'death' and 'dying': they wish to keep their mind free from negative thoughts, while at the same time they need to be true to their feelings. During The Creative Journey the experience of image-making is presented as a dynamic process, which may also become an experience of transformation of the initial mental image, through a combination of conscious and unconscious mental processes. Transformation is not an imposition: it is the 'freedom to transform' that is important, not 'how' the patient is going to transform the image. For example, during one of the workshops, an object is placed on the table, and the patients are encouraged not to copy it, but to modify it, according to their own free associations to the object. The possibility of a symbolic transformation from negative to positive is the theme of another workshop, based on two steps: the first image is about 'stress', which may include anything negative: confusion, deadness, tension; the second image may be a transformation, from confusion to clarity, from deadness to life, from tension to peacefulness. In this way the patients are given permission to really feel what they are feeling, but at the same time they are encour-aged to view their images – and their feelings and thoughts – as potentially transformable.

CONCLUSIONS

A common experience of art therapists who have moved from psychiatric patients to medically ill patients is the dilemma of how much space to give to insight-oriented psychotherapeutic work, and how much to supportive interventions. A second experience, which is strictly related to the first one, is the need to be innovative. I have mentioned three areas where I felt professionally challenged by the needs of this patient population, in comparison to the psychiatric population: a) the first area is a different kind of balance between mind and body, the strong connection between psychological and physical pain, and the need of the patients, and of the art therapist, to deal with both; b) the second is the appropriate use of creativity as a healing agent, which should not be forgotten, but at the same time should not take over the psychotherapeutic process: it should be used within it; c) the third area is the strong ambivalence of the patients about the existential issue of death, which emerges at the same time as a thought that they should not have, and as a thought that they wish to explore. These three points have obvious repercussions on the therapist, according to the therapist's own personal issues. This chapter supports the need to be innovative, and presents three areas in the work with cancer patients where I personally felt the need to review my way of functioning, and to work towards new types of interventions. I have enclosed a short description of the group art therapy intervention for ambulatory cancer patients which I have called The Creative Journey. The objective of the ten-week programme is to facilitate the patients towards developing and transforming personal imagery – not necessarily related to the cancer experience – with the aim of increasing their self-awareness, and strengthening their self-identity.

Paola Luzzatto PhD has a background in philosophy and comparative religions. She has produced television programmes and written books for children. She then trained in art therapy at Goldsmiths' College, London, and worked with a variety of adult psychiatric patients. Paola Luzzatto has had further training in both humanistic and psychoanalytic psychotherapy, and has published a number of articles on art therapy, on both clinical and theoretical issues. She now works at Memorial Hospital Cancer Center, New York, and has a small private practice.

Chapter 15

Sunbeams and icebergs, meteorites and daisies

A cancer patient's experience of art therapy

Barbara Morley

> I am afraid the piece of skin I removed from your leg has shown a melanoma but it is a thin one with a good prognosis provided the whole area is removed. I am asking ... the consultant surgeon here, if he would try and organise this for you as soon as possible.

And so I learned that I was a cancer patient. The letter arrived over Easter bank holiday weekend, with no further explanation that melanoma is a kind of cancer, and without any offer of medical or emotional support over the four-day break. I was completely alone with the news. I so clearly recall my initial reaction – a double sense of disbelief and acceptance. I had to learn to say 'I have cancer' and just practised doing so to convince myself that this was something I had to face up to. Was this going to be life threatening? It hung heavy over me at night alone. I knew that life would never be the same again.

Throughout the treatments I took a positive, holistic approach in my response to the diagnosis. Recognising that cancer is serious and that I must fight it played an active part in the healing process. I used many different techniques including osteopathy, homeopathy and flower remedies as well as more conventional medical care. Holding to faith in God and discerning something of his purpose for me through cancer was part of the healing process as was my daily journal in which I was able to record my feelings and determination in depth. My chief memory of this time, however, is of the vivid imagery I used to inform and assist the healing process. It is this personal discovery through working with images and how it formed such a crucial part in helping me cope with cancer that I want to describe here. Image is the word I use for vivid, intuitive mental pictures from which the painted pictures are created. Though I think very visually, the news that I had cancer did not evoke a visual image. I have no pictorial memory of the important moment when the news was given, and I have not found the need to create one. Of far more significance has been the imagery which accompanied the treatment and the healing process over a period of weeks resulting in a series of twenty-three pictures – and many captions.

The story of my cancer undoubtedly began many years before, my fair skin burning on summer beaches, moles and blemishes scattered over my body, the pressure of work in a busy public relations job, times of emotional stress and bereavement: all this surely contributed to the disease. More specifically I had recently returned from a week in the Mediterranean sun where I had burned quickly and been left with sun marks for months afterwards – which no one could explain, nor did I immediately worry about them. This was I believe the specific trigger for the melanoma to develop. After years of demanding work I had just begun a long-awaited career break. That release from pressure was a further opportunity for the cancer to develop: my body was telling me in no uncertain terms that I had been struggling too hard for too long and this was the dramatic and unanticipated result.

The noticeable change of a long-existing mole on my left shin made me initially curious and soon concerned. I was I think even at this early stage aware of the possibility of this being more than a blemish. A slight change of colour and shape led me to consult my GP who, without any fuss or indication of the serious nature of the potential diagnosis, arranged an immediate appointment with a dermatologist. Somewhere in the back of my mind was a book I had read many years ago. Written by Rosemary and Victor Zorza, *A Way to Die* tells the moving and tragic story of their 23-year-old daughter who developed a mole on her foot – that malignant melanoma proved fatal. I knew that this was not an issue to be trifled with.

My appointment with the dermatologist did not get off to a promising start. I was greeted with the memorable words 'It's your leg isn't it?' I felt offended at being treated as a piece of diseased flesh rather than a human being. A week later *the* letter arrived and my fears were confirmed. The following day – mercifully there was neither panic nor delay in the diagnosis or treat-ment – I had an opportunity to discover what would happen next in a meeting with the consultant surgeon. He assured me that there was a good chance of full recovery, the operation would include the removal of an area about $4 \times 2\frac{1}{2}$ inches from my left shin and a graft of skin taken from my right thigh. Five days convalescence was indicated. My reaction to the diagnosis was not as I recall discussed, although we talked in sympathetic and businesslike tones about the melanoma!

For two years I had been painting with a remarkable artist, teacher and art therapist. Her timely visit the day after my out-patient appointment gave me the opportunity I needed to safely and freely talk about my illness as cancer. I had come to know her as a safe, understanding and sympathetic confidante and I was sure that she would help me to find a constructive way forward. Her inspirational approach had helped me realise a creative potential I would not have dreamed I was capable of. Having disastrously failed art at school some 25 years or more previously, it took a long time before I had the courage to commit images to paper. I would never claim to be especially artistic in the conventional sense. I cannot paint or draw portraits, landscapes or still life. She encouraged me to explore a variety of media, large sheets of paper and total freedom of self-expression. I suddenly discovered the power and beauty of expressing myself in paint and crayon, charcoal and gouache, pencil and pastels, applying the materials with everything from toothbrushes to J-cloths, kitchen sponges to fingers – even paintbrushes! It seemed perfectly natural, having shared the news of cancer, to begin to explore the images it evoked through art therapy. I am someone who needs to know what is happening, to see the physical, emotional and spiritual interrelationships in my life, to approach any illness or disability by proactively participating in my own healing.

We began working with visualisation and imagery (in which she suggested that cancer was essentially cold and chaotic) – a technique with which I feel very much at home. The images may be contradictory, paradoxical or unpleasant, but they always provide visual clues to deeper levels of experience and understanding that I find ultimately provide a source of healing and growth. I have learned to accept both the inspirational and the seemingly unacceptable images since both provide a deepening insight into my self and my condition. At no point did I *consciously* decide what to depict. Rather I responded to visual images that simply emerged. I worked with them, sought to understand them, expressed them on paper, both in visual form and in accompanying poems or captions. For me the crucial thing is to convey as closely as possible the colour, shape, size and impression of thoughts and feelings that emerge in the image. The pictures then provide something which becomes a tangible reminder of the moment that I can return to as and when I choose.

By the time the cancer was diagnosed, I had been working with the art therapist for two years, establishing the confidence to work with images in the interval between meetings. Consequently our ninety-minute sessions were devoted entirely to sharing, reviewing and discussing the artwork that I had painted independently. Before having cancer we had already explored in considerable depth several major concerns and issues in my life, including the implications of giving up my career, the bereavement of being childless and specific family and personal relationships. As a result, the way I used art therapy in my response to cancer was part of a well-established pattern. Perhaps unusually therefore the experience of having cancer was not of itself the catalyst to exploring other major traumas in my life.

Whilst I did not feel the need to ask 'Why me?', I did feel both curious and ignorant and so I asked many other questions. I visualised my search for answers as an outwardly curling spiral of multi-colours, from which sprang yet more questions. The spiral was constructed so as to be awkward to read – a reminder that no answers were given without first asking awkward questions. Having given voice to the reality of suffering from cancer, I seemed to encounter powerful images on all sides. Visiting my local church early next morning, for example, I lit an intercessory candle and in committing the new scenario to God, sensed a powerful image of a bright flame cauterising, burning, obliterating, healing the cancer. I felt a deeply intuitive understanding that the cancer would be eliminated and I would be healed. I expressed it first in the form of a large bold drawing of a single flame in vivid shades of yellow and gold and second in more tactile form as a half relief in brightly coloured tissue paper. This was followed by an abstract expression of the glory of God shown in endless interlocking swirls and spirals of all shades of gold. It was very powerful.

Not all the cancer-related images were so positive; there was a thoroughly unwanted picture of the melanoma as a large cold grey pear shape. Though discouraging, I learned to recognise it as the unacceptable image of the disease. I learned not to reject, adapt or change any of the images; each had something specific to say as it was given. It was not pleasant, but it was valid. Letting the image speak for itself is always more challenging, more instructive and ulti-mately more rewarding.

Preparing for the operation in the week following diagnosis I was aware that as a single person leading a full and active life I had become very indepen-dent. I recognised that at least when I first came out of hospital I was going to need practical assistance as well as moral and emotional support. I would need to consider whom I should share this news with and how they might respond. I decided against telling people for whom the news would have been a great shock and emotional strain: I did not want to have to support others as well as myself. Still for some the news was more difficult to accept than it seemed to have been for me. Sharing my artwork with friends was a big help. When the subject of 'the big C' came up in conversation the images acted as a catalyst, a talking point and a way of sharing and exploring feelings and reac-tions. This was beneficial to all concerned, both demystifying the experience and enabling valuable sharing.

Entering hospital for the first time in twenty-five years required considerable mental, emotional, spiritual and practical preparation. I referred myself to the Cancer Support Centre at my local hospital and there found space and confi-dence to share the experience of being a cancer patient with a counsellor who had been an oncology nurse. This was invaluable, through her I discovered the BACUP booklet on malignant melanoma and from that learned more about the disease, potential causes and triggers, high risk groups and something of the pathology of the disease. I did not want a medical textbook but I did want to know in lay terms what was going on. Also when I reflected on how many people by the age of 44 have suffered major disability, incurable disease, severe trauma or death, I was able to put into perspective the fact that my cancer was treatable. I do not wish to dismiss the very real fears that a diag-nosis of life-threatening illness produces. Cancer is so often portrayed as the ultimate terrible condition that it can be difficult to remain hopeful.

All this was reflected in and expressed by the powerful artwork. The visual imagery of the flame remained particularly powerful and encouraging and was complemented the morning I went in for the operation. I was reading Psalm 18 which tells of God leaning down to pluck the psalmist from the waters at a time of great turmoil. As I read of the rescue the phone rang – to confirm that I was to be admitted. The timing was a perfect confidence booster. The imagery was of dramatic storm clouds, a bright gold light, turbulent waters and a figure, myself, reaching upwards to be held and rescued (Figure 15.1). I also recorded the images verbally in my journal – as a way of giving voice to events and encounters, feelings and reactions, reflections and aspirations. I wrote about the impression the images were making over the next three weeks using the most appropriate words, phrases and poems that sprang to mind as an elaboration of the pictures. These added another vital dimension to the power of the imagery. Words such as searing, cleansing, moving, glory, mutilated, inspirational, comfort and growth came to mind quite unbidden.

For me cancer is both cold and chaotic and the images that came to mind included much that is typically heat-giving and ordered as a way of expressing confidence and potential healing. I mostly used pure beeswax crayons in a wonderfully vivid array of colours as a practical solution to the problems of

Figure 15.1

'painting' in bed. One dramatic exception, however, was an iceberg made of crinkled layers of blue and white tissue paper, highlighted with gold. The iceberg represented the largest, coldest thing on earth, which I then symbolically obliterated with a 'meteorite' of bright blue, gold, red, orange and purple flames, representing unlimited heat and energy. The time, planning and creative energy devoted to this pair of images was probably greater than for any other. But I felt it was really important that I had something very tactile to work with and something tangible and dramatic to express the potential damage which the (cold) cancer might cause and the great sense of determination and confidence that I needed to draw on in order to tackle it effectively. Though now rather dusty and well past its sell by date, the iceberg-meteorite remains a special piece of cancer art therapy.

I was not an easy patient! Due to administrative confusion I was actually taken straight to theatre before being fully admitted to the ward. There simply wasn't time to wonder what was going to happen or become apprehensive. I recovered rapidly from the anaesthetic (with the help of homeopathic remedies) and was amazed to discover the extent of the bandaging. My left leg was heavily dressed and bandaged to the knee with dressings that were not to be touched for eight days. My right thigh was heavily dressed too over the donor site. Nursing staff told me that I must have a week's bed rest – a far cry from the consultant's suggestion that I would only need five days convalescence! Being confined to bed but reasonably alert, I occupied my time in expressing my feelings in vivid imagery.

The idea of cancer as chaos was particularly pertinent at this time: though on the surface everything had gone smoothly, the imagery that emerged intuitively showed a more chaotic form. I found myself using crayons of colours that I rarely use and really do not identify with – pale yellow, pink, beige, grey. The shapes were abstract and rather formless – lots of would-be hexagons which failed to make complete shapes and forms that ran off the edge of the page without obvious direction. Drawing in bed caused something of a stir among the nursing staff but regrettably there was no time or opportunity for any of them to discuss the images and the all important question as to how they reflected my feelings. I would have welcomed the opportunity to say how I felt about being a cancer patient with them. In reality as far as I recall the word cancer was not explicitly mentioned during my stay in hospital. I was on a general surgical ward rather than the oncology ward but even so . . .

The next day the pale chaotic images resolved quite spontaneously into clear jewel-like hexagons of favourite colours – cobalt blue and gold, jade green and burgundy. A real and immediate sense of healing was evident to me, evoking great optimism. The images were very beautiful. The shapes were not tight packed as a honeycomb but rather loosely clustered, complete in themselves yet allowing for growth and movement, a pattern of order in creation. Another powerful set of images revolved around the Genesis account of creation; of order emerging from chaos, or form from the void. Very simple globe shapes in primitive blues, greens and browns evolved into more creative and positive shapes which symbolised the uncertainty from which a new shape was emerging in my life.

That same morning I received contradictory messages about the length of my stay in hospital – the young houseman said I could go home, whilst nursing staff insisted on a week's bedrest. At 10 a.m. I was not allowed out of bed, by lunchtime I was allowed home! I felt confused, frustrated and impatient. On reflection the nursing staff realised the seriousness of a double operation which effectively incapacitated both legs. Certainly life at home in a two-storey house, living alone was very awkward for the first few days and I did need help to cope in purely practical terms. On balance, however, I think my convalescence was considerably helped by being in my own home. I felt the immense value of setting my own timetable and pace of life, having friends to visit and enjoying as much peace and quiet as I wanted, sleeping in my own bed and working as long and as often as I wanted with the powerful and creative imagery which continued to enlighten my healing. Despite feeling tired and physically uncomfortable the imagery was entirely related to healing from cancer. Powerful, elemental images expressing a fundamental sense of optimism, healing and new life far outweighed concerns about moving about the house or kneeling to light a log fire.

Although I had produced some pictorial representations of the images that emerged whilst in hospital, at home I was able to catch up on committing to paper a backlog of images. I drew a symbolic representation of the 'trigger' day when I burned in the Mediterranean sun, and made pictures of the biblical imagery of the canker being pruned from the vine so that the whole might better flourish. I also depicted my experience of taking a career break and letting go alongside the need to muster all my energies to fight this potentially fatal disease. I simply drew a block of pale tranquil blue colour, joined and infused by a vibrant and energetic red and linked the two in an uplifting wave which blended the blue and the red, the calm and the energy into a powerful yet quietly confident purple.

At the same time I worked with images that appeared contradictory: images of the sun giving searing heat to obliterate the cancerous cold, whilst also recognising the critical part the sun had played in provoking the development of the cancer. Cold was in my mind linked with the cancer, yet the visual experience of streams of cold rushing water cleansing and reviving were equally powerful, equally valid. I recognised that each image, each symbol was significant and valid in its own right and needed to be expressed to inform the healing process.

A week after surgery the melanoma site was re-dressed for the first time and I had the opportunity to see the wound. One nurse in particular took time to warn me about the depth and size of the wound – something for which I had not been prepared. I had believed that only skin would be removed; what I now saw appeared to be a deep crater. Logically I understood that if both the melanoma and the area that might have become diseased were to be removed then depth as well as breadth would be essential. But it was not a pretty sight – ringed in a web of black stitches, raw from recent surgery and stained with coloured dyes.

In time as I returned for replacement dressings I became accustomed to the sight – which was of course beginning to heal. I had also to deal with the donor site from which the graft was taken. This was raw, weeping and sore for several weeks. After the initial shock of seeing the wound I became constructively intrigued as to how my skin would reform. My osteopath provided a simple but intelligible account of the healing process. The donor site was growing by natural regeneration from below, whilst the melanoma site, the crater, was devoid of skin and flesh and the grafted tissue had to knit laterally with the host tissue.

The initial images of this main wound were of a crater filled with smoothly worn rocks. In one the rocks are baking under the heat of the sun, the warm, pink glow of which was comforting and restorative, recalling images of hearth stones for the baking of bread and all the associations of home and sustenance which that evoked. The next crater was filled with rocks tumbled by rushing water – sea water, clear blue and green, with the healing, cleansing properties of a salt solution. The healing process evoked images of daisies growing up through the grass and creating a new, living surface, and of a vibrant patchwork quilt (Figure 15.2), loosely stitched together to leave room for growth, soft and comforting in texture and coloured red, purple and orange

Figure 15.2

– colours of raw vibrancy. All the images were intuitive rather than based on meditation and the resultant artwork was all created as I worked on my own. However, regular meetings with my art therapist enabled the pictures to be shared, reflected on, discussed and the sense of my own understanding of the images affirmed. Undoubtedly our conversations over two years added new concepts and ways of thinking which were important at this time of intense creativity. It meant that in my immediate response to cancer I already had at my disposal a rich array of approaches, images and understanding with which to work confidently.

I maintained contact with the Cancer Support Centre at the hospital and attended a group there. It was very beneficial to relax, to share, to meet and get to know other people with cancer. I recall one meeting in particular, early in June – a time to be in summer dresses and sandals. My leg was still heavily bandaged, my mobility and energy impaired. The word that kept coming into my mind was 'mutilation'. I felt particularly hurt and mutilated. I knew that the removal of skin and flesh from my shin was minor in comparison with the life-threatening cancers and major surgery experienced by other members of the group. But for me the experience was one of mutilation, which I had explored in my paintings with the art therapist. Having gained the confidence to express this feeling I found that it liberated others in the group to share their own experiences of mutilation and physical and emotional hurt.

Throughout the two months of my convalescence (a far cry from the 'five days' I had originally envisaged), I continued to paint, but the imagery which specifically related to the experience of having cancer lasted only three weeks. In all I created some twenty-three 'cancer images' which form a discrete collection. Having access to the possibility of exploring the images in the secure and supportive context of art therapy sessions was invaluable. After this intense period I felt a clear need to move on to other subjects, other experiences, other images. The art therapy facilitated this process too as I let go of the concept of being a patient with cancer with my energy focused on healing. The images were and remain a crucial, tangible shareable way of expressing how I experienced cancer, gave me a voice in my own healing and have I think encouraged others to begin exploring their own creativity.

There are for me no rights and wrongs in the images or in the way they are expressed. The critical need is to work with the image that emerges – to let it grow into further explorations of words or pictures, ideas and feelings as appropriate. I have learned not to deny the paradoxes and contradictions – life is not consistent and logical! I focus very strongly on colour and the essential elements of the image – shape, form, size, texture and so forth: these seem far more telling than any ill-fated attempt to produce an exact 'picture' of the image in my mind's eye. Ideally I use large sheets of good quality cartridge paper and a rich variety of media and painting tools. Whilst incapacitated my freedom of action was quite literally restricted and the materials and form of expression reflected this. This is far less significant than the fact that these special images were recorded, worked with, shared and given expression. They provided my means of communication – with my art therapist, with fellow patients, with friends and relatives and with other professionals involved in my care. After more than two years I can still very clearly recapture and share the experience of being a cancer patient. I firmly believe that finding an external way of expressing my hopes and fears, confusion, cold and chaos, positive and healing experiences helped me find a way of recounting my story that could not otherwise have found a voice.

REFERENCE

Zorza, R. and V. (1981) *A Way to Die*, London: Sphere Books.

At the time of diagnosis **Barbara Morley** was taking a career break, having recently completed eleven years as a Regional Public Affairs Manager for the National Trust. Currently employed as a Community Arts Officer for the Community Council of Shropshire, Barbara continues to enjoy being creative and encouraging creativity in others.

Appendix I
Complications to grieving

1 Relationship between the bereaved and the deceased:

    a) Highly ambivalent relationships, especially where there are communication difficulties.

    b) Narcissistic relationships in which the deceased represents an extension of the self.

    c) Highly dependent relationships (children or adolescents, family members with learning difficulties, sick or elderly). This may include the loss of the primary caregiver/constant companion/emotional support, or loss of financial provision or home.

2 Circumstances surrounding the death:

    a) When the loss is unconfirmed and the bereaved is uncertain whether the deceased is alive or dead.

    b) Disasters in which multiple losses occur.

    c) Deaths from which no body is recoverable.

    d) Unanticipated deaths.

    e) Deaths by murder, suicide, self-neglect or other violent means.

    f) Absence at the time of death, did not say goodbye or attend funeral.

    g) The nature of the pre-death illness.

    h) The nature of the death itself (e.g. especially traumatic).

3 Life history of the bereaved person:

    a) History of complicated grief reactions.

    b) Multiple losses over relatively short period.

    c) History of depression, instability or mental illness.

4 The personality of the bereaved person:

    a) Those who avoid feelings of helplessness.

    b) Those who perceive themselves to be 'strong' people who do not break down.

    c) Those reluctant to face the facts of illness or death.

    d) Families unable to share their feelings.

5   Social factors:

   a) Where the death involves a relationship perceived as being socially unacceptable.
   b) The loss is socially negated – the bereaved and those around them behave as though the loss did not happen.
   c) The absence of a social support network, including poor communication in the family.
   d) The presence of an unhelpful social network.
   e) Existence of concurrent life crises or bereaved are ill too.

6   Children and young people – all the above plus:

   a) Excluded from or misinformed about the illness, funeral, etc. (explanations should be honest, open and age appropriate).
   b) Where no model is readily available for the expression of strong emotions (sadness, anger, guilt, fear).
   c) Where demonstrations of feeling are discouraged.
   d) Where decisions or actions are not explained to them.
   e) Unsympathetic response to behaviour or mood changes.

This compilation is based on Littlewood (1992) and supplemented by those factors isolated by the Counselling and Social Care Department, Mildmay Mission Hospital.

REFERENCE

Littlewood, J. (1992) *Aspects of Grief*, London: Tavistock/Routledge.

Appendix II
Psychological defences and the mourning process

Repression/suppression of emotion In the long term may result in an inability to express emotion in a healthy and appropriate fashion, withdrawal.

Denial/forgetting Refusing to focus on those aspects of the loss that evoke the greatest distress prevents the comfort that lies in sharing grief.

Projection/blame As an outlet for anger and/or guilt the focus shifts to a person or incident as the cause of death.

Reaction formation Masking feelings behind artificially 'jolly' behaviour.

Avoidance Of a specific type associated with the deceased, places or events associated with them (for example removing all physical reminders from the home). In the extreme this may manifest as phobic associations, panic attacks.

Displacement As the intense pain and anger is refocused on the self leading in extreme cases to suicide attempts.

Regression A reversion to a level of functioning that is not appropriate to the individual's particular age as a result of stress.

Confusion Seeming inability to focus on immediate reality.

Sublimation A redirection of the energy of grieving onto altruistic projects (for example fundraising).

REFERENCES

Freud, A. (1930) *The Ego and the Mechanisms of Defence*, London: Hogarth.
Klein, M. (1932) *The Psychoanalysis of Children*, London: Hogarth.

Appendix III
Childhood bereavement

Children of all ages experience grief in the same way as adults, as an intensely powerful feeling that can manifest itself in physical or psychological symptoms. The way in which these feelings show will vary according to the child's maturity. Below is a list of 'symptoms' of grief most commonly associated with children in different age ranges. These are *not* fixed, some children may show no outward sign or symptom of grief, others nearly all. It is important to stress that these signs represent a normal, healthy reaction to the loss of someone we love, rather than a cause for concern.

Pre-school child Very young children tend to be unable to verbalise their feelings so symptoms tend to be expressed physically as: regression to earlier behaviour (bed wetting, thumb sucking, etc.), clinging behaviour (often at bed time or when a carer leaves for work/shopping, etc.), withdrawal (disinterest in usual activities, extended sleep) or 'acting out' through temper tantrums, uncooperative behaviour (for example, overeating), or uncharacteristic aggression towards others.

Infant school child All the above plus an increasingly social aspect to behaviour (for example, lying or stealing in school), fear for self/others (possibly even to panic levels), magical thinking (whereby the child's logic may make connections between factually unrelated events) which enhances feelings of guilt, shame and blame caused by their distorted perception of the death (for example, 'I used to shout and made mum's head hurt' = I caused mum's brain tumour).

Junior school child All the above plus an increasingly cognitive approach leading to a seemingly detached curiosity about death or illness, isolation related to perceiving themselves as different, an overprotectiveness and associated insecurity towards themselves and others or over/under achieving in school.

Senior school child All the above plus a heightened sense of injustice, sensitivity to peer responses which may lead to isolation or withdrawal (even clinical depression) or 'acting out' through inappropriate sexual activity, substance abuse, aggression, rebellious or reckless behaviour and so on and changes in eating and sleeping patterns.

All children need to be included as much as possible in events that will so profoundly affect their lives, to be given accurate information and encouraged to express their feelings in their own way. The above list is far from exhaustive, and children's grieving will tend to be episodic (that is, seem to have ended only to reappear as they grow and their understanding matures). The complications to grieving listed in Appendix 1 equally apply to childhood grief. This should alert us to children for whom loss may become a long-term problem as the behaviours listed above (which are childhood manifestations of the defences listed in Appendix 2) become fixed and so prevent the child adjusting to their loss.

REFERENCES

Black, D. (1978) 'The bereaved child', *Journal of Child Psychology and Psychiatry*, vol. 19: 287–92.
Dyregov, A. (1990) *Grief in Children*, London: Jessica Kingsley.
Freud, A. (1974) *The Ego and the Mechanisms of Defence*, London: Hogarth.
Furman, E. (1974) *A Child's Parent Dies*, London: Yale University Press.
Klein, M. (1932) *The Psychoanalysis of Children*, London: Hogarth.
Pincus, L. (1976) *Death and the Family. The Importance of Mourning*, London: Faber & Faber.

Appendix IV
The Barcelona Declaration on Palliative Care

THE PROBLEM

Worldwide, 52 million people die each year. Approximately one out of ten deaths is due to cancer and millions more suffer from other life-threatening conditions including AIDS and diseases of old age. Of patients with advanced cancer 70 per cent have pain. In the developing countries of the world, people with cancer are only identified, if at all, after their disease has become incurable. Unrelieved suffering on this scale is unacceptable and unnecessary.

WHAT WE KNOW

In recent years, major advances have been made in pain and symptom management in people with progressive incurable diseases. Great strides have taken place in understanding the psychological, social and spiritual aspects of dying and death. Health professionals, family members, volunteers and others are working together to create dynamic partnerships for the relief of suffering at the end of life. Palliative care incorporates medicine, nursing, social work, pastoral care, physiotherapy, occupational therapy and related disciplines.

WHAT MUST BE DONE

Palliative care must be included as part of governmental health policy, as recommended by the World Health Organisation.

Every individual has the right to pain relief. Palliative care must be provided according to the principle of equity, irrespective of race, gender, ethnicity, social status, national origin and the ability to pay for services. The experience gained from the palliative care of cancer should be extended to the care of people with other chronic incurable diseases.

Inexpensive, effective methods exist to relieve pain and most other symptoms. Thus cost should not be an impediment. Governments should use knowledge about palliative care in a rational way by:

- Establishing clear and informed policies
- Implementing specific services
- Educating health professionals
- Making necessary drugs available
- Systematic assessment of needs in palliative care should precede the establishment of any service at the local, regional and/or national level.

Families and other informal caregivers are essential contributors to the delivery of effective palliative care. They should be recognised and empowered by government policy.

Barcelona, December 1995
World Health Organisation Cancer and Palliative Care Programme
Ministry of Health, Government of Catalonia
Fourth Congress of the European Association of Palliative Care
First Congress of the Spanish Society of Palliative Care

REFERENCE

'The Barcelona Declaration on Palliative Care', *The European Journal of Palliative Care* (1996) 3.1, p. 15.

Glossary of terms

This glossary is intended to provide a definition of terms which arise in the text for the non-specialist in art, psychotherapy and palliative medicine.

AIDS Acquired immune deficiency syndrome (as HIV produces a combination of signs and symptoms such as weight loss, fevers, diarrhoea, neurological damage, Karposi's Sarcoma and other cancers, PCP and other opportunistic infections).

Benign Encapsulated, non-invasive growth of abnormal tissue.

Biopsy Microscopic examination of tissue sample.

Carcinoma Cancer.

Chemotherapy Chemical agent infused via bloodstream or ingested to contain or destroy diseased cells (side effects may include nausea, hair loss or effects associated with depressed marrow functioning).

Convene A sheath for the drainage of urine avoiding male catheterisation.

Countertransference (a psychoanalytic concept) The therapist's emotional attitude toward the client.

Defences (a psychoanalytic concept) Techniques employed to protect the ego against anxiety.

HIV Human immuno virus (status positive means the virus is present in the bloodstream).

Homeopathy Method of selecting remedies based on the principle that 'like cures like'.

Karposi's Sarcoma Characteristic purple cancerous skin lesions.

Lymphoedema Swelling of a limb due to poor lymphatic drainage.

Malignant Growth of abnormal tissue which invades adjacent tissue or spreads via blood or lymphatic circulation.

Metastases Secondary spread of tumour cells via blood or lymph to any site in the body (especially bone, brain, liver, lung and abdominal cavity).

Mesothelioma Cancer of the lung, 90 per cent correlation with exposure to asbestos.

Motor Neurone Disease Degeneration of the motor nerves resulting in progressive weakness, wasting, spasticity and palsy (all systems are affected causing impaired speech and swallowing but with no diminution of mental functioning).

Palliation   Treatments and care programmes offered to patients for whom treatment of active progressive disease is no longer advisable. These include symptom control and measures which improve the patient's quality of life.

PCP   *Pneumocystis Carinii* pneumonia, acute infection of the lungs by a resident fungus which only becomes problematic once the immune system is compromised. The main presenting disease and most frequent cause of death in AIDS.

Prognosis   Forecast of the probable course and termination of disease.

Projection   (a psychoanalytic concept) The process of attributing aspects of the self (usually associated with past experience) to another person.

Psyche   (a psychoanalytic concept) The soul, spirit or mind.

Radiotherapy   Large doses of radiation from which malignant cells recover more slowly – treatment given to 50 per cent of all cancer patients (side effects may include hair loss, skin reactions and nausea).

Recurrence   Either of primary growth or new secondary spread of cancer.

Rehabilitation   Enabling a person to achieve their maximum potential for living.

Remission   Period of abatement of disease.

Respite   Daycare or admission to provide relief for carers.

Stoma   An opening (usually section of bowel) to the surface of the abdomen.

Symbol   The figurative representation of something; the unconscious substitution of one image, idea or activity for another.

Transference   (a psychoanalytic concept) The client displaces feelings arising from previous relationships (for example with parents) onto the therapist and/or the image in art therapy. Recognition of this process enables the therapist to identify and work with unresolved childhood conflicts.

Tumour   An abnormal mass of tissue growth.

Ultrasound scan   Visual image produced as inaudible sound waves are passed over and through the body.

REFERENCE

Kaye, P. (1996) *The A–Z of Hospice and Palliative Medicine*, Northampton: EPL Publications.

Useful addresses

The Creative Response
AIDS, Cancer and Loss
The Old Coal House
Station Road
Ardleigh
Colchester CO7 7RR

British Association
Of Music Therapists
25 Rosslyn Avenue
East Barnet
London EN4 8DH

American Association
Of Art Therapists
5999 Stevenson Ave
Alexandria
VA22304 USA

British Association
of Art Therapists
11a Richmond Road
Brighton BN2 3LR

British Association
of Drama Therapists
30c Bank Street
Kincarding
Fife FK10 4LY

ART THERAPY TRAINING ESTABLISHMENTS

City of Bath College
1 Avon Street
Bath BA1 1UP

Goldsmiths' College
University of London
New Cross
London SE14 6NW

Edinburgh University
Wilkie House
31 Guthrie Street
Edinburgh EH1 1JG

University of Sheffield
16 Claremont Crescent
Sheffield
South Yorkshire S10 2TA

University of Hertfordshire
Art & Design Building
Manor Road
Hatfield
Herts AL10 9TL

PALLIATIVE CARE RESOURCES

Hospice Information Service
St Christopher's Hospice
51–59 Lawrie Park Road
Sydenham
London SE26 6DZ

Hospice Arts
The Forbes Trust
9 Artillery Lane
London E1 7LP

Macmillan Nursing Services
Cancer Relief Macmillan Fund
15 Britten Street
London SW3 3TZ

Marie Curie Cancer Care
28 Belgrave Square
London SW1 8QG

Motor Neurone Disease Association
PO Box 264
Northampton NN1 2PR

ACT Association for Children
with Life-Threatening Conditions
65 St Michael's Hill
Bristol BS2 8DZ

CRUSE Bereavement Care
126 Sheen Road
Richmond
Surrey TW9 1UR

Terence Higgins Trust
52–54 Gray's Inn Road
London WC1X 8JU

Good Grief
19 Bawtree Road
Uxbridge
Middlesex UB8 1PT

Winston's Wish
Gloucester Royal Hospital
Great Western Road
Gloucester GL1 3NN

Corinne Burton Memorial Trust
Citroen Wells
Devonshire House
1 Devonshire Street
London W1N 2DR

The Omega Foundation
25 Middle Way
London NW11 6SH

TELEPHONE HELPLINES

Child Death Helpline
0800 282986

Lesbian and Gay Bereavement Project
0181 455 8894

National AIDS Helpline
0800 567123

Index

Page references in **bold** indicate glossary entries

abandonment 173
adaptive art therapy 94–6
adjustment 39, 41, 94
adolescents: griefwork groups 153–67
age differences 32
Ahmedzai, S. 22
AIDS **193**; art therapy 28, 29–30, 140; attitudes to 116; case studies 102–13, 116–25, 127–39, 140–51; death and dying 124–5, 150–1; palliative care 14, 22, 115; parental loss 157; physical health 148–9; *see also* HIV
AIDS-related dementia 121–2, 148–9
Aldridge, D. 8, 27, 30, 140
American Association of Art Therapists 195
anger 58, 61, 72, 73, 84, 133, 138
approach 53–4
Arguile, R. 2
Arnheim, R. 3, 8
art: in hospices 42–3; in hospitals 43–4
art-making process 4
art materials 3–4, 29, 77; symbolism 131
art therapists 6–7; facilitator role 140, 142; methods 7–9; responses 146–8; role 1, 7, 31–2; *see also* therapeutic relationship
art therapy 1–2, 48; aims 4–6; bereavement support 47–8; clients 27–8; emotional support 89, 93; group settings 82–6; history 26–7; in illness 44–5; location 3, 27–8, 28–9; modes of working 78–80; and palliative care 29–31, 33–5, 48, 49–50, 76; research 9; and spiritual needs 42; as staff support 45–6; training establishments 6, 195–6
art therapy groups *see* groups
Arts in Psychotherapy, The 140
artwork 33–4
Association for Children with Life-Threatening Conditions 196
auditing 23
Australia 7

BAAT *see* British Association of Art Therapists
Bach, S. 28, 33–4
BACUP 179
Baker, N.T. 20
Barcelona Declaration on Palliative Care 14, 191–2
Baulkwill, J. 28
beginnings 53
Bekter McIntyre, B. 27, 28, 30
Belfiore, M. 27, 31
benign **193**
bereavement 18–19; in childhood 189–90
bereavement support 16; art therapy 28, 47–8; *see also* griefwork groups
Bertoia, J. 28
Bion, W.R. 109, 127, 155
biopsy **193**
Birtchnell, J. 156
Biswas, B. 22, 23
Black, D. 156, 190
Blake, William 86
Blee, T. 5
Bloch, S. 155
bodies 170, 175; in artwork 34–5, 149–50
Boethius 75
Bohusz, Marian 43
boundaries 35, 64–5, 92, 155
Bowlby, J. 18, 157
British Association of Art Therapists 7, 26, 27, 43, 195; *see also* Creative Response
British Association of Drama Therapists 195
British Association of Music Therapists 195
Brook, Peter 113
Buildings for the Health Service (DHSS) 43
Bulgaria 7
Bussard, A. 140
Byers, A. 2

Cagnoletta, M. della 7
Camp, Karen 128, 130
Campbell, J. 57
Canada 7, 27
cancer patients 28, 75; art therapy methods
    78–80; case studies 57–62, 67–74, 82–6,
    90–2, 96–8, 106–9, 176–84; control 65;
    The Creative Journey 169, 173–5;
    creativity 171–2; negative thought
    172–3; palliative care 14; physical pain
    170
Cancer Relief Macmillan Fund 14, 196
cancer support groups 78, 184
carcinoma **193**
carers: informal 20, 22
Case, C. 2, 8, 28, 30, 147
Casement, P. 163
catharsis 5–6
change 6
chaos 181
charities 13, 14
Charles, Prince 43
Charlton, S. 2
chemotherapy **193**
Child Death Helpline 197
childhood 123–4
children: bereavement support 47–8; case
    studies 47, 50, 60–2; grief 153–67,
    187–90; literature review 28; parental
    loss 156–7; reading pictures 34; see also
    griefwork groups
chronic niceness 46
Clark, D. 23
colour 5
communication 5, 21, 57
Community Care Act 1991 23
confidentiality 33, 92, 125; and exhibitions
    80; griefwork groups 155–6
Connell, C. 2, 28, 29, 30, 32, 35, 94
control: cancer patients 65; over art
    materials 5, 171; within therapeutic
    relationship 72–3, 74, 148
convene **193**
Coplans, John 149
Corinne Burton Memorial Trust 27, 196
Cotter, Z.M. 13
countertransference 131, 150, **193**
Cox, Murray 66
Crane, W. 2
Creative Journey 169, 171, 173–4, 175
Creative Response 27, 195
creativity 4–5, 119, 171–2, 175
crisis model 39–41
Crouch, E. 155
Crowther, T. 13
CRUSE Bereavement Care 196

cultural differences 21–2, 32
cystic fibrosis 28, 50

Dalley, T. 2, 8
Dante 115
Davis, C.B. 28
death: AIDS patients 124–5; ambivalent
    thoughts 172–3, 175; anticipation 93, 96;
    denial 67, 115; near death experiences
    136; in poetry 81; as social experience
    150–1; talking about 44
defences 18–19, 188, **193**
dementia 121–2
denial 73, 172, 188; of death 67, 115
Department of Health and Social Security
    43
dependency 102, 109–10
destruction 122–3
difference 21–2, 32, 144
disease 39
disempowerment 61
domiciliary service 88–90, 99–100; case
    studies 90–1, 96–9
drama 150
Dulhoefer, S. 140
dying see death
Dyregov, A. 190

Edinger, E. 60
Edwards, G. 140
Eliot, T.S. 102
Embleton Tudor, L. 8–9
embodied images 136, 150
Emerson, Ralph Waldo 74
emotional support 16–17, 89, 93
empathy 44
empowerment 110
envy 146
Erskine, A. 34
euthanasia 13
exhibitions 80, 125, 138

facilitator role 140, 142
families 91, 98, 100
fear 117, 146, 173
Feldman, E. 28, 29, 30, 140, 149
Fell, Alison 103, 104–6
fight 111–12
Firth, S. 21
flight 111–12
Foulkes, S.H. 155
found images 66, 68–70, 74
Frampton, D.R. 4
funding 14, 23
Furman, E. 153, 156–7, 190
Furth, G. 28, 33, 34

gender differences 32
Germany 27
Gilbert and George 149
Gilroy, A. 9
Goldsmiths' College 27
Good Grief 153, 196
Gordon, R. 150
Greenblatt, S. 151
Greenwood, H. 2, 34
grief 18–19; children 153, 189–90;
    complications 186–7; staff 20
griefwork groups 153–4, 166–7; aims
    156–7; case study 153–67; sessions 154–6
Grigsby, J. 35
Grotawski, Zergy 113
group notebook 35, 77–8
groups 1; basic assumptions 109–13; case
    studies 82–6, 102–13, 116–25, 127–39,
    153–67, 169–75
Guardian 107–8, 140
guided concentration 173

Haiku 82
Hancock, B. 14
Hatoum, Mona 149
Henzell, J. 147
Herrmann, U. 27, 28, 125
Hill, Adrian 26, 169
Hill, O.W. 156
HIV **193**; case studies 116–17, 120–1, 125;
    dependency 110; palliative care 14, 22;
    Scotland 127–8; unpredictability 141; *see
    also* AIDS
HIV dementia 121–2, 148–9
HIV prisoners 127, 128, 138–9; case studies
    130–7
holism 14
home environment 28, 92–3; *see also*
    domiciliary service
homeopathy **193**
hope 30, 87, 94, 97
Hospice Arts 4, 196
Hospice Information Service 12, 14, 196
hospice staff *see* staff
hospices 12–13; and art 42–3; art therapy
    27–8; development 13–14, 23
Hospital Arts 4, 5
hospitals: art 43–4; art therapy 28
humanistic psychology 8
Hungary 7

illness 39, 44; crisis model 39–41
imagery 174, 176, 178, 184
individual sessions: case studies 53–62,
    64–74, 88–100, 140–51
Inscape 27

interruptions 61, 91–2, 155
intimacy 64
Italy 7, 27, 31

Jansen, T. 30, 32, 34
journeys 30, 65–6, 72, 74, 125
Judd, D. 28, 34
Jung, C.G. 77, 117, 166

Kanjiro, Kawai 67
Karposi's Sarcoma **193**
Kaufman, A.B. 28
Kaye, C. 5
Kaye, K. 35
Kaye, P. 15, 16, 17
Kearney, M. 42, 59, 60, 110
Killick, K. 2, 34
Klein, Melanie 8
Kübler-Ross, E. 44, 73, 94, 115–16, 136

La Rochefoucauld 62
Lago, C. 31
Laing, Joyce 130, 138
Lawrence, D.H. 81, 82
Learmonth, M. 94, 136, 147, 148
learning disability 26
Lee, C. 9, 149
Lesbian and Gay Bereavement Project 197
leukemia 27
Levens, M. 2, 34
Levine, Stephen 67
Liebmann, M. 62
life-threatening illness 12
lifestyles 22
liminal period 94, 151
literature reviews 27–32
Littlewood, J. 186–7
living-dying phase 94, 150–1
London Lighthouse 115, 124, 125
loss 18–19
Lunceford, J. 23
Lunn, S. 16, 28
Luzzatto, P. 2, 8
lymphoedema **193**

McIntyre, Sumaya 27
Mack, J. 160
McKeogh, M. 148
Macmillan Nursing Services 88, 196
McNeilly, G. 155
McNiff, S. 8
Mahony, J. 2
Males, B. 2
malignant **193**
Malitskie, G. 2
mandalas 117, 170

Mann, D. 4
Marcetti, A. 16
Marie Curie Cancer Care 14, 196
Marie Curie Centre 64
masks 161–3, 164
Maslow, A. 41
Maybe, The (Parker and Swinton) 149–50
Mayo, S. 28, 32
meaning 171–2
medical model of care 22, 38–9
meditation 173
Memories, Dreams, Reflections (Jung) 77
memory 35
mental health 26
Menzies Lyth, I. 130
mesothelioma **194**
metastases **193**
Mildmay Mission Hospital 186–7
Miller, B. 2, 27, 28
Milner, Marion 8
Moore, M. 28, 35
Morris, Margaret 113
Moss, V. 28
motor neurone disease 14, 28, **193**; case
    studies 55–7
Motor Neurone Disease Association 196
mourning 18–19, 188
multiple sclerosis 28
Murphy, J. 2
Murphy, Julie 138
mutilation 184
myths 112

National AIDS Helpline 197
National Council for Hospice and Specialist
    Palliative Care Services 14
National Health Service 13, 23
Neale, B. 20
near death experiences 136
needs 41–2
negative thought 172–3
Netherlands 7
Nightingale, Florence 43
North London Hospice 18
Nowell Hall, P. 8

Omega Foundation 196
one-off sessions 35, 59–60, 141, 145–6
open groups 82–6
Orlan 149
Orton, M. 30

pain: physical 29, 170, 175; psychic 170;
    spiritual 17, 41–2, 44; total 13
pairing 112–13
palliation **194**

palliative care 12, 13–14, 23–4; and art
    therapy 26–7, 29–31, 33–5, 35; auditing
    23; Barcelona Declaration 191–2;
    cultural and lifestyle differences 21–2;
    informal carers 20; loss and bereavement
    18–19; multidisciplinary team 15–18;
    resources 196; services 12–13; staff
    support 19–20
palliative medicine 22, 43
parent figure 131
Parkes, C.M. 18, 94
patient-centred care 14–18
Pattison, E.M. 94
PCP **194**
peer relationships 163
people living with AIDS *see* AIDS
physical care 15
physical health 148–9
physical limitations 29, 31
Pincus, L. 41, 157, 190
Plaut, F. 166
play 123
Plotinus 75
PLWA *see* AIDS
Pneumocystis Carinii **194**
poetry readings 80–2
positive thinking 172
Potter, Dennis 74
power 31–2, 61, 110
Pratt, A.J. 28
prison officers 129, 133
prisoners *see* HIV prisoners
prisons: art therapy groups 28, 127, 138–9;
    as environment 128–30; HIV 128
problem-solving 39–41
prognosis **194**
projection 188, **194**
psyche **194**
psychic pain 170
psychodynamic model 7–8
psychological defences 18–19, 188, **193**
psychological support 16–17, 89, 93

racism 21
radiotherapy **194**
recurrence **194**
reflective space 129
rehabilitation **194**
religion 17, 21–2
remission **194**
respite **194**
Rifkind, G. 2
Rosner David, I. 28, 29, 140, 149
Royal College of Physicians 22
Royal Marsden Hospital 75–6
Russell-Lacy, S. 34

Rust, M. 2, 8
Rutter, M. 156
Rycroft, C. 3

Sageman, S. 28, 29, 140, 149
St Christopher's Hospice 13, 42–3
St Helena Hospice 153–4
St Luke's Hospice 88
Samuels, A. 166
Saunders, Dame Cicely 13, 23, 42–3
Schaverien, J. 2, 8, 136, 150
Schneiders, J. 35
schools 28
Scotland 127–8
Scottish Prison Service 128
Seager, R.T. 20
searching 158
self-expression 174
sexual identity 123, 124
Shakespeare 81
'Ship of Death, The' (Lawrence) 81
Shorter, B. 166
sibling rivalry 131
silence 67, 147
Simon, R. 28, 30
single sessions 35, 59–60, 141, 145–6
Skaife, S. 31, 146
'Snake, The' (Lawrence) 82
social support 15–16
SOLAS 138
Sontag, S. 44
Sourkes, B. 28
space: reflective 66–7, 129
Spearman, John 28, 107–8, 140
Speck, P. 46
Spence, Christopher 115
spiritual pain 17, 41–2, 44
spirituality 17
Stack, M. 2
staff: attitude to art therapists 29;
    case studies 46; and griefwork groups
    155; multidisciplinary teams 15;
    relationship with patients 73; support for
    19–20, 30–1, 45–6; see also prison
    officers
Stedeford, A. 94
stillness 67
stoma **194**
Stott, J. 2
Strand, S. 2
Sue Ryder Foundation 14
Swinton, Tilda 149–50
Switzerland 7

symbol **194**
Szepanski, M. 2, 28

Terence Higgins Trust 196
terminal illness 12; art therapy 26–7
Terry, K. 2
theme-focused art therapy 94–6, 174
therapeutic relationship 31–2, 72–3, 76
therapists see art therapists
Thomas, G. 2, 28, 29
Thompson, J. 31
time 29, 64, 66, 140–1
Tipple, R. 2
total pain 13
transference 8, 131, **194**
transformation 174
tuberculosis 26
Tudor, K. 8–9
tumour **194**

Ulrich, R. 44
ultrasound scan **194**
unconscious 8, 171
United States: art therapy 27; art therapy
    research 9; associations 7, 195; hospices
    23

Vachon, M.L.S. 20
Van Duerzen-Smith, E. 141
Vasarhelyi, V. 7
visualisation 178

Waller, D. 2, 7, 26, 155
Walter, T. 19, 153, 166
Ward, B. 153
Way to Die, A (Zorza) 177
Weiner, A. 45–6
Wilkes, E. 20, 22, 23
Williams, K. 34
Winnicott, D.W. 8, 127
Winston's Wish 153, 196
Wood, C. 28
Wood, M. 2
Wood, M.J.M. 2, 28, 29, 30, 32,
    128, 140, 146
Worden, J.W. 19, 153
World Health Organisation 191–2

Yalom, I. 155

Zambelli, G. 30
Zorza, Rosemary 177
Zorza, Victor 177